MANAGING ENERGY RISK:

a nontechnical guide to
markets and trading

MANAGING ENERGY RISK:

a nontechnical guide to
markets and trading

**BY
JOHN
WENGLER**

DEDICATION

To Dragana, my love

CONTENTS

FIGURES

TABLES

ACKNOWLEDGEMENTS

Most authors save the most important acknowledgement for the end. But I want to start with a huge THANK YOU to Dragana Pilipovic, my lovely wife. Without her this book would not have been possible.

I next must thank Jeffrey Roark of Southern Energy for his glorious wit and experience. Jeff's comments could have been a book unto themselves and I feel very lucky to have benefited from his contributions.

Thanks to Bob Smock, Vice President, Group Publishing, and Director of the Global Energy Group, for PennWell, for suggesting the idea for this book several years ago and then harvesting the concept in 1999; Kirk Bjornsgaard, my PennWell editor, for his support and motivational emails; John Sodergreen of Scudder Publications and *The Desk* newsletter for his humor; SAVA Risk Management Corporation for allowing me the time to write the manuscript; and my friends and colleagues who provided the wonderful guest essays and interviews that appear within the chapters: Jim Clarke, Dunham Cobb, Ted Coates, Jeff Deneau, Adrian D'Silva, Tom Hahn, Glen Justis, Kevin Kremke, Greg LaFlame, Bob Smock, Karl Stanley, and Don Winslow. A special thanks goes to Andrea Kramer, a partner at McDermott, Will & Emery, for her contribution, both of a guest essay as well as the incredible outline of *Risk Management Policies and Procedures* provided in the Appendix.

I also want to express my appreciation to Professor John Bilsor and Ken Gibson of the Street School of Business, Illinois Institute of Technology, for giving me the climate to develop many ideas as an instructor.

Thanks to the people who responded to a questionnaire that I used to help write the final chapter on future issues: Barry Campbell, Energy Market Planning Manager, Nebraska Public Power District; Christophe Chassard, Global Head Structuring and Risk Management, RWE Energy Trading Limited; Chris Cramer, Risk Analyst, Duke Energy International; Jeff Deneau, Market Risk Analyst, NiSource Inc.; Samir F. Elia, Director, Risk Management, PG&E Energy Trading; Rob Gunnin, VP Risk Management, ICF Consulting; Jay Lindgren, Senior Quantitative

Analyst, R. W. Beck; Cliff McPherson, Lead Auditor, Northeast Utilities; David E. Mousseau, President, Strategic Energy Management Corp.; and Todd McRae, Market Analyst, TransAlta Energy Marketing.

I apologize in advance for any errors, omissions, or hyperboles that take away from my goal of advancing risk management in energy markets. All mistakes are mine alone and I would appreciate reader feedback.

I want to thank my great kids, Nevena and Sasha, for giving me space when I wanted it and diversions (especially soccer—Go Trevians!) when I needed it. Thanks to my parents Roman and Joan Wengler for the continued support. Finally, thank you to Dragana for being my love and my muse.

John Wengler
jwengler@rwbeck.com
or
authors@pennwell.com
www.pennwell-store.com
March, 2001
Winnetka, Illinois

FOREWORD

Jeffrey Roark,
Principal, Regulatory Affairs
Southern Energy

As a graduate student in electrical engineering at Auburn University in the mid-1970s, I sometimes led tour groups through our AC Lab, a dusty hall filled with electrical machinery collected over 80 years. The old machines, meters, and switchgear gave the appearance of an electric power museum, if not a 1950s horror movie. During one such tour, a prospective engineering parent asked me, "Why would you want to study power? Power never changes." Standing among the museum pieces, some still in use, I felt powerless to object, even though the term "Energy Crisis" had already entered the street vernacular several years earlier.

Twenty-five years of power industry experience later, I finally found the answer that I had needed on that day. The laws of physics never change. (We hope that this is true, even if what we know and say about the laws of physics changes rather often at the edges.) The Law of Conservation of Energy is immutable. (The Law of Conservation of Energy is the energy equivalent of "There is no such thing as a free lunch.") But as with any human economic endeavor, the power industry never stops changing. And as with the entire world economy and political structure, the pace of change in the power industry has accelerated to a dizzying deregulating open market whirl today. May it never end!

In 1995, I was one of the first three full-time inhabitants of Southern Energy's new Trading Center: a small corner office that only weeks before had housed a single occupant. As a 20-year veteran of tremendous change in the power industry, I found myself in yet another whole new world. My 1980s vintage MBA, though helpful, seemed like ancient history. I was in Risk Management 101 without a professor, a classroom, or even a book. Our one and only trader, Sean Murphy, had traded mortgages before, and he realized—electricity is different. We needed help! By chance, Sean found the names of Dragana Pilipovic and John

Wengler, of SAVA Risk Management Corporation, and invited them to come to Atlanta to talk with us about energy trading and help us explore the aspects of electricity that make it unique among commodities. A short few weeks later, they arrived in Atlanta. It was a pivotal moment for us all. John and Dragana, with knowledge and experience in oil and gas trading and risk management, were eager to learn about electricity. We were equally eager for them to learn about electricity and to help us out. Not only did I find in them a pair of professors for my rolling Risk Management 101, but I discovered that these were two delightfully intelligent and energetic people, and I have valued their friendship ever since.

Much has progressed since our first meeting. Southern Energy's Trading Center has grown to be the world's largest energy trading center, employing hundreds of employees, many of whom had not yet seen their twentieth year of life (much less of the power industry) when our "Corner Office" Trading Center first opened. In 1998, Dragana Pilipovic "wrote the book" on the subject—namely *Energy Risk*—with John's help of course. Energy risk management itself has become very hot news. After price spikes in eastern markets in 1998 and 1999 caused some notable bankruptcies, defaults, and early exits from electricity trading, the western price spikes in the summer of 2000 have even politicians demanding more forward hedging on the part of the local electric utilities. It seems that as an industry, and especially those living on the volatile margin, we learn through pain. (I am referring to both buyers and sellers of electric energy at the wholesale margin, as opposed to integrated utilities with rather stable average costs even in the face of wholesale price spikes.)

What better timing could there be for John's book on energy risk management aimed not at the quantitative whiz kids, but at managers of electric utilities? Regional transmission organization (RTO) formation is on the horizon. Every step toward competition adds risk to the energy supplier's business. California in 2000 has shown that we still have plenty to learn about risk management. And if today's popular backlash against competition in electricity is successful, it will have occurred because of a failure to grasp and embrace risk management principles.

The entire deregulation of the industry is an exercise in exposing risks that were hidden by regulation, and allocating, through markets, the various risks to those best able to manage them. Competitive energy suppliers risk billions of dollars on physical generating assets, and manage those risks through geographic diversity, fuel diversity, efficient plant operation, and trading and marketing of energy products. Transmission owners will manage the physical availability of their assets to maximize their profits. Users of the grid will find usage prices to be volatile, much like energy prices, and will manage their transmission price risk through tradable contracts, whether these are physical or financial. It is important that any company operating in this environment learn to analyze its risks and manage them appropriately. And, it is important that risk managers understand and internalize the concepts behind risk management in the electricity industry, rather than just learning the right things to do. Learning this stuff by rote is an instant recipe for learning through pain, because that which is right today will change tomorrow. We don't really know what will happen next. (This is much more fun than, "Power never changes.")

Complexity is not escapable in the electric utility industry. Efforts to ignore it fail. The Pennsylvania-Jersey-Maryland (PJM) independent system operator (ISO) tried to ignore it, and failed. New England tried to ignore it, and failed. California tried to overpower it with a "simplified" system, and failed. New York tried to embrace complexity, and found more devils in the details. But it always makes me smile when I see another one hit the dust. Folks, the complexity in power generation and delivery is real. It cannot be forced to look like or behave like gas or oil. And without regulation to cram all of the risks onto consumers, these complexities will continue to dog market participants until they deal with them explicitly. Unfortunately, we will likely find that consumers do not want to deal with the complexities or the volatility inherent in electric service.

This, I believe, forms the challenge for risk managers in our industry—to deal with and absorb the physical complexities and the concomitant financial complexities associated with electric service, providing price stability, efficiency, reliability, and simplicity to electric consumers. Given the unavoidable complexities, this is a tall order. The work has barely begun. Many practicing traders, marketers, and risk managers in electricity don't even understand their jobs yet. And though many are new to the industry, they are already actively resisting change from what they already know how to do. They want to settle in and do trading and make money; unfortunately, the final rules of the game are hardly in place.

This book, *Managing Energy Risk*, offers a valuable tool in meeting this challenge dealing with market realities. This book helps demonstrate how risk management *theory*, not just practice, can become second nature to those of us in this industry. These kinds of risk management ideas will help us absorb and control the many changes that lie ahead. Complexity in electricity risk management will increase. (In time, simplicity will return to consumers if they demand it.) But this time, if we listen closely to the market and respond wisely, we can make "good" with our new market opportunities, with its full complexity contained once more in an envelope of market-developed risk management tools and techniques properly designed around the physical realities.

This book is an introduction to energy risk management aimed at utility engineers and managers. For those engineers with an MBA or other quantitative business background, this book will help direct some of that educational experience toward a new way of thinking about the energy business. For those engineers, and especially managers, without a quantitative business background, I hope it encourages them to find an MBA program and place it firmly into their background. Of course, there will always be jobs in the utility industry in a quiet, sheltered environment with a relaxed pace of change and little exposure to risk. Unfortunately these are likely to be low paying, uninteresting jobs of lesser value. This book is for those who want to embrace the change and accept risk and risk management as means to a more exciting and better paying future in the electric utility industry. In fact, for many this will come of necessity, because the electric utility industry of the future will look very different from that of today.

Like the old AC lab at my alma mater, the electricity industry continuously collects new ideas to join the old ones. The secret to our success in dealing with new market challenges is how well we integrate new market-oriented ideas with our traditional engineering duties in generating power. Just as understanding physics is important for being an engineer, understanding risk management is increasingly important for being a manager of an energy business in the future. But the engineer with an MBA has an advantage—understanding of both physics and risk management. Though people have a natural preference for simplicity, the physical complexities of the electricity business have reasserted themselves time and again. Good engineers and good managers alike are needed to make sense out of the risks that are driven by the fundamentals, the ones that don't fit well into quantitative analysis. There yawns a gap that needs bridging, and in this industry it is uniquely important. Engineers can and do build bridges. In this book, may you sight your landing on the other side.

Jeffrey Roark
Jeffrey.Roark@southernenergy.com
Atlanta, GA
December 2000

Jeffrey D. Roark, a 29-year student of the electricity industry, is Principal, Regulatory Affairs, for Southern Energy, Inc., in Atlanta, GA. He holds Bachelor's and Master's degrees in Electrical Engineering at Auburn University, and an MBA from the University of Alabama at Birmingham. His experience in the industry includes transmission and generation planning in Southern Company's regulated business, as well as seven very interesting years of market analysis work in Southern Energy's trading, marketing, and asset development business in the United States and abroad.

EDITOR'S NOTE

by Dragana Pilipovic, SAVA

When John started writing this book, we agreed that the market needed a nontechnical guidebook for managers dealing with trading and risk management. Why not another technical book? Simple—the math scares off the average manager and prevents him/her from understanding risk and other issues. We were still left figuring out how to transfer our belief in the power of risk-related ideas. I felt a bit like Dr. Frankenfurter in the movie "Rocky Horror Picture Show" when he declared "I'll remove the cause, but not the symptom!"

At a coffee shop in our hometown, John and I ultimately landed on the notion of the *Risk Management Policies and Procedures* (RMPP) as providing the natural framework for this book. If it belonged in the RMPP or helped the manager understand the RMPP, then we should explore the topic. If a subject strayed too far afield, or did not have the simple benefit of being entertaining, that subject fell to the cutting room floor.

We had expected to use the "nontechnical" standard a lot more than we wound up doing. By keeping the focus on the manager's needs—in other words, using a mark-to-manager process— John typically found words and analogies to do the talking rather than relying on equations. That's the way it should be. The math can be left to the quantitative analysts working for the manager.

(A quick word for those quantitative analysts who are reading this book. For those of you working wonders in support of the trading desk, this is a great book if one day you want to be *in charge* of that trading desk. It's also a good book for understanding the reasons why quantitative analysis is important and how to make it better serve the industry.)

In editing this book, I looked for the right balance between the "big picture" and the kinds of detail that are absolutely necessary for true understanding. This book may be nontechnical, but the subject material remains very complex. It is my hope—and John's as well—that this book finds a comfortable spot among the great books on energy risk management.

Dragana Pilipovic
drag@sava.com
Winnetka, Illinois
December 2000

Dragana Pilipovic founded SAVA Risk Management Corporation in 1993 to provide analytic and risk solutions for the electricity and energy markets. In 1998 she published her groundbreaking book Energy Risk: Valuing and Managing Energy Derivatives *(McGraw-Hill.) She lives in Winnetka, Illinois with John and their two children.*

chapter 1

INTRODUCTION:
THE "TOP TEN CHECKLIST"
OF THINGS TO DO

Managing Energy Risk: A Nontechnical Guide to Markets and Trading introduces the issues that executives in the electricity and energy markets alike must understand in order to manage. This understanding may remain at a high level, with more emphasis on the business implications of choices rather than the more technical details. That's why managers hire teams of people including traders, risk managers, analysts, and the full risk roster. But as the sentry on watch in the uncharted waters of deregulation, a manager at a utility must stand upon certain core principles of market behavior and risk. This book's purpose is to define and explain these principles to help the manager control an otherwise perplexing and challenging enterprise. In writing this book, I kept the following picture of the target reader in mind: the reader is an engineer with an MBA who now manages a business unit that faces market price risk—or will so soon. With luck, this book will also benefit a much broader audience, from the boardroom down to new hires. Furthermore, the book can prove useful "horizontally" as managers move from a purely regulated environment to a deregulated one.

The manager's job is to manage. (A novel concept!) When managing a complex new business unit such as trading and risk management, the manager's secret weapon lies within solid "Risk Management Policies and Procedures" (RMPP.) The RMPP are written documents that articulate the corporate business plan as it relates to trading. A "policies and procedures" may suggest yet another boring legal document or bureaucratic nightmare, but a manager must consider the alternative of running a trading operation beyond management's control or comprehension. Think of *Risk Management Policies and Procedures* as equivalent to the U.S. Constitution, not just parchment and ink but a living document negotiated by the company's leadership and for the benefit of the shareholders. This book attempts to demonstrate the role of the RMPP in the daily responsibilities of a utility manager.

Throughout this book, I will generally use the word "utility" in the traditional sense of an electric company whose core competence is generating power. Unless otherwise noted, I will not necessarily distinguish between ownership structures—i.e., municipal vs. investor owned—because they share more risks in common than not. Likewise, for the purposes of explaining how managers should manage the risk process, I will not distinguish between such structures as an integrated generator-transmitter-distributor company or a chopped-up core company like a generating company (GENCO), or transmission company (TRANSCO), or distribution company (DISTCO). The only difference will be that some companies will be naturally "long" while others will be naturally "short"; in other words, some will need to sell power more than others, while others will be more likely to buy. Some might be long generation but short transmission. Some might be heavy into structured products for the sake of wholesale trading, while others might do so for purposes of marketing to sophisticated industrial end users. My point is that everybody needs to understand energy risk management and then be able to express their vision for what it means to their particular company and its business plan. While electricity examples dominate this book, the general concepts should be applicable to many other energy and non-energy markets.

This first chapter introduces the book in two ways. First, this chapter highlights the top priority issues facing the energy risk industry. The priorities appear in a "Top Ten Checklist" for managers with direct references to chapters and sections that provide greater detail. The second section summarizes the remaining chapters to help the reader skim the overall content.

THE TOP TEN CHECKLIST

The manager will either inherit an existing framework of policies and procedures or will need to draft some from scratch. To help the manager get to work, here is a Top Ten Checklist of things to do (see Table 1-1[1]), followed by more details about each priority and how they fit within this book:

1) Walk Before You Run
2) Balance "Wall Street" and "Main Street"
3) Learn the "Mark-to-Market" Mantra
4) Express Your "Risk-Return Strategy"
5) Line Up Your Political Sponsor
6) Hire Complete Roster, Not Just Quarterbacks
7) Brush Up on Risk Basics
8) Establish Risk Limits
9) Budget to Achieve Your Objectives
10) Network, Network, Network

Walk Before You Run

Start slowly. Energy risk covers vast ranges of complex issues, not even more complicated than the issues bankers worry about in money markets. Bank managers have learned about risk over several decades,

Task	Summary
Walk Before You Run	Learn and do things slowly (but surely) to avoid costly or embarrassing mistakes.
Balance "Wall Street" and "Main Street"	Combine the cultural benefits of both raw capitalism and the paternal conservatism of regulated utilities. (See Chapter 2.)
Learn the "Mark-to-Market" Mantra	Replace the traditional mindset of "cost-plus-return" with a willingness to consider market price information as the primary signal of future profit-loss scenarios. (See Chapter 2.)
Express Your "Risk-Return Strategy"	Clearly articulate your business unit's profit-loss appetite as a function of your overall business plan. (See Chapters 3 and 4.)
Line Up Your Political Sponsor	Identify individuals at the board level or in upper management who will back you and the concepts of proper risk management in good times and in bad. (See Chapter 3.)
Hire Complete Roster, Not Just Quarterbacks	Collect a team of people mixing the different specialties and personalities that you need to manage to success. (See Chapter 5.)
Brush Up on Risk Basics	Read this and other books (and attend industry events) to gather the bare essentials. (See Chapter 6, with more advanced material in Chapters 8-10.)
Establish Risk Limits	Map the corridor of what your traders, risk managers, and marketers "can" and "cannot" do by defining the "origination-to-settlement" lifecycle and the measurable limits within which employees may operate. (See Chapters 7 and 9.)
Budget to Achieve Your Objectives	Fight for the funding that is required to pay for the staff and systems necessary to achieve your business unit's "Risk-Return" objectives. (See Chapters 10 and 11.)
Network, Network, Network	Remember that you are not alone in terms of being new to the world of trading and risk, just as bank managers were equally new just 10 to 20 years ago

Table 1-1: The "Top Ten Checklist" of Things for the New Manager to Do

while it seems like the power executives must now pick up the concepts in just a few months. It's like jumping on a Harley-Davidson motorcycle without the benefit of first learning to ride a bike. So, despite the outside pressures, try to start patiently building solid practices to avoid costly or embarrassing mistakes. Reading this book is a good start.

Balance "Wall Street" and "Main Street"

Wall Street invented risk management. By "Wall Street" I mean New York's financial markets as well as those in Chicago, London, Hong Kong, and all other money centers. The utility should bring in people with Wall Street skills. But money market experts do not own an exclusive on the intelligence and common sense required to properly manage energy risk. Money market veterans may even pose a risk to the extent that they learned their tools in a very different marketplace. The utility's employees from "Main Street" understand the complexities of power. (In my database of U.S. power companies, I found at least seven utilities with an address on a "Main Street.") The smart "locals" compare well with those on Wall Street. The manager should consider hiring from within, training critical minds that could learn money market principles and still be able to see where updates are required to handle what makes energies different. A by-product of regulation, the utility's sense of paternal conservatism toward their service areas should be converted into marketing benefits. A more "Wall Street" approach can help spark this conversion, moving utilities and their customers from a sense of "mutual entitlement" toward market-based exchanges of real value. (See Chapter 2 for more details.)

Learn the "Mark-to-Market" Mantra

Under regulation, the utility's financial philosophy depended on cost-plus-return. Using the parlance of finance, this approach can be described as "marking-to-cost" where prices are "marked" or tied to a particular company's internal cost. With deregulation, the mindset must change from mark-to-cost to "marking-to-market" in which the market sets prices regardless of a particular company's costs. Under a mark-to-market process, market prices serve as the primary (if not exclusive) signal for current value and expectations. The focus moves from an individual company's cost and profit concerns to the aggregate cost and profit competition in the general market. Marking-to-market entails both pricing and processes; every employee from the trading desk to the salespeople should understand the concept. The clever manager should always ask "but is it marked-to-market?" (See Chapter 2 for more details.)

GUEST ESSAY

Kick Starting Risk Management at the "Reluctant Utility"

by T.C. Coates

The electric utility industry has a credible record for embracing and developing technological change to increase reliability and reduce costs in the physical realm. Yet it is surprising that technologically savvy utilities would be reluctant to embrace opportunities that a developing technology for energy risk management offers. What some energy industry market players seem to know intrinsically, others have yet to realize.

Energy risk management technology is essential to a company's long-term success in the market place. Even the most traditional of utilities must recognize that the skills and tools of energy risk management represent a new class of "technology" that must be incorporated into the company's already sophisticated non-financial technologies. For those utilities that continue to operate resources and manage their own wholesale power transactions, such new technology is not a luxury, it's required.

Spotting a Reluctant Utility

Even when the need is clear, managers/leaders with a vision for the value of energy risk management technology may find the challenge daunting in selling their vision in the halls of a reluctant utility. Let's be blunt: reluctance is a state of mind. Utilities are not reluctant, people are. You would think that everyone knows and is concerned about the effects of a changing, dynamic energy market. It is no secret that electricity prices are much more volatile today than last year or the year before. Thanks to rising volatility, utilities and their customers have traded sides on the issue of which party should have access to the market or be protected from it with long-term purchase/sale contracts. A utility slow to embrace and use a technology developed to clear away perceptions with valuable financial metrics will quickly lose its way in this new world of competitive energy markets.

Spotting the reluctant utility can be as easy as eavesdropping on internal conversations. See if any of these comments seem familiar:

- The sky hasn't fallen for us!
- Only those with a few rogue traders at the phone can get themselves in trouble!.
- *"Hey! We know our people and, after all, they're all good folks, not about to kill the golden goose."* (That is, we have good people and they wouldn't let us go down the tubes).
- Does anyone really know what is at risk here anyway?
- The benefits do not surpass costs of setting up a risk management program. We can't afford it.
- If you use the term "derivative" in front of a board of directors or a City Council, you're dead meat! Don't go there!
- This is just another consultant gimmick to fully employ themselves…again!
- I don't need finance type guys sticking their noses in MY operation! I know the market and their forecasts are always wrong.
- Heck, give me an accurate price forecast and anybody can do this stuff. Since nobody can, who are we fooling when we try to do this stuff?
- We're too small, just victims of the market.
- We have long-term contracts that protect us from the market. So why would we need a risk management program to protect us against the market?
- I can't beat the market anyway, so as long as I'm buying and selling at market, what's the problem?

If any of these attitudes and ideas don't seem a little unnerving, then there may be more than reluctance at work.

There's Hope for the Reluctant

"Kick starting" energy risk management in a reluctant environment will require a clear strategy and sound plan that deals with misconceptions, misinformation, fear, and cultural biases, but there is hope.

Luckily, the technology of energy risk management is evolving and maturing as the wholesale power market matures. The body of energy risk management expertise, references, and history is growing and is easily acquired. So, besides giving a pep talk and assuming there are resources and reasons, how best to kick start the reluctant utility? Assess your current condition by working through the following checklist:

- Can you answer in one sentence: What is at risk?
- Can you answer in one sentence: How do you limit risk?
- Ever hear of the risk/return trade-off curve?
- Have you assessed your tolerance for risk?
- Do you have a credit policy (limits on trading partners and traders)?
- How often do you mark-to-market and report your buy/sell portfolio?
- How often do you calculate Value at Risk of your buy/sell portfolio?
- How does management oversee/report on trading activities?
- What does management report and to whom?

Recommendations

- Take action immediately.
- Assess and acknowledge your current condition, including an initial articulation of your company's tolerance for risk.
- Take a leadership role and stop the buck.
- Establish a strategy/game plan for measuring risk, assessing your current risk position, and developing the action plan to do something about it.
- Decide upon and calculate a few metrics that get the ball rolling.
- At a minimum, start with basic pieces (credit limits/basic risk stuff).
- Develop worst case scenarios and reassess your company's risk tolerance profile.
- Find a way to routinely report and communicate.
- Don't give up.

Conclusion

Solutions don't have to be grand or elegant programs staffed by hundreds. Common sense is worth more than you think. Communication is worth even more. It is the key and the goal for all effective managers. But, you really do need to know what is at risk. And the only way to know for certain is to measure it. Just like in other parts of your organization, what gets measured, gets done, and usually gets done well. Continue to seek the truth about what is at risk and you will improve.

Finally, consider the idea that scare tactics won't work if you need support within the organization. Keep these horror stories about failures to manage risk to yourself and they'll keep you on track and motivated. Don't assume complexity is necessarily a good thing, especially within the management ranks. Keep it simple! (Does my boss really need to know about constant tenors?) Complexity may be worse than a scare tactic when it comes to glazing over one's eyes. Remember, at one time everything seemed more complex than it does today. When begun right, energy risk management just needs a not-so-reluctant champion (manager) and a little time.

Could this manager be you?

Ted Coates has more than 25 years experience in the electric utility industry, with senior management responsibilities for power production, maintenance, operations, planning, and power marketing. He has an exciting record of innovation that includes developing successful programs for integrated resource planning, decision and scenario analysis, reliability centered maintenance, and strategic capital asset replacement before they became mainstream. He recently retired after 24 years with Seattle City Light to pursue his passion for developing new technologies to support strategic planning, analysis, and power marketing as a consultant to the power industry. Ted was educated in chemical engineering and economics at the University of Washington and the school of real life. He can be reached at tccoates@prodigy.net.

Express Your "Risk-Return Strategy"

Risk and return. Unless you've found the perfect arbitrage, you can't have one without the other. The manager must be able to express the level of risk-adjusted profit and loss (P&L) that the company seeks; more to the point, the manager must be able to get this appetite for risk-vs.-return from the board—or recommend it to them. Without a risk-return strategy, the manager would be like the airline executive allowing the flight crew to fly wherever (or whatever) they want. (See Chapters 3 and 4 for more details.)

Line Up Your Political Sponsor

The words "risk management" or "derivatives" can suggest hocus pocus with images of rogue traders in the mist. The "D" word (derivatives) can raise fear in a board member's heart. Traders can hate risk managers for limiting their flexibility and enforcing accountability; upper managers can fear risk because they don't understand it. Like any other business unit, the manager sitting between the board and the desk must line up political support. "Derivatives is a people business," I once heard said. "People" means politics and the manager best not go it alone.

Political support can come from anyone in the executive suite. In addition, identify a flag bearer at board level, someone who will fully comprehend the RMPP. Wealthy individuals with their own portfolios (of equities, futures, and even options) qualify as good candidates. Remember, the worst time to be explaining "gamma" (See Chapter 9) is during a crisis when the board is looking for answers. (See Chapter 3 for more details.)

Hire a Complete Roster, Not Just Quarterbacks

Deregulation opens up new markets and the manager needs a full staff. A great trader plays the role of a football quarterback, but a good

The following books represent "must haves" on your office bookshelf. Even if you don't read them, these titles guarantee to impress visitors and job applicants alike.	
Bernstein, Peter, *Against the Gods: The Remarkable Story of Risk*, John Wiley & Sons, 1996.	The perfect holiday present for *your* manager. Fun-to-read introduction to how humans feel about risk. No equations! An audio version is even available.
Hull, John C., *Options, Futures, and Other Derivative Securities*, Prentice-Hall, Inc., Englewood Cliffs, NJ, 1993.	The Blue Book. The Basic Text. A well-written text for those wanting to understand derivatives theory by looking under the hood.
Jarrow, Robert and Turnbull, Stuart, *Derivative Securities*, South-Western College Publishing, 1996.	Written for MBA students, this encyclopedia of futures and options is a great reference for the generalist.
Pilipovic, Dragana, *Energy Risk: Valuing and Managing Energy Derivatives*, McGraw-Hill, 1998.	My personal favorite and a very successful book by my lovely wife Dragana! This book details how energy markets differ from money markets and provides new tools to handle these differences.
Wilmott, Paul, *Derivatives: The Theory and Practice of Financial Engineering*, John Wiley & Sons, 1998.	A comprehensive reference for generalists wanting to become specialists.

Table 1-2: The Manager's Bookshelf

coach (the manager) must also develop the complete team. The manager should blend skills (risk, marketing, engineering) as well as personalities. Traders with "Type A" personalities play an important role, but should not be allowed to bully risk managers or analysts who have "Type B" personalities. (See Chapter 5 for more details.)

Brush Up on Risk Basics

The manager may not be a risk manager but he/she should understand the basics of risk. This book attempts to introduce these basics. (If you are in a hurry, try reading the "Five- Minute Manager" in Chapter 6.) In addition, the manager should develop a personal library of books; Table 1-2 recommends the *Manager's Bookshelf* of must-have texts. The manager need not read all these books cover-to-cover; just keep them nearby for specific questions. (If nothing else, the book titles should impress visitors.) In addition, subscribe to as many risk magazines and newsletters as possible. The annual budget should be about $1,000 in subscriptions, but the insights can provide hundreds of thousands of dollars in risk protection. (See Chapter 6 for more details; more advanced information is provided in Chapters 8-10. Also see the bibliography and endnotes throughout the book for more references.)

Establish Risk Limits

Risk limits put the teeth into the RMPP. Like speed limits, risk limits provide objective measures against which to monitor employee behavior and evaluate potential deals. Setting risk limits can be very difficult, and utterly dependent on first stating one's risk-return strategy and then being able to quantify the boundaries in which that strategy is pursued. But hey! Who said business is easy? (See Chapters 7 and 9 for more details.)

Budget to Achieve Your Objectives

As part of political sponsorship, the manager should fight for the budgets required to achieve the company's risk-return strategy. The manager needs money for both people and technology. Hedging costs money, both directly for premiums and indirectly for opportunity costs. (See Chapter 10 for more details.) Our power trading markets started only a few years ago, and experienced veterans are few and very expensive. Training from within offers an excellent alternative, but the cost of education fees (and providing the time to learn) represents a very real budget and operating concern. The cost of technology can also be significant but the manager must always remember that one gets what one pays for (See Chapter 11). Finally, budgeting includes planning for profit and loss; if the firm wants to hedge against risk, the board must accept lower expected profits.

Network, Network, Network

Finally, the power executive must network to keep abreast with new ideas and avoid becoming overwhelmed by the magnitude and number of energy risk issues. We are all new to this market; it is natural for a manager to assume that no one else has dealt with the same problems and thus there exist no available solutions outside the company. The risk becomes that the manager believes that he/she must invent a new "wheel" to solve it when the solution might already be available. Of course, trade shows and seminars cost time and money. But isolation carries a very real cost. A utility committed to risk management will be committed to its managers and will be motivated to learn from market leaders.

ORGANIZATION OF THIS BOOK

Managing Energy Risk: A Nontechnical Guide to Markets and Trading is organized into four general sets of chapters. Chapters 1-5 cover high-level managerial issues, Chapters 6-11 go into greater details about the mechanics and principles of risk management, Chapter 12 discusses issues that will face the manager in the future, and the appendices provide greater details on the RMPP as well as a glossary.

The following is a synopsis of these remaining chapters:

Chapter 2: The Bull, the Bear and the Spark Spread

Chapter 2 discusses what constitutes a market and how the traditions of the American power industry have fostered the growth of effective energy markets. The chapter also endorses concepts such as "marking-to-market" and valuing physical assets as options as examples of the new kinds of thinking required to compete after deregulation.

Chapter 3: The Living Documents: Your Risk Management Policies and Procedures

Chapter 3 argues for the manager to use the RMPP document as a dynamic tool in the management of the trading and risk desk. Issues include the differences between Policies and Procedures documents, enforcement, and the *Five Questions the Board Should Ask (and Get Answers To)*.

Chapter 4: Starting with Your Risk-Return Strategy

Chapter 4 offers four types of "Risk-Return Strategies" that an energy trading organization could pursue to achieve their profit objectives. The trading strategies include that of Treasury, Speculation, Arbitrage, and Market Maker. The chapter concludes with how strategic conflicts can help explain the market horror stories of Orange County, CA, and Federal Energy Sales.

Chapter 5: The Risk Roster: Personalities and Specialties

Chapter 5 highlights the major positions that must be managed on the manager's risk team, including upper management, traders, risk managers, analysts, engineers, marketers, and support people. The chapter also introduces the "Concentric Circles" model for an organization that puts assets at the core of the trading, risk, and marketing operations.

Chapter 6: Energy Risk Boot Camp: "Must Know" Concepts for Managers and Directors

Chapter 6 covers the basics that every energy professional should understand about risk, starting with "The Five Minute Risk Manager" (which can be read literally in five minutes). Placed within the context of the *Price-Risk Pyramid*, the building blocks of forward prices, volatilities, correlations, options, and risk measurements are introduced.

Chapter 7: The Deal Process: From the Desk to Delivery

Chapter 7 tracks transaction flow from deal origination through delivery and payment, to give the manager a bird's eye view of the process. The chapter also notes where the RMPP can take effect.

Chapter 8: Portfolio Analysis: *What Have We Got? and What Do We Want?*

Chapter 8 introduces the full hedging cycle (with continuing discussions in Chapters 9 and 10) and its implications for the RMPP. The chapter explores how "payoff diagrams" allow us to determine today's value of positions and portfolios.

Chapter 9: The Essence of Risk: *How Might Our Portfolio Change?*

Chapter 9 surveys the risks within a power portfolio and how they can be measured and graphed for the benefit of managerial oversight. Special attention is given to how positions will change during price spikes. The chapter ends with discussion on how the manager can determine and set risk limits.

Chapter 10: Hedging: Navigating Toward Our Portfolio Objectives

Chapter 10 demonstrates how hedge trading alters the risk topography of a portfolio in order to conform to the company's objectives. Several case studies follow the full hedging cycle, using dynamic payoff diagrams.

Chapter 11: Critical Path IT Issues

Chapter 11 covers the inescapable issues involving computers and information technology (IT.) Issues include identifying your company's system needs and matching them with potential staffing and vendor strategies.

Chapter 12: Looking Forward: Management Issues in Risky Markets

Chapter 12 concludes *Managing Energy Risk: A Nontechnical Guide to Markets and Trading* much as the book began—with a "Checklist of Things to Do." This checklist covers the next generation of problems and issues that the power executive will face in the coming years.

Appendix: Items to Consider for Trading and Derivatives Policies, Guidelines, Controls, and Internal Procedures by Andrea S. Kramer, McDermott, Will & Emery

A leading expert in the field, Ms. Kramer outlines key issues for managers to consider when designing a RMPP that fits their corporate needs.

In addition, a bibliography and glossary appear at the end of the book.

Special Symbols

Several special symbols will highlight special topics within the book:

Java Moment. The "Java Moment" symbol marks a technically challenging concept. The novice reader might want to get a fresh cup of java (coffee, not programming language) because the topic deserves comprehension even by

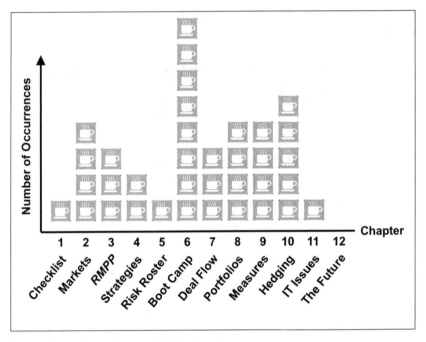

Figure 1-1: "Java Moments" By Chapter

a generalist manager. Spending time to understand risk represents a very real cost of deregulation, but hopefully the manager's time investment will yield significant future returns in terms of profits increased, disasters avoided, or efficiency enhanced. As Figure 1-1 depicts, "Java Moments" remain scarce in the early chapters and appear more often in the second half of the book.

| Marking-to-Market Concept |
| Markets Can and Do Change |

Marking-to-Market Concept. The theme of market-driven thinking percolates throughout the book. A "Marking-to-Market" concept box appears to help reinforce the application of this mindset. See Chapter 2 for a table summarizing these concepts.

RMPP Concept. If "marking-to-market" defines the spirit of this book, then helping to design (and implement) the *Risk Management Policies and Procedures* (RMPP) is a key practical objective of the book. The "RMPP Concept" icon signals a comment on this practical, hands-on task that typically falls within the purview of a higher-level manager.

These icons are offered for two purposes: First, to alert the reader to important concepts. Second, to help the busy executive skim the book or highlight specific sections. With luck, this book will become a reference for the broad and fascinating world of energy risk management.

ENDNOTES

[1] I first presented a version of this checklist at the PowerMart tradeshow in October 1999.

chapter 2

THE BULL, THE BEAR, AND THE SPARK SPREAD

TALE OF THREE STATUES

A statue of a large bull stands in New York's Wall Street neighborhood. In downtown Columbus, Ohio, the corporate headquarters of powerhouse AEP features an even larger monument—this one stylized from two huge, historic turbines.[1] As a corporation, Enron fits somewhere between these extremes of money and megawatts, two types of assets kept apart by regulation since the days of Thomas Edison. Fittingly, an abstract sculpture[2] sits in front of Enron's tower in Houston.

Enron's sculpture best represents the confusion of many power executives as they first encounter new market dynamics during the course of deregulation. Unbridled price competition may at first look appear amorphous, even frightening. But markets do have structure; prices do tend to follow some sort of understandable behavior; complex contracts can be digested in terms of simpler building blocks.

Like a tour guide, this chapter attempts to interpret power markets and their behavior in a deregulated market. In this chapter, I attempt to introduce the environment in which energy risk management is taking root in the world of electric utilities. I will paint in very broad strokes a general picture to support learning about risk management in a market-driven context. Jeffrey Roark of Southern Energy (who also wrote this book's foreward) provided invaluable historical insight, so much that I have decided to include many of these concepts in the text. (Any errors, however, are mine alone.) I will make the case that power markets can be considered true markets for two reasons: because deregulation promotes the kinds of price flexibility required by efficient markets and because even traditional, regulated power companies do bring nascent market skills that facilitate the industry's next stage of evolution. I will then switch from my pro-industry cheerleader approach (*We can do it, yes we can, if banks can do it, anybody can!*) to a schoolmarm mode (*You should do this, you should do that.*) Finally, I conclude this chapter with a case study on how market principles can be applied to a traditional power industry problem—the valuation and optimization of generation assets.

WHAT MAKES AN EFFICIENT MARKET?

In the context of trading and risk management, a market describes something containing enough participants—both buyers and sellers—to support meaningful activity (typically measured by liquidity or the volume of contracts being traded) of a particular asset. Is there an economist in the house? This section of the book does not portend to replace John Keynes or other market thinkers. Rather, this section on markets attempts to highlight the primary questions and most common concerns that I have encountered in the power industry over the past five years. Assets can be held in your hands (wheat, soybeans), traditional legal documents (stocks, bonds), or at-first esoteric constructs (SO_2 emission allowances, weather derivatives.) The role of the market is to allow price discovery by standardizing the defini-tion of what the asset is while the traders answer the remaining question of what the asset is worth. The degree to which the market achieves all of these objectives suggests the degree of efficiency of that market and its structure. (See Table 2-1.) In an efficient market, prices would "accurate-ly reflect relevant information."[3]

As in many other markets, electricity and other energy traders stan-dardize their markets as unique combinations of several categories.

Asset

An asset can be a deliverable, physical commodity (power, natural gas, crude oil, or some other commodity), or a paper contract that derives its value from such commodities without actual delivery. (This recalls the source of the word "derivatives"—an asset that "derives" its value from some other asset or assets). I use this word "asset" very generally in this book. In an economics textbook, one would expect clear delineation between such words as "commodity," "capital asset," "derivatives," etc.

The fact is, in reality, such delineations begin to blur; physical com-modities and generation assets begin to be valued as interchangeable with financial derivatives. It is exactly this kind of flexible viewpoint that I am trying to communicate in this book. The contracts can be relatively sim-ple or fall in the complex category of *structured products* such as the famous "spark spread" option, which derives its value from the heat-exchange rate between natural gas and electricity. In addition, physical generation plants or transmission lines can also be considered assets.

In terms of structure, the "assets" sit at the market's center (as seen in Figure 2-1). Different companies using and trading the asset revolve around the core. Some players have too much of the asset ("long") and primarily want to sell, others need it ("short") and want to buy. Still oth-ers are willing to buy or sell—some due to unexpected need or some due to speculative desires, buying or selling, whatever might be profitable. If the asset is risky—or becomes risky—the market structure will evolve to provide risk management tools. Figure 2-1 offers a simplified model for

Asset	The well-defined unit of value that is either delivered (such as a commodity or stock certificate) or represented by derivative contract.
Region	The geographic point or area relative to which the asset is valued. May be physically or financially settled. Could be defined as the spread between two regions (also known as *basis*.)
Standardized Contracts	Standardized contractual terms, such as for "on-peak" versus "off-peak" delivery in power markets. This includes both spot contracts (for immediate or next-day delivery) and forward contracts (for delivery at future time.)
Forward Contracts	The presence of standardized contracts available for multiple periods going forward in time. Can be for firm delivery (futures, forwards, and swaps), optional delivery (options), and/or variable volume (swing option) contracts.
Liquidity and Price Discovery	Adequate volume of standardized contracts being traded. Directly correlated with price discovery—the more, the better. Both sides of market—buyers and sellers—must be well represented and diversified to have good price discovery.
Central "Meeting Place"	The availability of a place or communication channel where market players know they can find pricing information and trading partners.

Table 2-1: What Makes an Efficient Market?

market structure, however, because the players themselves possess the assets. Figure 2-2 offers a more dynamic model in which certain players own assets and perform "bilateral" trading among themselves. An efficient market will contain a centralized exchange in which players can effectively trade without the risk or inefficiency of bilateral trading.

Consider the case of banking, where cash represents the central asset that institutions lend and borrow. Prior to the inflation of the 1970s, the cash in the vaults carried relatively low risk compared to the counterparty risk of borrowers. But when inflation started to corrode vault value, the money markets responded with risk management practices. In essence, the derivatives market started as a "defensive" or "asset protection" activity; only later did players come on the scene to play a speculative role of buying and selling risk.

We currently see a parallel evolution in the world of power—only here we see electricity replacing the bank's cash as the central asset. Power may not be stored in a vault as could cash or gold. (As throughout the book, I use the phrase electricity in a broad stroke to encompass the actual megawatts, the generation assets, the transmission lines, the financially-settled paper contracts, etc.) Otherwise, the parallels are intriguing: both banking and power were considered mature industries that suddenly faced new price risk, potential asset devaluation, and challenges to managerial leadership. The causes and dynamics of devaluation differ by market. Jeff Roark of Southern Energy put it this way: The banks' assets were cash, the thing traded. The power companies' assets threatened with devaluation were power plants, the assets used for the energy conversion and delivery service. The energy itself was no less valuable, but the assets used to convert it were. There were only two main reasons: a shift in generation technology cost, and a change from declining book-value pricing [steeply declining in real terms] to economic pricing [flat or mildly declining in real terms].

With all of its great strides toward market efficiency, perhaps the greatest threat to the efficiency of power markets is the lack of speculators who will buy and sell risky positions; in money markets, speculators require "deep pockets" or plenty of cash to ride out the inevitable losses in the pursuit of profit. In power, with the focus on the "juice," financial settlement is simply not always adequate—the true speculator must be able to deliver megawatts. This means the speculator's deep pockets must include cash, generator assets, transmission rights, and perhaps most importantly, experienced power people. Ironically, traditional utilities potentially best match this profile! Time will only tell how this evolution will complete itself.

Region

Due to obvious issues like transmission constraints, an asset's value will be a function of geographic location, delivery point, or similar regional definition. Geographic variation in value (also known as *basis* or *basis risk*) is typically a function of storability, portability,

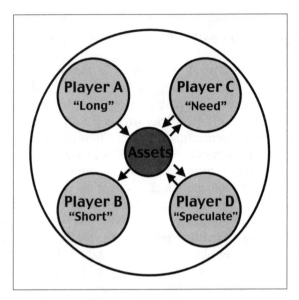

Fig. 2-1: What Makes an Efficient Market?

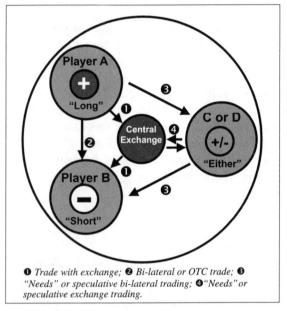

❶ Trade with exchange; ❷ Bi-lateral or OTC trade; ❸ "Needs" or speculative bi-lateral trading; ❹"Needs" or speculative exchange trading.

Fig. 2-2: Dynamic Structure of a Market

THE BULL, THE BEAR,
AND THE SPARK SPREAD

quality or differences in location of sourcing and delivery. Considering extremes, power jumps up as the classic "un-storable" commodity whereas a dollar is worth the same "from redwood forests to the Gulf Stream waters." But even currency has regional variation, as evidenced by the foreign exchange markets.

Standardized Contracts

Contract terms provide the specifics of the asset being traded. Power markets, for example, distinguish between "on-peak" and "off-peak" contracts. In trading parlance, the "on-peak" contract covers 16 peak hours during the business day (typically between 7 a.m. and 11 p.m., depending on the particular market.) The Monday-through-Friday contract is known as the "5x16" market, whereas the Monday-through-Saturday market, common in the western U.S. markets, is referred to as the "6x16" market. Likewise, the "off-peak" can be referred to as the "5x8, 2x24" market. The around-the-clock or "flat" contract is then "7x24"; one trader recently referred to the "8760" market— a phrase that comes from multiplying 24 hourly periods per day by the 365-day year! The contractual terms can be very detailed, but standardizing them is at the heart of efficient markets. (We will discuss these in greater detail in Chapter 7: *The Deal Process: From Desk to Delivery.*)

Forward Strips

A forward strip is a series of equivalent standardized contracts that differ only in terms of the period of forward delivery that they cover. While not all markets require tradable forward markets, forward markets (including options) are essential to commodities that are not easily storable and for players who want to hedge their future profit-loss scenarios.

Liquidity

As measured by quantity, liquidity is the relative number of units being traded of an asset in a particular market. A measure of quality, high liquidity is considered good, whereas illiquidity is not. Consider the case of selling your 1974 Chevrolet Vega Kammback station wagon. You park it in the driveway with a "For Sale, $500" sign on the dashboard. This is classic illiquidity, due to low traffic of prospective buyers and low volume of other Vegas being bought and sold. Later, you discover a "Used Vega Bonanza" event at the local fairgrounds where you join hundreds of other Vega sellers and prospective buyers. Now that's a market! (To see a photo of an actual Kammback wagon, see www.stationwagon.com/gallery/1974_Chevy_Vega.html.) High liquidity

 comes from large numbers of contracts being traded; as liquidity increases, the margin shrinks between the *bid price* and the *ask price* (known as the *bid-ask spread*.) Liquidity is also a function of contract evolution. Liquid standardized contracts are generally detailed enough to capture the majority of specific buyer/seller needs, while being general enough to appeal to a large number of market participants. During its early stages, young markets can be diluted by too many different types of contracts competing to become the standard, leaving the market fractionalized without common ground.

Price Discovery

Price discovery is the process of ascertaining the price of a particular asset. While the phrase comes from money markets, the concept of "price discovery" maintains its currency in commodity markets. If you are driving your car, and you pull up to an intersection with a different gas station on each corner, that's a case of pretty good "price discovery."

The quality of such price discovery is correlated with liquidity as well as the number of players in the market. There's safety in numbers because no single player can easily move the market. Finally, an aspect of price discovery involves the diversity of players. No single player should be able to exert "undue market influence." Market efficiency depends in part on a blend of buyers (who are *short* or want to buy the asset) and sellers (who are *long* or want to sell the asset.)

In terms of risk, this buyer/seller exchange allows one player to assume the risk of another—for a price. This is the speculator's role and should be respected as such, lubricating the market by allowing companies to free themselves of unwanted risk. In this sense, we should remember to not equate the word "speculator" with a negative image. Speculators are part of the risk management industry. As Southern Energy's Jeffrey Roark suggests: "The buyer of risk can follow different strategies: a) hold it in the hopes of profit; b) diversifying the risk within a portfolio; or c) otherwise managing the risk better than the one he/she bought it from. The whole point is that the various types of risk would end up in the hands of those best able to manage them, either through diversity brought about by the market reach of the trader, or by other physical or managerial means."

Price discovery depends upon finding an aggregate balance of supply and demand. An individual company's preferences may not necessarily correspond with the aggregate market. This issue is at the heart of a set of very common questions: *If power prices have such a strong tendency to spike, why would I ever want to sell my generation through a forward contract? Why wouldn't I hold onto the power and take advantage of the spot market?* If indeed you believe that markets are efficient, these forward prices will embed all potential price spike information.

However, if your company believes that markets are inefficient, the firm's trading strategy ought to take advantage of any perceived under- or over-valuations in the forward price market. The ultimate answer is a function of your business strategy. If your company's profit strategy is based on spot price trading, then don't sell forward. In fact, your company then believes that the market is undervaluing the forward contracts and is willing to take the "naked" price risks. If your company, on the other hand, wants to forego large potential profits in order to avoid large potential losses, it will lock in lower profits through hedging; then selling forward is appropriate.

Central "Meeting" Place

Finally, in an efficient market, the players will know "where to go" to find pricing information and trading partners. Trading exchanges like NYMEX represent the traditional face-to-face meeting place. The rise of communication technology allows more virtual meeting places, with brokers supporting over-the counter (OTC) markets by phone and fax. The advent of the Internet brings the e-commerce solutions of web-based brokerage and on-line trading services. Power pools and independent system operators (ISO) represent a special case of central trading platforms. The design of these platforms vary across the world; their relevance to increasing price discovery and liquidity will be a direct function of how much market issues influence their design. Perhaps the biggest issues to consider will be the impact of "auction" style pricing mechanisms and the imposition of market price caps. Auctions tend not to demonstrate the price behavior of open markets described in this book. In a mark-to-market environment, the price tends to reflect the average of the aggregated market's bid-ask spread; auction prices, on the other hand, tend to be skewed toward the extreme of the bidding process. Likewise, market caps tend to prevent the marketplace from seeing all the possible price outcomes. When managing price risk in such price-constrained situations, the manager is advised to adjust the assumptions, models, and procedures in his/her *Risk Management Policies and Procedures* (RMPP) accordingly.

GUEST ESSAY

Why Power is Different

by Donald Winslow, Enterprise Risk Manager
Pinnacle West Capital Corporation

Despite suggestions that electricity price risk is analogous to other commodity markets, power markets have several unique characteristics that require modifications to the conventional risk management paradigms. These differences arise from both the physics and politics of electricity. Three of these differences are the following:

- The value of power is highly dependent on time and location.
- The statistical properties of power prices are much different from other storable commodities.
- Unlike purely financial institutions, utilities must manage volumetric risk, i.e. large swings in the demand and supply of their product.

The Unique Character of Power Markets

Perhaps the most important economic characteristic of electricity is its inability to be stored easily. Thus, power is similar to airline tickets that are specific to a given time: the value of a ticket on a Friday afternoon may be much greater than on a Sunday morning. Unlike the market for more storable commodities in which storage dampens the peaks and fills the troughs in demand and supply, electricity is primarily balanced in real time in the spot market. Thus, in addition to a power market for energy, there is a value attributed to owning "capacity" in power markets which does not exist in other commodity markets.

The value of power is also specific to its location and transmission constraints. Crude oil is a global market because it can be transported efficiently, thus, there is a high correlation among crude oils delivered around the world. However, transmission of power is subject to physical and political constraints. In some cases, transmission between given markets does not exist; for example, virtually no power flows between the eastern and western interconnects in the United States. In other cases where transmission does exist, transmission losses can be cost prohibitive.

Finally, in some cases transmission capacity constraints may be reached only in peak seasons. For example, in the Western United States, as the North-South transmission lines reach their maximum capacity in the summer, the prices in the Northwest and the Southwest may diverge. In addition to the limitations due to physical constraints, the market rules vary significantly from one region to another. In the Northeast United States, for example, there are three regional pools, each with its own market structures and rules on transfers between pools.

This regional nature of power markets restricts the number of participants in any one market, causing the markets to be fragmented and remain illiquid. For example, forward quotes are typically only available for up to two years in most power markets. In contrast, natural gas and crude oil markets have forward markets that extend beyond 10 years. Thus, a utility attempting to purchase power for native load for the next five years may not be able to find a willing counterparty to sell it the power. Furthermore, if the volume the utility wishes to purchase is large relative to the volumes traded in the forward market, this single purchase itself could cause the market price to move significantly.

To further compound this problem, there is a lack of a robust market in financial risk management products with which to hedge physical and transmission risks. Although this market is starting to develop, the vast majority of the trades in power settle into physical delivery. This is in stark contrast to mature commodity markets where the volumes traded on the financial markets are on the order of 10 times the volumes actually physically delivered.

The Inelastic Behavior of Power Prices

Despite deregulation, very few consumers of electricity receive any specific price signals regarding the hourly value of power they are consuming. Thus, the demand for power is effectively inelastic, that is, the short-term demand for power may continue to increase despite the fact that the wholesale price may have increased dramatically. This situation is typical across the globe: deregulated markets in Australia, Chile, New Zealand, Canada, and the United States have all experienced price spikes in excess of $1,000/MWh.

As demand approaches or exceeds supply in power markets, the price regime changes. Instead of market prices reflecting the marginal cost of production, prices become related to the price required to convince a user to interrupt voluntarily. Whereas the cost of marginal production is typically less than $100/MWh, the price at which customers are willing to reduce consumption may range from $1,000 to $10,000/MWh depending on the user. This situation is similar to that of an overbooked flight. The airline can balance the supply and demand for seats by offering incentives such as travel vouchers in exchange for passengers choosing a later flight. As electricity providers begin to offer the same incentives, the elasticity of the power prices will increase.

This inelasticity in demand is one reason that electricity does not fit well into models originally developed for the financial markets. Whereas the classical Black-Scholes model assumes a "random walk," this is not appropriate in electricity. Electric price distributions are much more skewed than predicted by the lognormal distributions assumed in the Black-Scholes model. Electricity prices can jump from $50/MWh to $1,000/MWh and back to $50/MWh in a matter of days. A Black-Scholes-type model would not predict this type of behavior.

Not only do power prices have statistical properties different from other commodity prices, power markets require econometric models specific to each of their unique supply and demand characteristics. For example, in the Midwest, plant outages and transmission problems combined with warmer than normal temperatures to cause the prices to spike in the summer of 1998. These were relatively short-term phenomena that were followed quickly by prices of less than $50/MWh . In contrast, in markets such as the Western United States where hydroelectricity plays a significant role, a dry year can cause prices to remain on a relatively high plateau until the reservoirs are replenished. The statistical behaviors of prices in these two regions are dependent on their specific supply and demand profiles: power price models calibrated for one region should not be expected to apply to another region.

Volumetric Risk

At most financial trading companies, risk management typically emphasizes price and credit risks. Perhaps the biggest challenge unique to utility risk managers is "volumetric risk," having to cope with unexpected changes in volumes.

At the wholesale level, trading contracts typically refer to fixed volumes. In contrast, retail electricity consumers have an unlimited call on power at a fixed price. If the utility purchases only enough supply to cover its expected load but then higher loads are realized, the company will be forced to cover its shortfall in the market at the prevailing spot prices. These prices are likely to be driven higher by the fact that all the other utilities are experiencing high demand as well and will be purchasing to cover their needs also.

Plant outages provide another source of considerable supply uncertainty. Unlike airlines that can cancel flights because of equipment failure, utilities must go into the market to cover their plant outages. When this happens, prices can rise dramatically. Having an unscheduled outage of 500 MW in a tight market of 10,000 MW capacity may have a more dramatic effect on power prices than the loss of production from Kuwait and Iraq in the Gulf War had on oil prices. Thus, volumetric risk and the price risk are highly correlated in most power markets.

A final note on volume risk: despite its potential impact on a utility, volumetric risk is not usually included in most "Value-at-Risk" (VaR) measurements. These calculations typically focus on the effects of price changes for fixed volumes. The total risk of a utility is usually much greater than what is implied by considering price volatility alone. The manager should be alert to this potential omission and take measures to correct it, including using risk metrics that include volumetric risk.

Conclusion

The experience of other deregulated industries offers insights for risk managers within utilities. However, exclusive reliance on paradigms developed for other industries may give a false sense of confidence. Electricity has several fundamental physical and political characteristics that distinguish it from all other commodities. These traits give rise to unique risk management challenges for the industry.

Don Winslow is the Enterprise Risk Manager for Pinnacle West Capital Corporation, the parent company of Arizona Public Service, APS Energy Services, and Pinnacle West Energy Company. He has also worked in risk management positions at Cinergy, Enron, and Unocal. He received a BS in Physics from Georgia Tech and an MBA from Southern Methodist University. He can be contacted via donald.winslow@pinnaclewest.com.

IN PRAISE OF THE AMERICAN POWER TRADITION

A personal observation: very few people give much credit to American power companies when it comes to market issues! The general perception that utilities are backward, conservative, and bureaucratic is not entirely ill deserved; later sections of this book will chastise such unproductive attitudes, e.g., the "cost-plus-return" mindset. I believe, however, that a broader perspective will serve to back up the progressive members of the power industry and help their companies better face the brave new world of the marketplace.

So, to accentuate the positive, I can see open power markets benefiting significantly from the social contract between America and its power producers, the regulated solution which granted monopolies in return for the economic development benefits of electricity. These benefits include the following:

- First and foremost, we got the "juice"! No electricity, no Internet, etc.
- Second, while we Americans granted geographic monopolies to our generation companies, there were many such generation companies spread from sea to shining sea with no single dominant organization. Thus, our infrastructure featured *distributed generation*, with plants and wires in each major city and/or region. In the wake of various stages of deregulation, these geographically distinct entities would begin trading in each other's markets and emerge in the 1990s as the multiplicity of players required for liquidity.

Jeffrey Roark of Southern Energy provides this historical summary of deregulation: "In 1978, President Jimmy Carter started the ball rolling with Public Utility Regulatory Policies Act (PURPA), which created an automatic market for Independent Power Producers (IPPs) who qualified under the act. That act birthed the independent power movement, since it required utilities to buy from qualifying facilities at a fair price [avoided cost]. Only then did the market support anybody other than utilities building plants, and that fundamentally changed the construction market. Next, the construction market impinged on utilities' own expansion plans as regulators began demanding that they consider independent power producers as alternative suppliers. Initially this meant qualifying facilities (QF), because only they had the right to sell without being regulated as a utility. Then NEPA92 created the Exempt Wholesale Generator (EWG) entity—exempt from state regulation as a utility but able to sell in FERC-regulated wholesale markets. If the absence of market power could be demonstrated, then FERC allowed market-based rates. In addition to the EWG, NEPA created power marketers as legal entities in the wholesale market. NEPA92 also required open transmission access. Boom! In a few years you had many buyers and sellers of various types in the wholesale market, and a method for moving power across utilities. In summary, the electric utilities had a solid monopoly until PURPA, which cracked it open. NEPA92 broke the bottle forever, and let the genie go. Among other things, it was gracefully gradual."

This distribution of assets and ownership contrasts with England and much of continental Europe where generation was generally concentrated into one-per-country companies. Germany is a major exception to this rule. Most cities had its own local generator (and brewery). Thus, even following liberalization, European markets did not enjoy the same number of diversity of players, as did the American. Neither the United States nor Europe could have anticipated this impact, but it certainly can help to understand why our traded markets had a more dynamic liftoff.

- Third, U.S. power companies had a head start with trading (or at least sharing) power well before deregulation, with such experience setting the stage for today's markets. Roark describes the "traditional interface-oriented business structure" in which interconnected utilities would sell power based on cost-plus-return rather than a forward price. There were schedules for short-term firm, short-term non-firm, long-term firm, and long-term non-firm. There were also provisions for seasonal exchanges and inadvertent needs.

The U.S. power market also inherited a market-structure from central-ized generation points (such as the Palo Verde, AZ, yard with generation assets owned by multiple companies) and pre-defined regions. After the blackouts of 1965, the power industry created the "reliability regions[4]" of the North American Electric Reliability Council (NERC). These regions followed natural transmission costs, with sub-regions (called "coordinat-ing areas") around major generators. These regions formed nascent mar-kets in which utilities would trade electricity with each other both for prof-it and to fulfill their end of the social contract: reliability. Within this "brotherhood of reliability" —to coin a phrase— electric utilities formed early counterparty relationships. The NERC regions also help increase the "liquidity" of information about transmission and generation expansion plans. During early stages of deregulation, these NERC regions and coor-dinating areas provided convenient monikers for individual markets, giv-ing name to some of the first widely traded, over-the-counter North American power markets. Certainly NERC probably did not foresee the role that their regions would play in deregulated markets, but the industry can certainly be credited for taking advantage of a natural opportunity.

Natural gas markets followed a slightly different history, with markets defined less as regions and more as delivery points relative to a single, major hub. NYMEX's fabulously successful natural gas contracts specify delivery at the Henry Hub in Louisiana. Local gas markets are then quoted as basis spreads to this NYMEX point. Interestingly, when NYMEX first launched their power contracts, they defined them likewise as delivery points (namely California-Oregon Border—or COB—and Palo Verde, AZ).

- Finally, our current process of unwinding electricity's social con-tract for energy supply is no different from similar first-regulate-then-deregulate cycles of other industries. Power executives can take comfort by remembering the bumps experienced by banking, airline, telecommunications, and other deregulated industries.

ENGINEERS, THE MINUTEMEN OF DEREGULATION

One more positive legacy from the traditional American power industry is the "engineer with an MBA." There were many such professionals working for utilities when deregulation first came. Many individuals offered the kind of progressive vision and management to make the transition. Please note that I am painfully aware of many engineers who do not fit this romantic vision; I suspect that the engineers who thwarted market-driven principles were actually bad engineers too!

Engineers constantly face dynamic changes in attitudes and technology. My father Roman Wengler is a hydroelectric engineer. He tells stories of how the design industry originally resisted thin double curvature arch dams as an alternative to the traditional thick concrete gravity dams. Progressive engineers followed the vision of new solutions while others resisted them. The same story holds for new risk technologies; progressive engineers evaluate them fairly in order to determine their effectiveness. Bad engineers reject them out of hand.

Progressive engineers and similarly technical staff like schedulers, transmission planners, economists, etc. can be credited as the "Minutemen of Deregulation" for they were on the front-line when wholesale trading began and, thanks to their relatively conservative cultures, helped stabilize what could have been a far rougher ride into the modern age. (I would have clearly preferred saying "Minuteperson" but something would have been lost in the translation.) Unlike their European counterparts, American engineers tend to be very business-oriented, as symbolized by their strong representation in MBA programs[5]. Engineers are comfortable with trade-offs in technological decision-making; they use equations to build reality and are not intimidated by computers (or software experts.) It's a lot harder to sell vaporware to an engineer than it is to an English major.

My colleague Parks Mitchell of TVA attended an early seminar that SAVA offered on *Pricing OTC Energies* in 1996. He told the story of how he had taught himself options theory. When he was looking at the famous

Black-Scholes model, Parks said, "That's just heat-exchange theory. Next problem!"With many in upper management only vaguely aware of the implications of trading and price risk, the engineers became the *de facto* risk managers.

In a related matter, utility folks tend to have grown up in the same communities where they now work. For an engineer or other local professional, the power company represents one of the largest "high tech" opportunities. I have personally seen a sense of local commitment by many individuals in the power industry. This certainly makes for a pleasant work environment and may have inspired better stewardship of early trading and risk management efforts.

To temper this glowing view of engineers, it must be said that engineering should not be considered to be the badlands for socially dysfunctional people, where "nerds" can hide. Engineers—particularly those in business units with market price risk—should be expected to be open to new ideas. A lingering addiction to fundamental modeling to the exclusion of quantitative methods, first pioneered in finance, represents a common trend among the remaining engineers who do not accept risk technology. Perhaps my personal experiences were skewed by the fact that the "best and the brightest" engineers gravitated early to the growth and salary opportunities in the trading arena.

MARKING-TO-MARKET: THE REVOLUTIONARY CULTURE OF DEREGULATION

 "Marking-to-market" means the process of valuing a position or portfolio against market clearing-prices. Marking-to-market (MTM) includes looking to market intermediaries such as brokers and trading exchanges for aggregate price signals (see Table 2-2), and then using this information as a reference point.

An example of marking-to-market happens at futures exchanges; counterparties must maintain "margin accounts" as partial guarantees in case positions start losing value. Each day the positions are "marked-to-

Marking-to-Market Concept
Definition

market." Losers must pony up more cash while winners can withdraw from their margin accounts. With the market's role as third-party benchmark, the mark-to-market process helps companies oversee their traders. It is natural for traders to have educated opinions—even instincts— about market direction that differ from the mainstream market. If the company is willing to speculate on these trader opinions, then so be it. In either case, marking-to-market will help keep things honest and true to market reality. I doubt there is a single manager out there who wants to register a huge profit—based on what are trader's views—only to be followed by posting huge losses—based on marking-to-market reality.

Chapter	MTM Concept
2. The Bull, the Bear and the Spark Spread	Definition
	Alternative to mark-to-cost
5. The Risk Roster	Risk manager develops inputs
	Responding to client needs
6. Energy Risk Boot Camp	Market prices drive analysis
	Quantitative vs. fundamental Modeling
	Convergence to market inputs
	Option-implied volatilities
	Mark-to-model approximations
	Real prices and role of modeling
	Market-driven VaR
7. The Deal Process:	Price discovery phone calls
8: The Portfolio Process:	Treating assets as options
	Markets can and do change
9. Measuring Risk Measurement	Volatility measures risk
	Deltas can and do change
10: Hedging	The need for quality hedges
11: Critical Path Risk IT Issues	Market price signals to system

Table 2-2: Applications of Marking-to-Market

From the point of view of a utility manager worried about his/her trading operation, "marking-to-market" or MTM captures the truly revolutionary potential of deregulation. As a central concept, MTM is so central to this book that paragraphs applying the concept will be highlighted with a "Marking-to-Market Concept" flag (as we see in the next paragraph.)

Marking-to-Market Concept
Alternative to mark-to-cost

As a revolutionary concept, MTM can help expand the traditional utility of the traditional mind-set of "cost-plus-return" or "marking-to-cost." In effect, this perspective places the market at the core of all thinking and appears throughout the trading and risk management process. (Table 2-2 summarizes some of the MTM concepts that appear throughout this book and references the specific chapters.) In a way, the regulated power players performed mark-to-market, but only sequentially, through the following over-simplified rate case cycle:

- The regulator allows a reasonable rate of return.
- The utility calculates costs and multiplies by rate of return; submits original request.
- The regulator debates, alters, and approves rates.
- Some months later, somebody—whether it is the utility or the consumer—discovers that it is getting hurt by the rate structure. They appeal the rate case. Many utilities performed continuous analysis using revenue models, a form of managerial hygiene suggestive of "continuous hedging" or "continuous hedging analysis."
- Repeat.

In deregulated markets, this process happens far quicker—at least one would hope it does—with greater economic efficiency. To the degree that public safety and to a lesser degree reliability remains a political priority, certain regulations should remain in place. But when it comes to contract valuation, it should be marked-to-market!

RISK-ADJUSTED EXPECTATIONS OF CHANGE, NOT SINGLE POINT PREDICTIONS

Market prices for forward contracts (including both swaps and options) represent *risk-adjusted expectations* rather than *predictions* of what the spot price will actually be on the day of delivery. Forward prices are certainly dependent on the projected spot price, but we must also adjust our expectations for the risk of unforeseen changes in the marketplace. "Risk-adjustment" means taking the expected spot price, for example, and adding such market factors above and beyond as these:

- Cost of risk—an insurance premium, if you will, for contracting today instead of waiting for exposure to the spot market
- Cost of money—which is simply the market's lending rate
- Cost of carry—the cost of holding the asset between now and the delivery date
- Additional real-cost advantages of holding the commodity today rather than in the future, which have to do with the fact that the commodity is used for consumption. (These advantages, together with the cost of carry, are embedded within the concept of "convenience yield"–the net benefit of holding the commodity outside of financing costs.)

Financial modeling of market prices is commonly referred to as *quantitative modeling*. "Quants" use stochastic calculus and applied statistics to characterize market price behavior. Three such quants did such a good job with the famous Black-Scholes option equation that they earned the Nobel Prize in Economics in 1997[6]. In contrast, utility engineers under regulation developed a different tradition of models known as *fundamental modeling*. Fundamental methods do not model the prices directly but rather the market fundamentals in order to generate such prices. Also known as "structural modeling," fundamental models attempt to predict production units and/or marginal costs by modeling the fundamental factors which drive the physical power system. Again, here we see the contrast between risk-adjusted expectations and predictions. Deregulated utilities should keep their fundamental models to capture their cost behaviors, but also add quantitative models to explain market price behavior. (See Chapter 6 for more on this important topic.)

Markets can and do change. What are normally stable prices can suddenly swing wildly, as stock investors experienced in 1987 and more recently in the spring of 2000. Markets themselves can grow and die. Consider the historic Chicago Board of Trade (CBoT). (If you're ever in downtown Chicago, a visit to the CBoT's Visitor's Gallery at 141 W. Jackson is a guaranteed hit, especially at the close of the trading day.)

In 1999, two new power contracts started trading in the CBOT's old German Bund[7] pit. By 2000 the pit was again left fallow, as the once-promising power contracts withered away. Money markets can be equally fickle. The once-dominant 30-Year Treasury Bond is slowly being "replaced" in popularity by the 10-Year Treasury Bond[8]. CBoT officials are even considering switching the pits in which these contracts are traded.

We can find an excellent market drama in the over-the-counter (OTC) electricity market. The Pennsylvania-Jersey-Maryland (PJM) market started as a tight pool of generators operating in an area later codified as a NERC reliability region. In the 1990s this wide area gave root to an active OTC trading market. (Contributing factors included the relatively large numbers of generators on the supply side, dense populations, and large industrial end users providing attractive markets on the demand side, and the widespread drive toward deregulation on the political side.) PJM trading was liquid enough to support strips of futures and options extending 18 months to two years forward. Even NYMEX was beginning to seriously consider launching a contract for the market in the mid-1990s. Suddenly, transmission issues and the local desires of generators fractured the market into hundreds of sub-markets through a structure called Locational Marginal Pricing (LMP.) LMP effectively put an end to the original broad PJM-traded market, but set the stage for more effective trading in the future, including the PJM contract that the NYMEX did ultimately launch.

CASE STUDY: ASSETS AS OPTIONS

As the proverbial Bull and Bear of the marketplace shatter the crystalline calm of the power industry, the manager will do well to blend the positive legacies of the traditional "Main Street" with the risk-oriented, quantitative tools applied on "Wall Street." In fact, quantitative techniques can help solve long-standing engineering problems. Case in point are the valuation and optimization of physical generating assets[9].

The hot topic in power is "real options." Physical assets always carried "optionality value." With "real options," the idea is to value physical generating assets as their equivalent financial options or derivatives—and book them into an enterprise-wide risk management portfolio. "Assets as options" solves a major need and may well spark the interest of traditional utility managers to boot.

In the world of regulated electricity there was no price risk. Historically, utility managers simply justified their prices to regulators using a cost-plus framework. Any cost risks were passed on to the power users, leaving the spread between price and cost for the most part risk-less and positive. As a result, generators applied a business strategy of cost-minimization approach to plant running operations. But deregulation is forcing these same managers to move from "marking-to-cost" to "marking-to-market." These same managers must now be market-driven while remaining cost-conscious.

Based on the experience of the last several years of OTC trading, the wholesale side of the electricity markets can tell you that, while the valuation of traded electricity products remains a factor, the demand side brings many issues into the price equation. Cost-plus frameworks are no longer relevant in the price discovery process except as a possible lower bound benchmark. Similarly, valuing generation plants outside the market perspective leaves out the marked-to-market value of a plant. Ultimately, the marked-to-market plant valuation might cause non-efficient plants to be seen as unprofitable as the cost cannot simply be passed on to the user.

The same principles apply to retail contract valuation. The load of a 24-hour casino represents the "ideal load" that replicates a swap: it burns a steady number of MWh day and night, 365 days a year. On the other extreme, consider a retail contract with an aluminum plant. The smelters show a variable load volume and shock the local system when starting up. In this case, the retail position valuation should incorporate both market price volatility as well as the high load volatility.

Finally, the new (FASB) 133 Financial Accounting Standards Board standards may prove to be both a "stick" and "carrot" to motivate certain power companies to capture and value their generation assets as options. FASB 133 will most impact those companies that created trading desks to hedge their physical position. FASB 133 may force the utilities to articulate their assets as underlying positions that required such hedging. In other words, these companies will need to justify treating market products on their trading books as hedges (instead of investments) only if they can prove that they are indeed exactly that. This means that they must be proven to be offsets to their existing long electricity positions. And this, ultimately, brings us to the inclusion of utility's generation plants into the marked-to-market portfolio for valuation and risk reporting purposes.

ENDNOTES

[1] Untitled, George Greenmayer, 1983. AEP's dedication brochure provides the following description: "The two turbine rotors mounted on five granite piers...were integral parts of two pioneering generation units...The north side rotor in the AEP sculpture was taken from the turbine installed in 1957 as part of Unit 6 at the Philo Plant...This pioneering 120,000-kilowatt unit, while small in today's terms, was the first in the world to operate at a stream pressure above the 'supercritical' level." Thanks to AEP.

[2] Iron Laces, One, Louise Nevelson, 1980. Prior to installation at Enron's Allen Center location, the sculpture was exhibited in New York City's Central Park and at the

Storm King Art Center in Mountainville, New York. (Marzio, pp 3.)

[3] Jarrow and Turnbull, pp 670. For those really interested in "efficient market" theory, also see Hull (pp 191) who describes a "Markov process" as a "particular type of stochastic process where only the present value of a variable is relevant for predicting the future. The past history of the variable and the way in which the present has emerged from the past are irrelevant." Hull further goes on to explain how the theory fits with reality: "The Markov property of stock prices is consistent with the weak form of market efficiency... The very fact that there are many, many investors watching the stock market closely and trying to make a profit from it leads to a situation where a stock price at any given time impounds the information in past prices."

[4] "On November 9, 1965 a blackout left 30 million people across the Northeastern United States and Ontario, Canada without power. In an effort to prevent this type of blackout from ever happening again, electric utilities formed the North American Electric Reliability Council (NERC) in 1968 to promote the reliability of the electricity supply for North America." (Source: www.NERC.com.)

[5] At my alma mater, Northwestern University's Kellogg Graduate School of Management, one third of the new business students during 2000 held bachelor degrees in engineering or science. (Source: www.kellogg.nwu.edu.)

[6] Fisher Black, Robert Merton, and Myron Scholes received the 1997 Nobel Price in Economics "for a new method to determine the value of derivatives." (Source: http://almaz.com/nobel/nobel.html.)

[7] According to Joseph Poncer of the CBoT, the Bund contract traded at the Chicago Board of Trade between 5/9/97 and 12/17/97.

[8] Gunset, George and Barnhart, Bill, "Long bond now falling short: Former king of the pits is on road to obscurity," Chicago Tribune, May 21, 2000.

[9] Elements of this discussion first appeared in Dragana Pilipovic's and my article "Assets as Options" (Derivatives Strategy, December 1999.) We later expanded on the concepts in a seminar by the same name in November 1999 and September 2000.

chapter 3

THE RISK MANAGEMENT POLICIES AND PROCEDURES

THE LIVING DOCUMENTS

To the power executive, the trading floor can at first seem like a mutation between the Wild West and the bridge from *Star Trek*. (I have heard an incredible story of a trading manager throwing a phone as a motivational technique.) Traders hunker down at monitors, sometimes shouting into two phones at once. The Weather Channel flickers on multiple televisions. The hum indicates that something is very different on that floor of the traditionally regulated utility—the vanguard of deregulation.

RMPP And like a sheriff in the Wild West, the vice president (VP) in charge of trading risk management must apply various techniques to bring law and order. First, he/she must show leadership. Second, he/she must have the political backing of his/her superiors. Finally, he/she must have the law, otherwise known as the *Risk Management Policies and Procedures* (RMPP). The RMPP documents express the corporate vision as it relates to trading and risk management. These documents define the "thou shalts" and the "thou shalt nots" for traders, analysts, risk managers, and marketers. Sometimes the process of formulating these rules can be as important as the documents themselves. The RMPP offers a pro-active alternative to reactive "screech-mark" risk management—dramatically putting on the brakes in response to unexpected conditions.

The RMPP envisions the ultimate benchmarks, the rule of law. Its protective coat spreads wide, protecting the shareholders from inappropriate trade losses, shielding the VP from second-guessing from above and below in the organizational chart. Not least of all, a good RMPP gives direction to the trading desk. Considering the alternative—a weak RMPP – the risk includes the trading floor unwittingly (or consciously) setting corporate policy, from the bottom up.

Trading floors in the 1990s did tend to operate without formal RMPPs in place. Fortunately for much of the American power industry, as I suggested in Chapter 2, the engineers and local employees who had come up through the ranks of the utilities tended to be self-governing. With dramatic exceptions, the market players acted like consenting adults, thanks to a strong knowledge of power fundamentals and general culture of risk aversion.

Think of the RMPP as being like the Constitution of the United States. The Constitution is a living document, created through a negotiated process, offering both the letter and spirit of the law. Not static, the Constitution offers opportunity to be amended and a judiciary to interpret the rules in place. True, Constitutional law can be dry, even boring, but this parchment and ink serve as the bedrock of American society. So too does the RMPP process risk being bogged down by bureaucratic details and even political struggles. Within your company, certain individuals may benefit by obfuscating trading and risk management, while others may not want to risk displaying their own ignorance. The RMPP provides a powerful tool for distinguishing who is with the program or perhaps in conflict with the new ways of doing business.

I recently heard the RMPP characterized as a "cage that we keep traders in." For that particular company, the cage analogy was perhaps relevant; perhaps their strategy heavily depended on aggressive trading "tigers," who needed strong limits. But other companies might consider

Fig. 3-1: The U.S. Constitution offers a great analogy for Risk Management Policies and Procedures (RMPP) , which is a living document defining the rights and responsibilities of the trading community. (http://www.law.emory.edu/FEDERAL)

other analogies. For example, the RMPP could be designed as a NASCAR racetrack on which traders could seek to attain maximum speed and optimal performance under agreed-upon constraints. For those with more alpine tendencies, the RMPP could be the grand slalom course where trader flexibility and endurance would be measured. The basic concept here is that RMPPs should reflect the character of the company.

While RMPP issues appear throughout the book, this chapter attempts to put the process and document into a general context.[1] The topics to be covered include:

- Key assumptions about your Board and upper management
- The difference between policies and procedures
- General outlines
- Measurement means enforcement
- The five questions the Board should ask (and get answers to)
- Who should write the RMPP documents?

A wonderful resource is available in the Appendix: *Items to Consider for Trading and Derivatives Policies, Guidelines, Controls, and Internal Procedures* by Andrea S. Kramer, a partner at McDermott, Will & Emery in Chicago. A leading expert in the field, Ms. Kramer outlines key issues for managers to consider when designing a RMPP that fits their corporate needs.

Key Assumptions About Your Board and Upper Management

This book and chapter are written with three critical assumptions about your Board of Directors and upper management:

- Assumption 1: The company is capable of expressing its vision or wishes to figure out how to do so.
- Assumption 2: The company will enforce its RMPP once written.
- Assumption 3: Upper management will provide political cover for a risk manager who implements and lives by the RMPP.

Assumption 1

The company's leaders understand the company's primary business, how trading supports that business, which profits are desired and which risks are unacceptable, and are capable of expressing the company's vision. If these conditions are not present, at least, we assume that the company's leaders wish to achieve them. As suggested by the earlier discussion about "marking-to-market" (see Chapter 2), the principles of market behavior can be a powerful compass as utilities chart their way into deregulated waters.

This is not to say that every Director must read and understand Dragana Pilipovic's book *Energy Risk* and every other title on my recommended *Managers Bookshelf*. Instead, I am suggesting the following:

- At least one Director should be recognized as the "designated driver" for trading and risk management. This Director should understand the majority of the RMPP. (If someone with direct energy trading and risk experience is unavailable, good candidates include bankers or the independently wealthy. The rich tend to have portfolios and read the *Wall Street Journal*; one would hope they know about futures and options.)
- Next, the Board must be able to state its profit objectives. Does it expect the trading operation to beat the market, posting returns that outpace the Dow Jones Index? Or does the board expect the desk to play a loss-leader role, hedging away dramatic risks at the cost of profits? (See Chapter 4)
- My final suggestion is the most subversive: The "Gamma Criterion." As will be articulated in Chapter 9, every member of the Board must understand at least the concept of "gamma" and the risk concepts necessary to understand the concept. (Gamma is one of the risk sensitivity measures known as the "Greeks.")

Admittedly, I expect this proposal to fly like a lead zeppelin[2]. I've mentioned this idea to dozens of audiences and encountered the

groans of the cynical and the moans of the overworked. But I am
sorry! Does one expect the Board of a nuclear utility to have no
detailed knowledge of public safety operations? Do they simply
take the word of management that everything will be okay?
Looking at a different industry, do the Directors of an airline
ignore standards for pilots, equipment, and maintenance?
Deregulation brings radical changes—needing to actually understand energy risk is one of them.

Assumption 2

The company will enforce its RMPP once written. Such enforcement begins with understanding the RMPP. (See Assumption 1!)
Other factors include
- Drafting the RMPP for enforceability: The RMPP should be comprehensive without being cumbersome, realistic in its expectations, and meaningful in terms of how the company's operations
  actually occur.
- Funding execution: The Board must be willing to fund the personnel and systems necessary to fulfill its expectations. If the
  Board expects the VP to hire a Director of Trading with at least
  three-years of energy desk experience, the Board had better
  budget for a six-digit salary. Good trading and risk systems cost
  a great deal of money. Don't forget support: trading desks require
  information technology (IT) support that can be costly, and seem-
  ingly unimportant, but is in fact worth every penny in terms of
  workplace efficiency and crisis prevention.
- Punishing non-compliance: if the policy states that a trader must
  not do something, and the trader agrees to that policy and still
  violates its terms, then the punishment should be exacted. If a
  rogue trader is allowed to continue unabated, the responsibility
  for resulting losses jumps upstream to management.

GUEST ESSAY

Items To Consider for Energy Trading and Derivatives Policies

by Andrea S. Kramer*, Partner, McDermott, Will & Emery

I work with a wide range of energy trading companies at various stages in the development of their trading operations and derivatives activities. Some have multi-hundred page manuals, while others simply have short, high-level policies in place. Although they all have very different ways of approaching and handling their policies, procedures, and internal controls, no matter what stage of development they are at—and no matter what their approach is to their policies—there are general themes that must be addressed by all of them.

In this essay, I highlight some general policies that are of interest to all energy trading companies and derivatives users. For a more in-depth discussion, you can refer to the detailed outline that I prepared as the Appendix to this book.

In this essay, I identify the key objectives of risk management policies, which includes the need for involvement of—and buy-in—by the company's Board of Directors (the Board). I also discuss the need for a Risk Management Committee (RMC), a risk manager, and qualified traders.

Next, I discuss the need for adequate guidelines, measurement, and reporting of established risk exposures. Further, I address the importance of adequate legal review, accounting policies, and tax policies. And finally, I highlight the objectives of internal controls.

The high level objectives of a company's Board should be reflected in its risk management policies. Typical objectives include setting the company's overall direction with respect to the identification, measurement, monitoring, and control of risks from trading activities and derivatives use. And, the Board's objectives are then reflected in policies that are implemented by the company's senior and middle management.

Board Responsibilities

The Board should set out the company's risk management objectives. And the Board should periodically approve, at least annually, the policies adopted to reflect these objectives. To meet its obligations, the Board must understand the company's trading activities, derivatives use, and the attendant risks of trading and derivatives. In fact, the Board should ensure that the company's risk monitoring and risk management operations have the necessary authority and resources to accomplish the company's objectives.

To meet its obligations, the Board should address five key considerations. First, the Board should approve specific activities and designate authorized individuals. And if the Board limits permitted activities, the restriction should clearly state its application to specified products, markets, and activities. Second, the Board should identify and establish qualitative and quantitative limitations and guidelines to manage overall risk exposures. Third, the Board should approve the significant structural elements of the company's risk monitoring and management systems. Fourth, the Board should identify the scope and frequency of risk exposure reports. And fifth, the Board should authorize procedures to assure that there is an adequate review of trading and derivatives activities.

The Risk Management Committee

A critical component of any risk management program is the Risk Management Committee (RMC). It often establishes the risk management responsibilities and monitors all trading and risk management activities. It is typically the RMC's responsibility to assure that the company has the necessary management skills to manage its risks, reviewing risk management methods and evaluating the assumptions used to measure risk and limit exposures.

Often it is the RMC that proposes, at least on an annual basis, to the Board an acceptable level of risk exposure based on the company's business and financial strategies. And new products and markets typically go through a formal RMC review, which allows the RMC to develop appropriate policies and controls and to integrate the new products and markets into the risk management and measurement systems.

It is the RMC that regularly reviews all reports, policies, strategies, and compliance matters, allowing the RMC and senior management to evaluate the company's overall risk profile and risk exposures. Trading risks, profits, and losses are reported, often on a real-time basis but at least daily, to the managers who supervise—but do not themselves conduct—the trading activities.

The Risk Manager

In my experience, most energy companies appoint a Risk Manager to have hands-on responsibilities in managing risks. To be effective, the Risk Manager must have sufficient authority and stature in the company to provide an effective, independent assessment of risk exposures. The Risk Manager is typically a member of the RMC.

The Traders

A key component to the success of any energy trading program is the company's traders and trading support personnel. This means that trading employees should be properly trained, with the appropriate level of trading expertise for their responsibilities. The company should implement or provide access to training programs to assure that its traders understand the nature of the relevant markets and their responsibilities to the company. They must understand the company's risk management guidelines. And they must understand the management control procedures to document, record, and report all of their transactions.

Perhaps it goes without saying, but employees with trading authority must have a working knowledge of the trading markets. They must be familiar with all physical products and derivatives that might be used by the company (or for which they have trading authority). They must have a solid understanding of the company's specific risk exposures and hedging strategies.

Traders with discretionary trading authority need to clearly understand their trading limits and all restricted activities. Restricted activities often include a prohibition against disclosure of confidential or proprietary information; a prohibition against trading for the employee's own account in products traded by the company; noncompetition agreements;

and a prohibition against conflict of interest situations (including clearly specified limitations on incentives, gratuities, travel, and entertainment received from third parties).

To provide trading employees with guidance as to their trading activities, many companies I work with establish an Employee Code of Conduct. In the Appendix, I set out those topics often covered in an Employee Code of Conduct, including authorized transactions; prohibited activities; requirements to report violations; prohibitions against conflicts of interests; limitations on personal trading; requirements to report all transactions; and restrictions on disclosure of confidential information.

In addition, many companies I work with obtain written acknowledgements for their employees to demonstrate that the employees understand the company's policies and requirements. Employee acknowledgements are important for two reasons. First, the company may need to prove it has adequate controls in place if it wants to avoid penalties and sanctions for trader misconduct. And second, employees need to understand that if they breach company policies they will be disciplined, which can include a prohibition against trading, suspension from duties, and immediate discharge from employment. In these acknowledgements, employees frequently agree to the following:

- Obtain, read, and understand company's policies;
- Comply with the policies;
- Meet with senior management (or attended a training course or seminar) at which their responsibilities are discussed;
- Acknowledge that policy violations can constitute grounds for immediate termination of employment and criminal prosecution;
- Abide by limitations set on gratuities and travel and entertainment;
- Respect the confidential and proprietary nature of information used in the trading and risk management activities and to maintain this information as confidential and proprietary;
- Report any violation of company policies;
- Acknowledge that all conversations may be monitored, recorded, and transcribed and that all trades will be conducted on recorded lines;

- Trade only authorized products for the company's account, complying with all personal trading restrictions and limitations;
- Abide by any noncompetition agreements; and
- Assume the responsibility to maintain and update company policies in their files and records.

Risk Exposure Guidelines, Measurement, and Reporting

In implementing its risk management policies, a company should establish guidelines as to their overall risk exposure on physical and derivatives activities. These guidelines set the appropriate risk limits within which the company operates. The company can provide specific risk exposure limits or specific quantitative limits. The company's risk exposure guidelines should address the degree to which derivatives risk exposures should be aggregated (for purposes of risk monitoring and risk management) with the risk exposures arising from other trading activities. They typically identify the level of exposure, the maximum loss that can be incurred, and the amount of exposure that can be encountered in times of unusual market or financial conditions. These risk exposure guidelines are often measured on a value-at-risk basis (which quantifies the risk to earnings at a particular confidence level, that is, the maximum probable loss in normal market and operating conditions); stress testing (which attempts to capture unexpected stresses to the markets and operations); and the measurement of option sensitivities to market prices, rates, volatility, and time.

Legal Review

To protect itself, the company should provide for a legal review of its trading policies and procedures. Agreements should be reviewed, on a periodic basis, for changes in market practices and applicable laws. Transactions need to be evaluated to determine whether they are permissible under applicable laws and regulations. In addition, applicable bankruptcy or insolvency laws need to be considered because they can limit or alter contractual remedies. Key elements of a legal review should also include an evaluation of counterparty capacity and authority to enter into transactions. Procedures should be established to monitor and address the risk that transactions will be unenforceable if the documentation is inadequate; the counterparty lacks the requisite legal authority to enter into a transaction; or the counterparty is subject to other legal restrictions.

Accounting and Tax

It is important for the company to set out its accounting and tax policies to assure adequate compliance. In working with energy companies, I often find an enormous amount of effort is devoted to financial accounting compliance, without the same effort devoted to the tax rules. This is a mistake, because there can be enormous tax consequences if proper tax elections and identifications are not made.

Accounting policies should also address the appropriate financial accounting treatment for trading, hedging, and derivatives activities. They should require a periodic compliance review. Accounting policies should also address, for example, the appropriate procedures to determine realized and unrealized gain and loss; immediate recognition and deferral policies; and the reconciliation with general ledger and cash positions. The methodology should be defined for measuring value, market risk calculations, stress testing, reporting, procedures for exception and violations, and market risk management reporting. The company should establish systems and procedures to mark-to-market the value of its products, positions, and portfolios on a timely basis. The frequency of required mark-to-market calculations should be based on the volatility of the relevant market and the company's risk profile.

For statistical and simulation models, verification procedures should be established to compare model predictions against actual market performances. Any deficiencies in the company's models should be immediately identified and corrected.

To assure that transactions obtain the most favorable tax results, tax policies and controls need to be implemented. In addition, the appropriate tax treatment of various transactions needs to be verified and required identifications complied with. This means that all hedgers for tax purposes must comply with same day tax identification requirements and authorized tax accounting methods (to clearly reflect income). And further, "aggregate hedgers" must implement required tax aggregate hedge policy manuals and other documents required for U.S. tax purposes.

Internal Controls

Internal controls should be in line with the scope, size, and complexity of the company's authorized activities, as well as the nature and extent of its risks. An independent validation process should be in place for company-wide measuring and limiting risk. Internal controls should be in place to assure that there is an adequate separation of function and duties, so there is a complete separation between the company's trading operations and its trade capture and risk management operations. Trading positions should be valued without the input of trading personnel, with particular care given to valuing illiquid and long-dated contracts through independent sources.

To protect the audit trail and to control positions, deal input, edits, and audits should set out how trades can be amended—and by whom. Computer systems should have a lockout feature and audit function (using passwords) to limit access to deal and system data. Policies should set out how trades can be reversed and how exceptions and changes to open transactions must be reported and monitored. Adequate lockout functions can help assure that trade blotters and computer-tracking systems accurately reflect the company's transactions.

Operation policies should establish independent monitoring, providing appropriate checks and balances for all risk monitoring activities, which should be independent from those business and trading units that create the risks being monitored. These policies should establish the analytics to track position patterns and single day valuation. They should also track variations in patterns. And, further, they should confirm, on a regular basis, the valuation of illiquid and long-dated contracts and positions, including the reconciliation of cash and general ledger positions with the mark-to-market values. And finally, they should establish checks and balances to protect against irregularities or inconsistencies in risk measurement and to ensure that trading and derivative risks are uniformly and accurately identified and evaluated.

Ms. Kramer is a partner in the international law firm of McDermott, Will & Emery, resident in its Chicago office. She is the author of Financial Products: Taxation, Regulation, and Design *(Panel Publishers 3d ed. 2000). Ms. Kramer may be contacted via akramer@mwe.com.*

Assumption 3

Upper management will provide political cover for the VP in charge of trading and risk management, and the VP will provide political cover for lower level risk managers. Continuing the Wild West analogy offered earlier, the sheriff's authority must carry the implied threat of the cavalry coming to lend back up. The risk managers need the rule of law to do their jobs, to execute the corporate vision.

THE DIFFERENCE BETWEEN POLICIES AND PROCEDURES

 Table 3-1 suggests some differences between *policies* and *procedures*. While some companies legitimately write their RMPP as a single document, these differences justify creating two documents. The first difference alone would support this bifurcated approach: A "policy" expresses the highest level view, the kind of corporate strategy that should be defined by the shareholder's representatives. A "procedure" is how the lower levels of management and line-item staff are to execute the Board's policies. Other distinctions might prove useful.

Responsibility. The Board is responsible for drafting, approving, and monitoring the *Policy* document. For full Board participation, the issues expressed in the *Risk Management Policies* should be no more detailed or technical than the Board is willing to understand or for which to assume

Policies	Procedures
Highest levels: Strategy	Lower levels: Detail
Responsibility: Board	Responsibility: Risk Committee
Do's and don'ts	Processes and prevention
Limits	Methodologies and enforcement
Authority	Accountability and protection
Like the Constitution	Like the Legal Code

Table 3-1: Differences Between Policies and Procedures

responsibility. The *Procedures* represent the delegated portion of the equation. The Board would make the executive decision to delegate ownership of the *Procedures* to a Risk Management Committee (RMC) comprised of select Directors, upper management, and staff. In effect, the *Policies* state *What We Want* while the *Procedures* define *How We Get There.*

Macro vs. Micro-Management. The *Policies* document dictates "do's" and "don'ts" expected of the trading operation. For example, an important control issue is whether or not the desk may trade in options. Some firms allow buying call options but not selling them. The determinant issue in setting such policies will be for the Board to understand the kinds of trading activities required to achieve the corporate risk-return appetite. With the *Policy* document defining what tools are available, the *Procedures* manual focuses on the processes for using the approved tools.

Limits. Trading and risk limits add dimension to the general risk-return objectives. The *Policy* document should contain highest-level benchmarks against which business units are collectively measured. If necessary, appendices can be added to provide specific per-business-unit limits. In addition, the *Policy* document should clearly state what measures will be taken if limits are exceeded. On the other hand, the *Procedures* manual controls which methodologies and systems measure activities and mark them against the *Policy* limits. Likewise, if the *Policy* states the punishment, the *Procedures* must dictate appropriate enforcement measures. (Imagine a government setting highway speed limits and then assigning bicycle cops with radar guns.)

Governance. The Board can express its authority by taking ownership of the *Policy* document. (Of course, it is their choice to abdicate that responsibility, but that would be a powerful signal to the shareholders.) The *Procedures* manual distributes both accountability and protection to the management and staff.

Returning to our earlier analogy of how the Constitution symbolizes the *Policies* document. The *Procedures* manual is like the Legal Code, all the detailed laws for day-to-day issues. Like the Legal Code, all *Procedures* must be consistent with the *Policies*. Corporations are not democracies, so we cannot truly extend this constitutional analogy to recreating the three branches of government. We can however adopt the concept of "checks and balances" in which profit seeking and risk control are understood and discussed in terms of their tradeoffs.

GENERAL OUTLINES

RMPP outlines vary throughout the power industry according to the business plan, structure, and culture of each company. Tables 3-2 and 3-3 suggest very general outlines for the *Policies and Procedures* documents. These outlines are offered to suggest sample organizations for discussion purposes only. (Also see the Appendix for an outline of issues for the design of the RMPP.)

Chapters	Purpose
1. Business Plan	Restate corporate objectives and articulate the tactical role trading operations will contribute to reach these objectives. State the general risk-return strategy or blend of such strategies.
2. Governance	Grant the authority to define, change, audit, and enforce the *Policies*. Can include definition of and delegation of certain authority to a Risk Management Committee or similar entities. Can include the granting of authority relating to the *Procedures* manual.
3. Statement of Portfolio and Risks	Define the scope of the aggregate portfolio to be controlled. Inventory the financial and physical positions that comprise this portfolio. Positions may be organized into sub-portfolios or "books" according to market, asset type, business unit, etc. For the portfolio or books, identify the profit-loss expectations, the inherent risks, and which risks will be managed.
4. Approved Risk Management/ Hedging Tools	List approved risk management methodologies, measures, and models. Also list positions (primarily derivative contract types) allowed to be used in hedging or to modify portfolio in order to achieve business objectives. Section may also disallow certain kinds of transactions.
5. Appendices	Include support documents, as needed, possibly including Per Business Unit Limits or perhaps even the entire *Procedures* manual.

Table 3-2: Sample Outline for Risk Management Policies

Chapters	Purpose
1. Purpose of *Risk Management Procedures* Manual	Re-articulate highlights of *Policies* and establish role of the *Procedures* manual in achieving corporate objectives.
2. Authority and Enforcement	Establish chain-of-command and authority for writing, reviewing, and enforcing *Procedures*.
3. Deal Process Operations	Track the full deal contracting process, from motivation, origination, settlement, and (if necessary) delivery. Each step may be defined in terms of authorization, valuation, risk assessment, and limit checking.
4. Portfolio Management Operations	Track the full process of portfolio management cycle, including initial portfolio analysis, objective analysis, hedging analysis, portfolio modification due to hedging, and final portfolio analysis. Include statement of cycle frequency and define reporting requirements. (See Section 3.6 on *The Five Questions the Board Should Ask (and Get Answers To)*
5. Appendices	Can include Signature page to be signed by employee stating that he/she has read the *Risk Management Procedures* and accepts the legal requirements stated by corporation; Standard contracts for wholesale trading (also known as "Master Agreements"); Standard contracts for retail marketing; Glossary of Terms; etc.

Table 3-3: Sample Outline for Risk Management Procedures

MEASUREMENT MEANS ENFORCEMENT

A common complaint about risk articles, books, and seminars centers around the math—or more to the point—there being too much of it. The actual Black-Scholes equation[3] can induce dazed looks. Likewise, phrases like "gamma" or "intra-market correlations" do not appeal to the generalist. While the manager should not be expected to become an avid student of quantitative methods, he/she must appreciate that mathematics (and statistics) provide the tools for measuring value and risk. Why? In a trading environment, measurement means enforcement of risk limits.

As will be discussed, risk limits can be categorized many ways, but one distinction would be between *notional* aggregations and *calculated* measurements. Notional aggregations simply add up values, such as the total number of contracts open in a particular book. Another common measure is the Total Notional Volume of a book. For a book with only fixed-price, fixed-volume swap contracts (a.k.a. firm contracts), the Notional Volume would equal the total megawatts in a swap contract.

The notional for an option contract (or contract where the quantity or load is allowed to vary) is a bit deceptive and suggests the limitations of using only notional limits. The notional equals the total amount of power that the buyer *might* purchase; but if the holder of the option decides not to execute his/her option (or take full load,) the realized amount would be zero. This non-linearity of options suggests the need for risk managers to limit both notional values and calculated measurements such as the "Greeks."

As will be discussed in Chapters 8-10, comprehending the strategic implications of risk measures like the "Greeks" or "Value-at-Risk" (VaR) does require some math or statistics. The same holds true for understanding—and hence approving—alternative methods of valuing energy derivatives[4]. As a matter of course, the VP of trading and risk management should be required to have a passing knowledge of what works, what doesn't, and why. Otherwise, the company might be in the position of an airline hiring a chief pilot who isn't quite sure how those big metal planes float in the air.

THE FIVE PORTFOLIO QUESTIONS THE BOARD SHOULD ASK (AND GET ANSWERS TO)

The RMPP covers a great deal of topics, including the very broad topic of portfolio analysis. Portfolio analysis involves a broad spectrum of risk management methods, ranging from valuation, risk sensitivity analysis, and hedging analysis. The Merriam-Webster Dictionary third definition of the verb "to hedge" is "to protect oneself financially by a counterbalancing commitment." The same applies to energy trading. One does not hedge to increase return but to offset the risk of some other position. From this perspective, the phrase "hedge fund" seems an oxymoron.

In fact, the cycle of portfolio analysis forms the core of risk management. Summarized in Table 3-4 are five questions for this hedging cycle. The details of answering these questions will be explored in Chapters 8-10.

What does our portfolio look like now?

The Board needs to know the aggregate value of initial portfolio. This involves ensuring that all positions are captured in the portfolio and then marked-to-market using appropriate valuation models and inputs. (See Chapter 8 for more details.)

How might our portfolio change?

Risk can be defined as a measurement of change. Risk sensitivities such as *delta* (Δ) and *gamma* (Γ) —collectively known as the "Greeks"—measure how much the portfolio value might change given a single-unit change in the valuation inputs. (Such an input, as in the example of *delta*, includes the forward price.) The "Greeks" are relatively easy to calculate and can be applied against the portfolio's forward strip of time. As another benefit, the "Greeks" provide measurements that in turn can be used to calculate optimal hedging strategies. Value-at-Risk (VaR) represents another measure; VaR provides a single-figure estimate of possible losses given certain probability assumptions. (See Chapter 9 for more details.)

| 1. What does our portfolio look like now? |
| 2. How might our portfolio change? |
| 3. What do we want our portfolio to look like? |
| 4. How will we achieve and maintain our desired portfolio? |
| 5. Have we achieved our portfolio objectives? |
| REPEAT! |

Table 3-4: The Five Questions for Portfolio Analysis

What do we want our portfolio to look like?

The answer should already be available in the *Policies* document, ready to act as the benchmark. The profit-loss margin (P&L) can be calculated by comparing the portfolio's value to previous data; in turn the P&L may be measured against the policy limits. The same holds true for the risk measurements.

How will we achieve and maintain our desired portfolio?

If the portfolio does not conform to the policy limits, the risk manager must order hedging to bring the portfolio into compliance. Hedge trading responds to conditions, must be performed repeatedly, and should decrease the risk (measured by the statistical concept of *variance*. (*Variance* is a statistical measure of how data within a distribution are dispersed around the mean. The square root of the variance equals the *standard deviation*.) Again, the *Policies* pre-approve the kinds of hedge tools that may be employed. (See Chapter 10 for more details.)

Have we achieved our portfolio objectives?

The final step in the cycle is the simple comparison of the hedged portfolio's risk topography to that of the desired portfolio. Since hedging is never a perfect process, the manager may need to approve any minor deviations from compliance.

This process should be repeated with a *Policy*-specified frequency. End-of-day analysis is common, but every company will follow their own hedging cycles. In some cases liquidity and deal flow might define the optimal frequency. The portfolio analysis process is analogous to shampooing one's hair: lather, rinse, and repeat!

GOVERNANCE ISSUES

Risk governance can take many forms, starting with leadership of individuals. As mentioned, the Board level almost requires at least one strong advocate at the table. Personally, my own observations over the past few years fail to identify any clear patterns within the executive suite. In the 1990s, Chief Financial Officers (CFO) and Treasurers seemed more focused on the traditional financial management issues while energy trading risk grew organically at the staff-level. In 1999, business cards with the title "Corporate Risk Manager" started to appear. In early 2000, I learned of a utility in which the energy risk managers actually took over the fixed-income book! At the next level, one or more VPs oversee trading, risk management, marketing, or other related business units, depending on the particular organizational chart.

One relatively consistent structure involves a Risk Management Committee (RMC) or some similar body. The RMC can play a primary managerial role, advising the Board and overseeing the trading operations. Some advanced companies appoint specialist sub-committees such as a Risk Valuation Committee to provide more technical oversight over such things as credit or modeling risk.

WHO SHOULD WRITE THE RMPP DOCUMENTS

Like the Constitution, a committee should write the Risk Management Policies and Procedures. Certainly, individuals will arise in Jeffersonian roles, writing compelling first drafts. Writing a complete RMPP is a monumental task, however, so bringing in outside attorneys and management consultants can be incredibly helpful. These experts specialize in drafting comprehensive documents. The secret is for the company to be able to both pose and answer the questions. The VP of risk management should play the role of editor, pulling together component parts and making sure that the RMPP documents transcend mere boilerplate to become the living documents envisioned in this book.

Unfortunately, many companies will appoint the risk manager as the RMPP's sole author. This scenario correlates highly with upper management's fear of understanding trading and risk management. The danger here is that the risk manager should not be the one defining corporate strategy. There is no surprise, then, that the resulting RMPP commonly remains just ink and paper: documents that nobody heads or reads but behind which management can hide when facing their boards. Ideally, the Board and upper management work in partnership with the risk manager or consultant, with the executives providing the vision and the "risk professionals" providing the technical details to help convert that vision into reality.

ENDNOTES

[1] While writing this chapter, I first presented some of the concepts as the keynote address of the *Energy Price Risk Forum* in London, May 2000, sponsored by IIR Ltd.

[2] To paraphrase drummer Keith Moon of the *Who* when he heard that Jimmy Page and Robert Plant were forming a band.

[3] The Black-Scholes Equation first appeared in *The Journal of Political Economy, May-June 1973*. The equation is also documented and discussed in numerous books including those in the *Manager's Bookshelf* (Chapter 1).

[4] As Dragana Pilipovic argues in Chapter 1 of her book *Energy Risk*, energy derivatives are different enough from their money market counterparts to justify the need for energy-specific valuation models.

chapter 4

STARTING WITH YOUR
RISK-RETURN STRATEGY

JUST ASK, "WHY?"

A well-known bumper sticker suggests that we "Just Say No!" When it comes to setting strategy, perhaps the energy manager should adopt a similar motto, "Just Ask, Why?" The company's objectives contain the answers to "why?" because the answers lead directly to specific strategies for the trading operation. These objectives and related strategy serve as the ultimate standard for decision-making. This chapter will focus on the *Four Risk-Return Strategies*[1], a framework developed by Dragana Pilipovic and me, for articulating, comparing, and defining corporate objectives.

Why focus so much on strategy? First, that's what managers are paid to worry about. Second, members of the Board and upper management tend to have a sense of direction but need new frameworks with which to express them. This direction is requisite for the design of a meaningful *Risk Management Policies and Procedures* (RMPP.) Finally, a strong strategic compass focuses decision-making when imperfect information is available. My favorite analogy is NASA's race to the moon. President

John F. Kennedy set the objective: Beat the Russians. The engineers did not start with the perfect Apollo spacecraft with low-resistance Teflon shields. The Mercury capsule sported corrugated metal, with bolts and washers exposed *on the outside*. In energy risk, the lesson is that we too must do the best we can with what we have. We should focus on our priorities and improve the details when and as we can.

At the corporate level, the energy company's objective will probably be some combination between profit and public service. As legacy of regulation's social contract, reliability concerns can strongly temper profit seeking. (Even privately held players may emphasize reliability as part of their product quality positioning.) In terms of profit, the question becomes how much profit relative to some standard index. *Should our utility beat the market? If so, then by how much?*

THE FOUR RISK-RETURN STRATEGIES

 During deregulation, some power companies will seek their fortune in a variety of ways: mergers and acquisitions, telecommunications, bandwidth trading, etc. This chapter, however, will focus on the core business of power and how the trading operation fits within the power strategy. As in Table 4-1, we can categorize our alternatives into the *Four Risk-Return Strategies* as follows:

- Treasury Strategy: eliminating risk to avoid potential losses.
- Speculation Strategy: assuming risk to increase potential profit.
- Arbitrage Strategy: exploiting risk-free opportunities.
- Market Maker Strategy: exchanging and balancing risks between other parties.

These strategies represent generalizations, but in these extremes we find important contrasts about objectives. Conservative companies

Strategy	Risk	Potential Profit	Potential Loss
Treasury	Eliminate; high risk aversion	Reduce or cap upside	Reduce or cap downside
Speculation	Assume; risk seeking	Maximize	Maximize
Arbitrage	Exploit; look for profitable trade-offs between risk and return	Guarantee	Lower or, in the case of pure arbitrage, none due to risk-free exposure
Market Maker	Exchange; risk aversion with highly controlled risk taking in order to offer services to clients	Limited to fees or bid/ask spread	Limited by back-to-back trading or aggressive hedging

Table 4-1: The Four Risk-Return Strategies

should see themselves in the Treasury strategy or perhaps the Market Maker role. These strategies consciously attempt to reduce risk. The Speculation strategy should appeal to high-growth oriented firms. On its surface, the Arbitrage approach holds the greatest appeal. Unfortunately, pure arbitrage is hard to find. Statistical arbitrage does require enough liquidity to offset the majority of risks and still leaves some residual risk.

While each strategy is unique, most companies will follow a hybrid approach. This is perfectly acceptable as long as the firm can distinguish which trades are being entered for what purpose. One solution is to organize one's portfolio into strategic books; the delineation could be by contracts or underlying assets. For example, the desk may have 100 megawatts to trade from a generation asset. Perhaps 60 MWh should be hedged, with 30 MWh available to the marketing department, and 10 MWh available for speculation. Again, this kind of book balancing should be defined in the RMPP. It is really no different than budgeting between the business units.

The Treasury Strategy

The name for the "Treasury Strategy" was inspired by the role of the treasurer's department in a corporation. The objective of this strategy is to prudently manage resources in support of the company's core profit units. This strategy can be likened to buying insurance, paying cash or value upfront in order to hedge against potential problems in the future. In this respect, the "Treasury" strategy could be alternatively named the "Hedging" strategy. But this would be misleading, because any strategy will use hedging to contain its risk frontier. As will be explored in Chapter 10, hedging is the process of keeping the portfolio on track, so while a conservative company might be doing more hedging than a speculator, both companies will be hedging.

The Treasury book should be a cost-center operation; its role is to support the company's other business units (such as generation, transmission, distribution, etc.) that are dedicated to profit making. At non-financial companies, the treasury department theoretically should not be a moneymaker. Shareholders presumably invested into those companies for their core competence such as steel making or power generation, unless the non-financial companies had advertised their expertise at financial investing. Otherwise one would presume that shareholders seeking financial expertise would have invested elsewhere. This approach applies equally to financial risk and reliability risk.

Certain utilities continue to put a premium on being naturally "long" on power, thus always have the juice available to deliver to clients. Such reliability could be a natural selling point for the utility's clientele and the investor community; it could also be a hedge against the political risk of a "black out." In terms of governance, the managers of the Treasury book should be rewarded for prudence rather than be punished for showing low profits or even modest losses.

The Speculation Strategy

Fewer words incite fear as does "Speculation." Unlike the Treasury function, the speculation strategy consciously looks for risky trades, because if the company wants larger profits from the desk it must take on greater risk. Here we can see a case in which "risk management" does not equate to "risk reduction." Speculation is not necessarily a "bad" word. Here the company states that the trading desk should make money by taking on responsible risks. The stakes will be high, as can be the possible rewards. The potential losses are also high, but the management should not be punished at the first sign of trouble. In terms of marketing, talented trading firms might specialize in taking on the risk undesired by more conservative firms and then managing these risks better in their portfolios. Speculation requires deep pockets and an iron stomach to succeed.

Setting aside reserves could be considered part of a Speculation Strategy if the company does so for purposes of taking advantage of unexpected market moves. Setting aside reserves also could be a hedge against unexpected internal needs, so we can see how the same "position" can play different roles in different strategies.

The "Do Nothing" approach suggests a unique case of Speculation. Consider the traditional company that actually distrusts trading and risk management. Upper management read the articles about the "D" word (derivatives). What happens is that trading is de-emphasized; managerial emphasis or political cover is not granted to risk management. Ironically, this null-approach to risk more resembles Speculation in its carelessness than it does Treasury in its conservatism.

INTERVIEW

Thinking Beyond Rate-of-Return

An Interview with Jim Clarke, Karl Stanley, and Jeff Deneau of NiSource's Risk Management and Capital Allocation Group

NiSource Inc. acquired Columbia Energy Group during 2000 as part of a major corporate initiative. The risk management group, lead by Jim Clarke, played a key role in supporting the acquisition and the integration process that followed. This interview explores how their risk management strategies helped meet the corporation's objectives.

The participants included Jim Clarke, VP of Risk Management and Capital Allocation, who prior to joining NiSource in 1998 was associated with various hedge funds and trading groups in Chicago and New York where he was Head of Risk and Investments; Karl Stanley, Director of Risk and Capital Allocation; and Jeff Deneau, Market Risk Manager. Located in Merrillville, Indiana, NiSource is a holding company that includes Northern Indiana Public Service Company.

Question: *What is a "risk management mindset"?*

Jim Clarke: A "risk management mindset" is portfolio management. This mindset finds value beyond the constraints of traditional financial analysis. In the old days, cash flow was king. Utility decisions relied heavily on pro formas filled with fixed cash flow and rate-of-return expectations. Since deregulation suggests that precious few cash flows will be "fixed," every utility must learn to manage uncertainty and take actions to minimize downside and maximize the upside. We, as a utility, must therefore know how to balance risk and reward. We must recognize the existence of risk, then determine how best to manage (eliminate or minimize) that risk through the use of the appropriate derivative and insurance products.

A risk management mindset also sees opportunity. By that I mean we know where we want to take risk and in what manner. We believe we have an edge in certain markets and we don't in others. We then come to a decision on what is the best strategy and what financial or physical products should be used to take advantage of that edge. Being prepared to take or mitigate risk. Not just finding risk and hedging it but being compliant and competitive at the same time.

Question: *Why did NiSource's management look to the risk group for support during the Columbia acquisition?*

Karl Stanley: Upper management looked to our department to contribute this "risk management mindset" during our company's acquisition of Columbia Energy Group. Through our portfolio management approach, we try to make the company aware of the financial equivalent of all that is being looked at. Not throwing traditional valuation methodologies out the window, but combining them with a market-based view of the integrated business.

Question: *What specifically did the energy risk group offer that was different from a traditional financial analysis?*

Jeff Deneau: When we acquired Columbia, we began refocusing our corporate identity from being a Midwestern electricity-gas-water company to becoming an energy portfolio company, with assets throughout the eastern United States that we could optimize based on market opportunities. Upper management looked to our group to provide three major pieces to the merger and acquisition puzzle:

- Identify value based on market opportunity
- Demonstrate how business units can employ the "risk management mindset," and,
- Integrate the merged assets into NiSource's coordinated risk management portfolio

Question: *How do you find value based on market opportunity?*

Clarke: We perceive an integrated energy company as offering the marketplace far more value than a traditional utility. (Our battle cry is "a coordinated portfolio approach!") In helping to value Columbia, our job was to identify how integrating different energy assets in different geographic regions would add value beyond the pro forma statements. To answer this question, we have to get an understanding of the financial equivalent of what we have and can create and then we looked to the markets for information regarding forward prices and volatilities. We looked at the possibility of integrating some of the businesses and exposures of the entities that would make up the new NiSource. We saw opportunities for which the traditional financial planning and evaluation people do not look. These are opportunities in coordinating some of the Columbia assets with NiSource assets as well as changing some of the strategic assumptions of how we should look at the opportunities of the unregulated businesses. While others were looking for bottom-line cost savings we are looking for the top-line growth opportunities based on what is working in the markets today.

Stanley: For example, an asset might not have guaranteed cash flows today. Traditionally, we would perceive this as an "out-of-the-money" option. However, we now recognize that though it is out-of-the-money, it is an option nonetheless. There is extrinsic value in that option, found in volatility of cash flows. There's value in that probability of change. One needs to have an appreciation and understanding of the optionality of that asset. As Jim was saying, when you buy a company, there are certain synergies—but expense cutting does not necessarily lead to growth. When it comes to long-term growth, you have to think about how the assets can work together and be optimized to take advantage of market opportunities such as unexpected price movements or supply-demand constraints.

Question: *How can the risk mindset help departments not directly performing trading?*

Deneau: We want every department to understand their potential for risk and reward. We see risks that others might not see, or haven't been trained to see, and we also see enterprise-wide business integration opportunities. After all, from a portfolio management perspective, everything is a trade – whether it is a natural gas future or an entire business unit. As the risk group, it is our responsibility to make each unit aware of their market presence.

Question: *Can these principles prove helpful even before deregulation?*

Stanley: Yes. Most of our business units are still in the regulated world but they are certainly changing their ways of thinking about problems and solutions. It's a matter of changing the "we can't do that" mentality to a "how can we do it?" approach. In the old days, the more customers a company had, the better. In a risk-adjusted approach, however, we can suggest how different kinds of customers represent different value potential. If one parameter is the volatility of customer load, this approach can help distinguish a steady-load customer as adding less strain on our obligations than would a variable load customer. Sometimes less is more. It's all about "price discovery" and applying the idea to other business units.

Deneau: In thinking about customers, we remain committed to our obligation to serve. One change, however, is capitalizing on duty to serve. For example, when thinking about building a power plant for a customer, why not build in extra capacity that could act as an "option on reliability" or on a merchant opportunity in the future? In essence, we're trying to prepare the company for deregulation by positioning our "port-folio" before that day arrives.

Stanley: Again, we are trying to replace the old "we can't do that" approach with one that asks "how can we do that given the existing market parameters?" This approach performs best when different business units can communicate about market changes and collaborate on how to respond.

Question: *A person awakening from a regulated mindset might have problems distinguishing between an entrepreneurial and risk management mindset. Both approaches are fueled by the market. How would you distinguish between the two?*

Stanley: In any decision, a person will continually assess their potential risks and rewards. An entrepreneur might do this assessment intuitively, but the risk analyst will bring numbers to the table. We in the Risk Group do not have the luxury of taking a subjective opinion of the future to the market. We have to have the analyses to back up our opinions. Quantifying risk and its impact on value—that is how the risk management mindset helps the traditional utility go beyond a traditional analysis.

Deneau: Traditional analysis looks at "predictable" cash flows—so adding the risk component really throws a monkey wrench into traditional pro forma. By thinking about market uncertainty, we are adding the third dimension to a typically two-dimensional study.

Clarke: It is basically a "How" story. How are you participating in the market? We are here to make sure that we are competitive and compliant. We know the risk appetite of the company. We know what kind of risk the company wants to take and what it does not. There are only two ways to participate: take positions and hope the market goes your way or make markets. Hoping is for suckers. This company does not want to hope. This company wants to find out where we can take what we naturally have or have created to the market with an edge. I sometimes hear utility executives say that we are trading around assets. I assume that there is a cost structure edge in having those assets—either owning them outright or in the cost of controlling them. A risk management mindset is the discipline of understanding the financial equivalent of those assets and knowing what to pay for their ownership or control.

Now participating in markets by making markets is different. Embedded in making markets (a ready bid and offer) is risk management. The information you need to confidently make a market is the same raw material the risk manager needs to assess risk: historical data. The discipline of a risk mindset allied with the right assets and people is pivotal.

Stanley: Look at where Wall Street is rewarding people: capital follows success. In the energy markets, success can come from acquiring assets and customers, but you better know what to pay for the assets, how to manage the risk, how to be compliant, and how to participate in the market. In the future, the value of these assets will derive from diversification and the ability to participate in market opportunities. If you don't optimize your assets, somebody else will either beat you in the market or simply buy you.

Deneau: Like we've said: "A coordinated portfolio approach."

Clarke: We understand that the world is changing and we are changing with it. Just look at the evolution of our group—we started with risk management for just the trading groups. Our point of difference is taking a financial equivalent look at what we have, thinking about the value of change, and being able to quantify the numbers - seeing opportunity, as well as risk, with an eye to the market.

Now we are the "Risk Management and Capital Allocation" group, a central and high profile group at NiSource. Entrepreneurial, yes, and our tools are market experience, market analysis, and risk analysis. Our job is to look at our total asset portfolio, identify potential market value, and manage potential market risk. Our goal is to get the most out of our portfolio of businesses, both now and in the long-run. Because the people who are, long-term, the most successful at participating in markets are the people who best know how to manage risk.

For more information, contact Jim Clarke (jmclarke@nisource.com), Karl Stanley (kestanley@nisource.com), or Jeff Deneau (jwdeneau@nisource.com) of NiSource Inc. © Jim Clarke

The Arbitrage Strategy

"Arbitrage" describes an illusive ideal: a deal with guaranteed return with zero risk[2]. For example, in 1996-97 we saw a brief arbitrage opportunity in the power markets. Quarterly prices were not priced in accordance to their increment monthly prices. One could buy the third quarter swap for a lower price than the three July-August-September contracts. (Thus fulfilling the dream of buying low and selling high.) Like all arbitrage opportunities, this anomaly disappeared. In fact, in an efficient market, arbitrage does not exist; but even in a young market, any arbitrage opportunities generally do not endure long.

Profits from the Arbitrage strategy rely exclusively on being smarter, faster or more patient than your competitor. Put in other words, Arbitrage relies in part on the market being dumber, slower, or downright foolish. There are opportunities to be sure, but the power executive had better be prepared to pay top dollar for traders and analysts qualified to recognize and exploit them.

Special cases of the Arbitrage strategy involve situations that are not completely risk-free. In the early financial option markets, for example, statistical arbitrage generated huge profits for traders with better valuation methods. This competitive advantage derived from illiquidity and inexperience; as markets matured, statistical arbitrage waned.

Power markets face a parallel: utilities that are "long" generation assets possess the competitive high ground. (The same holds true for all physical assets including transmission.) While market prices do indeed represent the best impression of aggregate risk-adjusted expectations, certain utilities may have better internal supply information than the aggregate. Generators and producers also have the option of not selling forward, holding certain units or portions of units off-market to take advantage of spot price opportunities. Finally, generators have the basic asset-based arbitrage: capturing on the differential between the market prices and production costs.

The Market Maker Strategy

The Market Maker Strategy suggests opening a bank of telephones and coordinating a fleet of marketers. The trading strategy implies taking all comers, providing price quotes to buyers and sellers alike in the full diversity of products as the target market requires. The profit strategy suggests charging fees or some differential—the bid/ask spread—in the robust tradition of the middleman. Moving away from the "trading desk" point-of-view, the Market Maker Strategy also correlates directly with retail or marketing functions. Within this broad definition, a Market Maker could be moving financial contracts or actual power needs, even the generation plants themselves.

A successful Market Maker Strategy requires a large existing client base. In this regard, for the company considering this strategy, the emphasis is on the word "existing." If the company boasts a large client base, very serious thought should be dedicated to answering the questions as to "why" the base remains large and "whether" choice will lead to client retention or loss. Consider an example from banking: a huge competitive advantage of Bank of America (BOA) was its widespread coverage of individual deposits in the American west. The huge amounts of cash aggregated from all those depositors gave BOA leverage in money markets that smaller banks could only dream about. The utility manager would be wise to understand the implications of this asset-driven advantage: if you have it, don't squander it. If you don't, then figure out how to get around it.

In terms of designing its "product line," a Market Maker might wish to convert its ability to ensure "reliability" from a government concern into a marketing concern. Note how even the concept of "reliability" can be recast as a function of strategy. The Market Maker uses reliability as a product enhancement while the Treasury strategy uses it to attract investors looking for stable earnings.

Can a company make more money by being the "reliability" company like certain blue-chip insurance companies, or is it more profitable to be a cutthroat company that drops delivery (contractually-allowable, of course) in return for lower prices. As with any strategy, the Market Maker also would be actively hedging as well; one unique aspect, however, will be more-frequently-than-average "back-to-back" trading. Back-to-back trading is essentially a special case of 1-to-1 or 100% hedging. In the ideal, a Market Maker's preference would be to have "empty books" at the end of a trading day.

Utilities concerned about client retention might find this approach of value. When approached with a "mark-to-market" sensibility, however, these same utilities might want to consider some clients unworthy of retaining. High volatility, high load customers may be "too expensive" or even impossible to maintain using standardized contracts. (The impact of generation operations can be large, and satisfying load during high price peak periods can be very risky.) Low-bidding competitors may temporarily steal such high volatility, high load customers; but the real costs of serving these expensive clients may be the weight that finally sinks the competitor's ship. Valuing certain retail contracts using the real options approach may lead to higher bids; the greater the volatility, the higher the option price. At the same time, proper valuation may identify competitive bid situations as well. In essence, relying on better retail valuation combines the "Market Maker" and "Statistical Arbitrage" Strategies.

Another potential competitive advantage stems from developing a "structured products" desk, with marketers and derivatives specialists customizing or "structuring" non-standardized contracts for individual clients. Whether or not a market maker offers structured products is really a matter of strategy and expertise. In one sense, market makers should stick to standardized products that can be moved easily between parties. But young or illiquid markets may either have few standardized contracts or too many customers who believe that they have unique needs. Offering product structuring may be a basic servicing requirement for a Market Maker to get his/her foot in the door; with luck, the strategy can be profitable as well.

For example, a Market Maker could approach the high volatility, high volume customer with the following proposition: "We'll meet the fixed-price bid of our competitor; we'll also meet your full load-requirements with the exception of two days during the summer peak months." Called a "load-curtailment contract," this structured product attempts to exchange price and volume risk between buyer and seller. Should the Market Maker become too much ("long") or too little ("short") in terms of financial or volumetric exposure, the firm must give away some of the fees or potential upside through hedging. Ideally, the Market Maker performs "back-to-back" trading, immediately trading off any exposures and pocketing the differential in fees. If the Market Maker can do enough of these deals, profit margins may be accomplished along with portfolio balancing.

The mortgage origination business offers an effective analogy: Mortgage bankers find the clients and sell the loans. Rather than holding them through term, however, the originators sell them "upstream" to larger banks or Fannie Mae. These large institutions then package mortgages and sell them in the Collateralized Mortgage Obligation (CMO) market. By the way, this modern practice evolved from a regulatory origin: Fannie Mae was once exclusively government controlled and banking was once far more regulated.

Another potential market maker strategy would be credit-risk trading. In this strategy a company could buy or sell contracts from counterparties with lower credit ratings, then beef up the positions with credit-enhancements. This strategy could be very dangerous, to be sure, and requires significant market expertise to properly evaluate and value the credit risk potential of counterparties. Full disclosure would be necessary to avoid the risks of the firm unwittingly taking on unexpected credit liabilities.

HEADLINE STORIES ABOUT CONFLICTING STRATEGIES

"There's no such thing as a bad boy," said Spencer Tracy's character Father Flanagan in the classic movie *Boys Town*. The same could be said of the "D" word—derivatives; there is no inherently bad thing about them. The source of horror stories can be traced to conflicts between objective and strategy. Should the company want to gamble on speculative trading, with the blessing of the shareholders, then so be it. (This is the utility-as-equity-fund model.) The Board sets objectives and approves strategy, the managers oversee the strategy, and the desk makes the trades. But as we see in Table 4-2, strange and terrible things can happen when strategies go awry.

Case	News Story	Possible Prevention
Orange County (California)	Treasurer tried to make money	Limits against speculation. Proper risk capture; managers asking the source of profits
Federal Energy Sales - City of Springfield (Illinois)	Market maker trades with market via municipality	Enforcement by municipality, diligence by market

Table 4-2: Headline Stories Due to Strategic Conflicts

First we'll consider Orange County, California.[3] To make a long story short, Orange County is the poster child for speculation disguised as treasury strategy—the proverbial wolf in sheep's clothing. The government of Orange County assigned the treasurer's office the objective of managing cash. Traditionally, cost increases were met with tax increases. This should sound eerily familiar to the traditional cost-driven utility manager! But, when California passed the famous Proposition 13 that severely limited such increases, County Treasurer Robert Citron found himself in a conflict of wanting to generate profits (the speculative strategy) through the office assigned a treasury function.[4] Under such financial pressure, it's little wonder how the Orange County Treasurer would respond positively to the lure of derivatives markets. Things went very well until 1994. Prior to 1994, Citron's policies were doing very well and very few demanded an explanation. Unfortunately, the County Treasurer bet the wrong way on interest rates and lost $1.7 billion. The astute power manager should learn from this—demand explanations about unexplainable profits, because the reasons may pose equal threats of unexplainable loses.

Our second horror story hails from the immediate world of electricity trading. A small power marketer, Federal Energy Sales, in the summer price spikes of 1998, played the role of the straw that broke the supply chain's back. Prices were spiking due to a midwestern heat wave. Demand outpaced supply; prices reached monumental levels. (One trader told me that she saw a $10,000/MWh price.) High prices triggered calls by option holders who bought the contracts as hedges against temperature events. And since the credit chain is only as good its weakest link, when

Federal failed to deliver on its derivative obligations, the first well-publicized "Great Credit Risk Crisis" for power markets was born.

Federal was among the hundreds of power marketers approved by the Federal Energy Regulatory Commission in the 1990s. Some power marketers were the deregulated vanguard of still regulated generators. Others, like Federal, consisted of a few employees. Strategically, in the end it was either a speculator that lost its gamble or a market maker that simply failed to hedge its exposures. It could be argued that it remained true to its strategy, but paid the price for failure of execution and risk-limit setting.

The real moral of the Federal story lies with its counterpart, the City of Springfield, Illinois. Like Orange County, Springfield was a governmental entity with objectives that would suggest a Treasury strategy. Springfield had rules regarding energy trading, yet the trading desk broke those rules by trading with Federal. (In fact, Springfield's senior electric-power marketer took time off and worked for Federal!)[5] The biggest problem involved Springfield's role in what is known as "sleeving," in which a middleman trades positions from an undesirable party with an unsuspecting third party. In this case, major power traders had already disqualified Federal from their list of approved counterparties, yet Springfield remained in good standing. (Government units tend to carry the implied "full-faith-and-credit" guarantee.) Springfield acted as a middleman, backing deals with the unsuspecting market with deals from Federal.[6]

In the end, effective management and enforcement offer the best insurance. A well-written RMPP is only as good as management's ability to monitor the desk, understand what is happening, reward strategic accomplishment, enforce limits, and punish transgressions.

Consider this headline: "Wisconsin Fund Posts $95 Million Loss From Unauthorized Use of Derivatives."[7] The key word "unauthorized" suggests that policies were in place for authorized derivatives trading but monitoring and enforcement were not.

ENDNOTES

[1] Dragana Pilipovic and I first collaborated on this framework for the *Risk on the Slopes* seminar that SAVA Risk Management Corporation offered in Aspen, CO, February 1997. The framework first appeared in print in Dragana Pilipovic's book *Energy Risk*, Chapter 11.

[2] Jarrow and Turnbull offer this definition: "Arbitrage is any trading strategy requiring no cash input that has some probability of making profits, without any risk of loss" (p. 33).

[3] For the full story, I recommend Professor Philippe Jorion's excellent book *Good Bets Gone Bad: Derivatives and Bankruptcy in Orange County*, Academic Press, 1995.

[4] Jorion, 1995, p. 12.

[5] Baily, 1990.

[6] Kranhold and Ershviller, 1990.

[7] Knecht, 1995.

chapter 5

The Risk Roster: Personalities and Specialties

The Major Positions on Your Team

Like any business leader, the VP in charge of trading and risk management must hire a full team of personalities and specialists. While an effective VP must understand many core principles about energy risk, delegation to staff is required. The different roles on the risk team require different abilities and psychological profiles. The specifics of each member of the risk roster will vary by the character of the company. Does the company own generation? Is it regulated or not? Does the portfolio also include natural gas and other markets? Is the firm even an electric company—could it be an industrial end user or even a bank? With this type of variety in mind, this chapter suggests some general outlines for how to arrange the staff and the roles that each position can play on the energy risk management team.

Perhaps the key position to the reader of this book is the job of the VP of Trading and Risk Management. This VP may or may not be the "top risk manager;" instead he/she could be a generalist who happens to be in charge of that particular business unit. Regardless, each VP will have different duties, but the following roles will be invaluable:

Translator. The VP must be able to translate between the highest level and lowest levels of the corporation. He/she must convert corporate vision into trading and risk terms, and vice versa. In addition, he/she must be able to translate sophisticated concepts to people of varied experiences and skill sets. Patience becomes a fundamental prerequisite.

Facilitator. The VP will be charged with a variety of projects in which nobody else could possibly be interested. Take the unheralded job of drafting and maintaining the *Risk Management Policies and Procedures* (RMPP). The VP will need to facilitate input and feedback from a variety of people who may actually be downright hostile to the entire process. It matters not whether that hostility stems from ignorance or indolence by those who resent outside control.

Gladiator. Perhaps the hardest task for a VP is to be challenged by an aggressive Director of Trading or a trader with Type A personality. This is equally true even if a risk manager sits between such a bulldog and the VP. The VP must still step in to provide political cover for the risk manager. Prior to playing this role, however, the VP should also remember Task #5 in Chapter 1's "Top Ten Checklist"—confirming his/her own political sponsor.

For the new VP who may not have much expertise with trading, a common mistake is to assume that Wall Street or financial traders make better candidates for hire as compared to hiring from within. True money market folks bring the requisite skills for managing risk, but the assets that they manage (cash) behaves very differently from the assets that utilities manage (electricity.) New hires from Wall Street must exhibit a willingness to understand just how various energy derivatives differ from their money market cousins. Hiring from within helps increase the chances that the "juice" will be understood. As suggested in Chapter 2, utilities throughout the United States have many intelligent, progressive people who decided to live and work in the same communities where they grew up. They may well be natural traders or risk managers, given the opportunity.

INTERVIEW

Baptisms by Fire: How People Succeed in Emerging Markets

An Interview with Adrian D'Silva, Director of Capital Markets, Federal Reserve Bank of Chicago

The electricity market exploded onto the scene during the 1990s like a volcano long dormant in a regulatory mountain. Many in the power industry struggled with their personal "baptisms by fire"—often believing their problems were unique and singularly insurmountable. In fact, what electricity leaders experienced mirrored similar struggles by those in numerous other new markets that emerged worldwide since the 1970s due to the revolutionary impact of derivatives.

After a distinguished career in and around the world of risk management, Adrian D'Silva of the Federal Reserve Bank of Chicago offers a unique perspective on how individuals adapt to and succeed during market creation. D'Silva is Director of Capital Markets Supervision. He is responsible for all capital markets-related activities in the Chicago District and for research and publications on capital markets issues. He also leads the system-wide Competency Center on Merchant Banking. This center is responsible for coordinating the supervision of all Private Equity and Merchant Banking activities throughout the entire Federal Reserve System. Prior to joining the Federal Reserve in 1995, Adrian managed the derivatives trading activities of Harris Bank, First Chicago, and Morgan Stanley in London, Chicago, Singapore, Hong Kong, and Tokyo. Adrian holds a BS in Sociology, Anthropology, and Political Science from Iowa State University and a Masters in International Management from the American Graduate School of International Management (Thunderbird).

Question: *Many new markets emerge from previously, regulated markets. When derivatives began to revolutionize banking and foreign exchange, what kinds of people arose from the ranks to provide leadership in the face of new market conditions?*

D'Silva: In the early days of the interest rate swaps market, we had a variety of people involved. In the beginning we had people with accounting and credit backgrounds, because the initial risks being taken were more related to credit. But as the market evolved and we began to take on more market risk, we started to use people with trading experience. Also, in the early stages, the people involved needed to be multi-dimensional, i.e. we all had to be involved with a variety of issues—accounting to credit to legal. As the market grew, we became more segmented. The managers who were successful were those people who understood the relationships between the different parts of the business.

Question: *A manager from a Japanese electric utility recently asked me how his company could identify who—if anyone—they could raise from within the company to become risk managers as their market deregulates. How would you answer this manager's question?*

D'Silva: I would suggest that he put together a team of people who had a basic understanding of the various parts of the business. They need to figure out what kinds of risks that the company would be comfortable with. They could start by talking to people in other markets where electricity has been deregulated. The first thing that his team needs to do is research, research, research! They are in a unique position in that they can learn from the experience of other people.

Question: *Still thinking about the Japanese utility—if they were to hire a trader from the Tokyo stock markets, how best could they "tame the tiger" and integrate his/her pure-market perspective with the realities of a traditionally regulated utility culture?*

D'Silva: Looking back over the past few years, as various embryonic or emerging markets have started, the first thing most people do is hire traders from another market. This has worked sometimes, and the key to success has been when the traders have spent time to really understand the underpinnings of the new market and become more integrated with the different parts of the business.

Question: *The international power market has looked to the United States as an example of how to effectively develop and manage new energy trading markets. How should other countries adopt US-style trading while adjusting for any potential cultural differences?*

D'Silva: The basic structures may be similar when you look at the economics of various markets. The important things to consider are probably the differences—credit, legal, regulatory. This is especially important where there may be various degrees of legal certainty. For example, the enforceability of contracts. We need to remember that the non-market risks (legal, operations, etc.) are probably greater.

Question: *What makes a good trader? Would you agree that a "trader is born, not made"?*

D'Silva: That has been the eternal question. I don't think there is a universal answer to this. I think it depends on the market. I also think that it depends on the level and type of risk. As markets evolve, this type of risk changes and will require different types of personalities. A couple of observations: first, my first boss in the trading business had the following philosophy: "hire three, fire two in six months." This was because he did not know how people would react once they actually started trading. I agree that as you start to build trading operations in these embryonic markets, you have to cull the traders very quickly. My second observation is that the best traders I have known have come from a variety of backgrounds. They have ranged from music, accounting, fighter pilot, and professional gambler.

Question: *Likewise, what makes a good risk manager? In your experience, do the best risk managers come with trading experience or is there some other kind of experience that is a better indicator of success? Within emerging markets, have the best risk managers arisen from within the ranks of the preexisting industry or have they been imported from other markets?*

D'Silva: I feel very strongly that the best risk managers have quite a bit of trading experience. I don't think they necessarily need to have experience in the same markets that they are managing—this is especially difficult in embryonic markets. The best risk managers have to be able to sense if the risk being taken is commensurate with the reward. Over the past few years, some of the best risk managers have been those with some trading backgrounds but also with substantial quantitative skills. In reference to whether they need to come from the industry or need to be imported from another market, as I said earlier the best solution is a team of people who have complementary skills and knowledge, since it is very difficult to find a single person with all the requisite skills and knowledge. Because of this, I am a big proponent of the team approach to risk management.

Question: *Are there other emerging markets that you see on your radar screen that might be of interest to electric utilities?*

D'Silva: One of the newer markets that I think is going to grow substantially over the next few years is market or markets related to carbon emissions. This is a potentially huge international market and is fascinating, because it will not only have market risks but also legal, environmental, regulatory, and—maybe most importantly—political risks.

For more information, Adrian D'Silva can be contacted via Adrian.B.DSilva@chi.frb.org.

THE CONCENTRIC CIRCLES MODEL OF ASSET MANAGEMENT

The banking industry simultaneously experienced the thaw of regulation and a super-heated rise of derivatives trading. (This should sound *very* familiar to utility folks!) Two organizational frameworks evolved that should be of great interest to energy executives: the Concentric Circles Model of Asset Management and the Front-Middle-Back Office approach.

 The Concentric Circles Model (see Figure 5-1) emerged naturally from the early days of inflation. Prior to inflation, banks kept large amounts of assets (cash) and applied them to the core competence of lending, profiting from fees and the differential between interest charged and interest paid. Inflation changed all this; assets in the vault lost value. Hence the creation of the risk management function. Power companies can directly draw the analogy between banking's cash assets to their own portfolios of trades and generation assets. In the banking world, one can envision the center of the circle to be a vault with cash or gold, or more broadly, as the general

Fig. 5-1: Concentric Circles Model

money supply. For power companies, the center of the circle would be generation assets or the general flow of traded power. It should be noted that the engineers who balance load and run the generation assets are key players at the core of the circle. Surrounding the assets, the first concentric ring includes traders, who both use and protect the assets in accordance to corporate objectives. The outer ring includes the marketers, who represent the assets to the outside world of clients. The marketer's job is to match what the company has to offer with what the client base desires. Finally, the middle kingdom comprises risk managers and analysts who play multiple roles in all directions. They must simultaneously aid traders and marketers alike. Risk managers, additionally, must also limit the traders. Many engineers would belong in this middle ring as well, especially those charged with modeling generation and optimizing assets.

The Front/Middle/Back Office Model

The players laid out horizontally in the Concentric Circles model can be rearranged vertically, stacked up in an alternative framework called the "Front-Middle-Back Office" model. These offices also evolved naturally in the money markets. Here, the traders and marketers occupy the Front Office, making deals and representing the company. With time the Front Office wished to delegate some of its work and the Back Office was born. Traditional Back Office tasks include deal confirmation and accounting. The Back Office also took up the role of controls and risk management. Finally, with the advent of sophisticated derivatives and the need for extensive modeling, the Middle Office appeared. In reality, few power companies have trading operations large enough to be organized formally into distinct front, middle, and back office operations. In very small operations, the same person might be performing all three functions! The model can still be used to help describe the kinds of processes required and delineate responsibilities among staff.

A whimsical analogy for this model is one of those long "hook and ladder" fire trucks, also known as tiller trucks, with the long ladders. These trucks extend so far that they require two steering wheels—one in the front and another in the rear. In this analogy, the traders sit in the Front Office, with the best view of the road ahead. The risk managers hang on in the back, using their steering wheel to negotiate tough corners and keep the truck from flipping. Both "drivers" keep communicating. Perhaps sometimes the trader sees the fire and sets the direction, other times the risk manager calls out the directions. While at opposite ends, these two players should not be at odds, with coordination increasing the chances of success.

The Role of the Trader

Traders come in many forms. Some just have the right instincts; bringing pure value from the "gut" feelings and experiences. Others are more cerebral or quantitative. What binds traders together is they are *born*, not *made*.

As a function of the *Risk Management Policies and Procedures* (RMPP), the VP should give the general objectives to the trader. One trader may be assigned to spot- or short-term trading as part of the group dedicated to ensuring reliability or the group focusing on managing price risk. These groups may be distinct or integrated, purely based on how the company is organized. Another trader may be given a more aggressive role of seeking profits. Perhaps the trade order comes from the risk management staff that requests that a particular position, asset, book, market, or time frame to be hedged.

 When managing traders, managers share a common dilemma with coaches in the National Football League or other professional sports—how to command respect while giving staff the freedom to do their jobs. Good quarterbacks (the trader) must be good followers on the field (the desk) to execute the plays (the trade orders) sent in by the head coach (the VP) or the coaching staff (the risk managers.) In this analogy, the upper manager will be similar to the football coaches who rely heavily on both their offensive and defensive coordinators. (The playbook would be the RMPP, designed as an expression of general strategy and specific do's and don'ts.) Likewise, good quarterbacks also must be independent leaders to earn the loyalty of the athletes (the rest of the traders) and make quick decisions if conditions change unexpectedly.

Each VP will find his/her own solution to managing the quarterback, but here are some suggestions.

- Show respect for the irreplaceable skills that the trader offers.
- Understand the basics of trading and risk in order to see through any smoke or obfuscation that the trader is blowing your way.
- Enforce the RMPP in a consistent and continuous manner.
- Fire any trader who deserves it. Traders can sense fear and cowardice. That's their job! That's why you hired them! But remember, a good gladiator kills the lion first or suffers the alternative.

The Role of the Risk Manager and Analysts

The risk manager's role can vary, but like traders, personality is a key ingredient. Effective risk managers should be pleasant, intelligent people whose confidence resists intimidation. To the trader, the risk manager may seem like a parsimonious party-pooper. To the Board of Directors, the risk manager may appear like a dour technician speaking in foreign tongue. A thick skin, calloused by confidence and experience, is recommended for the job.

The risk manager must employ a variety of tools to measure risk and by extension play a jack-of-all-trades role. Risk analysis requires valuation tools, so risk managers often play a leading role in discussing, developing, and approving valuation models. The manager should make sure that his/her risk manager can make the distinction between good "risk management skills" and the ability to create quantitative models. A risk manager should be more focused on making existing tools "sing" rather than on building those tools. The quantitative analyst or modeler should delegate the task of building such tools.

Marking-to-Market Concept

Risk Manager Develops Inputs

Risk managers must also compile or coordinate inputs for mark-to-market analysis, and thus get pulled into the world of market analysis (quantitative and/or fundamental.) Many companies rely on traders to develop market inputs such as forward prices, volatilities, and correlations. Unfortunately, this allows the traders to inject their opinions to the inputs, thus defeating a major purpose of a mark-to-market process. Risk managers should certainly collaborate with the trading desk when analyzing inputs, but a certain degree of autonomy is important.

Risk managers require power computer tools, with the line between IT and risk management systems blurring easily. Finally, risk managers work so closely with traders that sometimes it is hard to distinguish the roles. Maintaining the distinction is important, however. When hiring a risk manager, the VP will do well not to assume that a good trader will be a good risk manager, and vice versa.

In the Concentric Circles model suggested above, analysts join risk managers in the middle ring. From a trading point of view, engineers and economists belong in this category as well. These professionals provide the analysis that the traders and risk managers utilize in valuation and risk management. Often these analysts, engineers, and economists display the ideal skills and personalities of a good risk manager, reinforcing their natural alignment.

How does one distinguish an analyst from a risk manager? First, one looks for managerial authority—risk managers have it, analysts don't. Second, risk managers focus exclusively on risk issues, whereas "analyst" is a broader term, supporting not only risk analysis but also projects for other "circles" in the Concentric Circles model. In this view, pricing specialists and quantitative analysts are not risk managers. Pricing and quantitative experts tend to be extremely proficient in technical and statistical skills, but may not have the managerial or business experience necessary to manage corporate risk.

The Role of Marketers and the Structured Products Desk

Marketers represent the interface with the client community. Marketers must understand the product being offered, the desires of the client, and how to profitably match these two needs together.

Communication and interpersonal skills are paramount, but the marketer should be intelligent enough to understand the basics of trading and risk. Come to think of it, marketers are born not made too!

Until 1999, the words "Structured Products" did not appear in energy job titles. Like many energy risk roles, the Structured Products character first appeared on Wall Street. Part marketer, part "quant," the Structured Products person was charged with the job of customizing derivative contracts for individual or complex needs. Consider the example of home mortgages—a consumer may choose a fixed-rate or a floating rate. A structured products person would have thought of this kind of choice and figured out the valuation such that the originator would be indifferent to either choice.

| Marking-to-Market Concept |
| Responding to Client Needs |

"The consumer is always right" is the marketing equivalent of marking-to-market. Deregulation provides choice to consumers whereas, under regulation, the "social contract" between utilities and government made decisions on the consumer's behalf. The flipside of choice is that it becomes the customer's responsibility to know what each wants—and to pay the consequences. In many deregulated states, many consumers expected their electricity bills only to go down. Many were surprised when some bills actually went up due to market conditions. The degree to which marketers can quicken this match marks a successful operation.

Special Teams

When football first began, players played both offense and defense, but specialization gradually took place. Today's teams will hire people to do just one thing or play on a special team. Likewise, the VP of energy trading will rely on important specialists to augment the Concentric Circles. These players would surround the circle itself in Figure 5-1. Some of these teams include the following:

Director of Information Technology (IT). The IT director must play the role of "Scottie" of the original *Star Trek* television show and movies.

He/she keeps the machines going, maintains huge databases, manages software vendors, and carefully responds to the other personalities on the ship.

In terms of personality, the IT director and staff should not be allowed to simply be technically proficient. They should demonstrate strong communication skills (e.g., be able to talk to people and hear their concerns) and be required to create good documentation of their work. In addition to their technical training, these professionals should be also as trained in the world of "the market" as any of the other members of the team. IT personnel should be expected to understand risk management to the same degree as upper management. This is essential to keeping the focus on the correct priorities.

Consider a true story. My firm was in a meeting with a prospective client and their current software vendor. A trader asked where in the interface he/she could tell if a particular option was a "call" or a "put." The other vendor's lead programmer actually replied, "We don't care if it's a call or a put!"

A different firm in the late 1990s offers a favorite example of the progressive role that IT can play on the trading floor. Every computer person had to go on the floor on a regular basis, sit at the desk, and make a trade. After the first trade the computer person received a football helmet. After each successive trade, they got a sticker for the helmet just like football players get in high school or college to reward sacks, touchdowns, etc.

Lawyers. All trading relies on contracts; hence the need for lawyers is obvious. Lawyers also play a key role in drafting, monitoring, and (especially) enforcing the RMPP.

Auditors. As trading operations grow and managerial oversight increases, the role of auditors will increase. The fundamental challenge to the manager is to ensure that the auditors will actually understand what they are auditing! Energy risk professionals have a hard enough time understanding these markets and tools, so it would be unnatural to expect that a generalist auditor will be prepared to replicate the work. The manager should attempt to communicate with the audit team and provide any educational documentation available.

Consultants. As with any business, good consultants are worth every penny they charge. A good consultant should have knowledge that is not available in-house, but that knowledge is only valuable if the utility knows how to ask the correct questions. I have been a consultant and have known many excellent consultants. Their value is to supplement, not replace managerial vision. Due to a dearth of experienced energy risk managers, locationally-challenged utilities often hire outside consultants as energy risk managers who then commute to their cities. But this should be a short-term strategy. The role of risk manager is far too central to the entire risk team not to invest heavily in your own employee.

RMPP

The Committees. As this chapter suggests, risk management involves many different people cutting across multiple disciplines. The manager can utilize different kinds of committees. As suggested in Chapter 3, each company should create a Risk Management Committee with its first charter to create the RMPP. This group should become a standing committee in order to monitor compliance with the RMPP and adjust the document to fit new realities. Other committee tasks could include setting credit policies, monitoring counterparty exposures, reviewing valuation models, interviewing key job applicants, designing and promoting in-house risk-related seminars, and communicating risk-related issues to the Board of Directors. (Alternatively, sub-committees or other standing committees could be created for these tasks.) Another possible group could be likened to a "loan committee" at a commercial bank, where managers get together to discuss and decide upon individual loans. Using this model, the firm could create a "Structured Products Committee," which would be charged with reviewing and approving either large-scale or customized product offerings.

chapter 6

Energy Risk Boot Camp: "Must Know" Concepts for Managers and Directors

Overview: The Five Minute Energy Risk Manager

Welcome to the *Energy Risk Boot Camp* designed as a primer for new recruits and a refresher course for veterans. Unlike ones previous, this chapter shifts upward in terms of technical sophistication. The intention is to challenge the manager, to introduce and explain the kinds of risk terminology and concepts necessary to control trading and risk operations. For this reason, the reader will encounter a significant increase in "Java Moment" icons as we cover some difficult territory.

This first section, the *Overview* for the chapter, can be read in five minutes (see Table 6-1 for summary.) Mastering these subjects may take years, so let's get started!

Elapsed Time 0:00: Key Assumptions Before Starting

Marking-to-Market Concept
Market Prices Drive Analysis

The market is liquid and efficient. Market prices contain all (or most) of the information needed for valuation and risk analysis—and thus market prices drive the entire process. When creating valuation models we can assume that we can create equivalent portfolios – one comprised of forward positions and another consisting of holding the asset, whether that asset is a financial product, a commodity, or even a physical generation asset that has "optionality value"—even if storing an asset like electricity is difficult, costly, or impractical.

0:35: Forward Price Behavior

A forward price represents the price one would contract today for delivery of and payment for the asset at some future time. Forward prices represent the single string of the risk-adjusted expectations of spot prices along all points of future time. Compared to money markets, energy forward prices exhibit a "split-personality[1]," in which longer-term prices behave differently from spot prices. Over time, spot and short-term prices do revert to the more stable long-term "equilibrium" prices; this process is known as "price mean-reversion." Energy markets, therefore, require a two-factor "price mean-reversion" forward price model, thus disqualifying such single-factor models as the lognormal model long popular in money markets. If you haven't already, you are simply going to have to memorize the phrase "price mean-reversion" and keep reading why the concept is so important to the power and energy markets! In addition, power and natural gas markets exhibit dramatic seasonality that requires attention.

1:21:Volatilities

If forwards represent a market-defined path of risk-adjusted expectations for spot prices, volatilities measure the certain range or band in which that path may actually occur. Each forward price displays a unique volatility. With the exception of volatility spikes for each seasonal peak period, the volatility "band" tends to be very wide in the short-term and narrows down going forward. Many volatility methodologies have been recommended, including historical analysis and forecasting, but the ideal mark-to-market approach is to back-out or "imply" volatilities from market-traded options.

2:23: Correlations

Just as the "hip bone is connected to the thigh bone," correlations express the conditional value relationships between all the complexities of the power and energy markets. There are many different correlations that impact contract valuation. Correlations within the same market—such as the correlation between spot price and the one-year forward price—are called "intra-market correlations." (These correlations dramatically impact the value of daily- versus monthly-settled options.) "Cross-market correlations" capture how prices in one market vary with another, such as how power relates to natural gas. (This directly influences the value of the spark spread options.) Other correlations include those between volume and price.

3:08: Options

Option contracts offer choice and protection, analogous to an insurance policy. We value options as a function of today's expectations of forward prices, volatility, and correlations. In a broad analogy, insurance policies contain parallel features to options: a premium is paid for both contracts; certain rules are set for making a claim (an "execution" for an option) at which time a predetermined deductible (a "strike price" for an option) is paid; and so on. Energy options differ greatly from traditional money market options; they can be simple "vanilla" contracts, more "exotic" or "structured products," or they can even be "real options" like generation plants. The most famous option valuation model, the Black-Scholes Equation, must be modified to handle power price behavior and contract specifications.

4:10: Risk Management

Risk management plays the function of navigation among changing seas: it charts a desired direction, measures the probable impact of

Elapsed Time	Topic	Summary
⏳ 0:35	Forward Price Behavior	Represents the market-defined string of the risk-adjusted expectations of spot prices along all points of future time.
⏳ 1:21	Volatilities	Measures the expected range or band within which that forward price path may actually occur as it converges into spot prices.
⏳ 2:23:	Correlations	Expresses the relationships between variables such as prices and volume of various power and energy markets.
⏳ 3:08:	Options	Offers choice and protection, analogous to an insurance policy. Valued as a function of today's expectations of forward prices, volatility, and correlations.
⏳4:10:	Risk Management	Plays the role of navigation among changing seas: it charts a desired direction, measures the probable impact of change, determines present location, and then orders corrections in the form of hedging.
⏳ 5:00	Finished!	

Table 6-1: Summary of the Five-Minute Energy Risk Manager

change, determines present location, and then orders corrections in the form of hedging. For the risk navigator, the primary instruments include the "Greeks" such as *delta* (Δ) and gamma (Γ) (which measure the sensitivity of a contract or portfolio to change in certain inputs over the entire forward term) and Value-at-Risk or "VaR" (which provides a single figure estimate of possible losses.)

5:00:

Finished!

GUEST ESSAY

The "D" and "H" Words

by Glen Justis, R.W. Beck

The "D" and "H" words. Of course, I am speaking of "Derivatives" and "Hedging." These words seem to create fear in the minds of executive management in many organizations. Interestingly, often these same organizations are those that are most in need of expanded financial risk management, which, in most cases, involves hedging and the use of derivatives to some degree.

One of my favorite books that explains risk management is Peter Bernstein's, "*Against the Gods*."[2] For me this is surprising since I've never really been that much into history. *Against the Gods* is a wonderfully detailed review of the history of risk management. Make no mistake; this book is a challenging read and is full of complex discussions on the evolution of statistical theory. In reality, though, the book is really about humankind, and how we think—rationally and irrationally—about risk and reward. In his book, Dr. Bernstein makes the observation that, "The revolutionary idea that defines the boundary between modern times and the past is the mastery of risk—the notion that the future is more than a whim of the gods and that men and women are not passive before nature." This observation puts into context both the historical significance of risk management in an objective sense as well as its bearing on the nature of humankind on a more personal level.

How does this relate to the "D" and the "H" words? The application of hedging techniques and use of derivatives in commerce has been around as long as, well, commerce itself. A *derivative* is a financial contract whose value is based on the value of some other more basic underlying variable, usually the price of a commodity or other contract. While many tend to think of derivatives in the context of exotic financial instruments used by traders to make money, derivatives were created as a vehicle to reduce risk. The fact that derivatives are traded in search of profit is a secondary, yet critically important part of the equation that allows risk management tools to exist such that price and risk become readily observable.

Valuation is truly the key here. As my friend and colleague Dr. Jay Lindgren of R.W. Beck once pointed out to me, "If you can't value it, you can't manage its risk (other than simply by not playing the game)." Through the open trading of derivatives, other market participants cannot only place a value on future price behavior, but can also trade away price uncertainty to the advantage of both parties. This is what I find appealing about the practical application of financial risk management—it allows for win-win transactions between parties that create greater efficiency and net wealth in the economy.

Like derivatives, *"hedging"* is a word that is sometimes confusing. After all, how does a "hedge fund" managed by such industry giants as John Merriweather and Myron Scholes lose $4 billion dollars? In this case, the term "hedge fund" is a misnomer. The collapse of Long Term Capital was a case of speculation gone bad, pure and simple. The true definition of a hedge, from my perspective, is that a hedge is designed to *reduce financial risk*, rather than increase it.

In order to survive in the competitive energy industry, market participants must either learn to successfully manage new risks, or avoid managing such risks by eliminating them through substantial organizational change. If leadership chooses not to manage risk, this strategy generally means selling off assets (and risks) to more risk-capable organizations. Another approach is outsourcing. While this strategy is not necessarily bad, the objective of most businesses is not just to survive but to thrive in their existing line of business. Thus, the alternative is to embrace and to benefit from modern financial risk management techniques that enhance risk-adjusted return. This is what hedging is all about. The key to enhancing risk-adjusted return is the valuation and management of optionality in both the inherent and transactional positions of an organization.

Glen Justis is national leader of R. W. Beck's energy risk management consulting practice. Prior to joining R. W. Beck, he worked for Ameren Corporation in St. Louis (formerly Union Electric Company) in power

*marketing, trading, and risk management. Mr. Justis holds a Bachelor of
Science degree in Nuclear Engineering from the University of Missouri-
Rolla and a MBA from Webster University. He may be contacted by email
at pjustis@rwbeck.com.*

HOW PROBLEMS FIT WITHIN THE PRICE-RISK PYRAMID

Learning the energy risk management in "five minutes" is appealing
but unrealistic! While the reader is again directed to the *Manager's
Bookshelf* (see Chapter 1) and other books, the balance of this chapter will
provide a few more mission-critical details that the manager should understand. This chapter is based in part on the *PowerSuite™* User Manual,
which I wrote for SAVA and reassembled here with its permission.

Understanding risk management can take years of learning and experience. To help facilitate this learning, my colleague Dragana Pilipovic and
I have developed the *Price-Risk Pyramid* (see Figure 6-1.) This pyramid
places the interrelated energy risk concepts in relation to each other.

The *Price-Risk Pyramid* symbolizes a comprehensive framework
through which to discuss analyzing, valuing, and managing energy derivatives. As Figure 6-1 suggests, the concept is that proper energy risk analysis is only possible with the integration of risk analysis, option valuation,
volatility analysis, and forward pricing. The upper layers depend on the
lower layers, just like the "FDA Food Group Chart"[3] that appears on cere-
al boxes everywhere—grains along the bottom, fruits and vegetables in the
middle, meat and dairy at the top!

The *Price-Risk Pyramid* is comprised of three layers, with each higher tier dependent on the one(s) below:

- The "markets" or price behavior level is on the bottom and provides
  the foundation of all risk analysis. This level incorporates forward
  prices, volatilities, and correlations. (Note here that a forward price
  is different than a forward contract!) This layer can incorporate both
  price and load behavior. It can also be called the "inputs" layer.

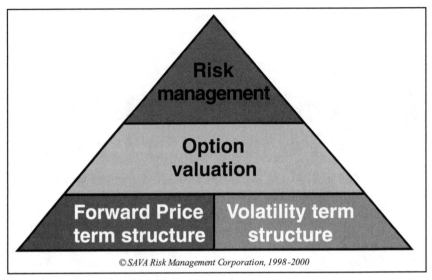

© SAVA Risk Management Corporation, 1998-2000

Fig. 6-1: The Price-Risk Pyramid

- The valuation layer resides in the middle. This stratum supports option, forward contract, swap, and other position valuation using inputs from the markets layer. Thus, the valuation tier can also be labeled the "contracts" or "positions" layer; it could also be known as the "derivatives" layer. Here we value positions that "derive" their value from the underlying input layer.
- Risk analysis sits on the top. This layer includes risk management, risk sensitivity analysis (a.k.a. the "Greeks"), hedging analysis, Value-at-Risk (VaR), etc.

The inter-dependencies within the *Price-Risk Pyramid* are crucial to properly managing energy risk. The markets layer serves as the foundation. Forward prices, volatilities, and correlations are the primary inputs to the upper layers of valuation and risk management. The middle layer therefore can be designed to focus on optionality and product structuring issues. Finally, at the top level, risk management becomes a relatively straightforward process of utilizing the lower levels of the pyramid. From the vantage of this high level, the risk manager is free to focus on the business issues of expressing and meeting risk objectives.

Using the *Price-Risk Pyramid* approach provides several benefits:

Building Block Approach. The pyramid approach allows a building block approach for solving complex problems. The classic Black-Scholes and Black models incorporate assumptions about both price behavior and contract-settlement specifications within the same model. I liken this combination approach to the "printer/fax/copier" machines available. While this "three-in-one" peripheral offers convenience, none of the functions are "best of breed." By separating and understanding the various effects of these layers, the analyst has greater flexibility for capturing the kinds of complex price behavior that characterize the power and energy markets.

Modeling Consistency. Modeling consistency helps avoid arbitrage between the various layers of risk analysis and between different business units. One would expect that the highest level of risk management—such as Value-at-Risk (VaR) analysis, for example— would be based on the same inputs and would use the same inputs as would the valuation models used by the trading desk.

Integrated Systems. From a systems point of view, the power of the pyramid rests within its ability to provide a blueprint for development, implementation, and integration. For example, the analytics group could be charged with responsibility for maintaining the forward price curves, while the trading desk would perform contract valuation. This way the traders could view, but not alter, the underlying forward price inputs. Many companies perform this step in opposite fashion: the traders create the forward price curve and give it to the analysts. There is a potential conflict of interest here, as the risk manager should be using a mark-to-market forward price curve to provide an independent benchmark against which to judge traders. Certainly traders should provide input to the curve building process—validating how it looks, helping provide access to market quotes, and even providing educated guesses on values of illiquid positions. But the manager must ensure the independence of his/her risk management process and should be sure to install checks and balances in building forward price curves, not to mention volatility matrices, correlations, and other data sets managed at the input layer.

Key Assumptions Before Starting

Using risk methods, models, and mathematics for trading and risk management requires us to make assumptions. As Jarrow and Turnbull write, "(t)he quality of any theory is a direct result of the quality of the underlying assumptions" (p. 34). These assumptions are embedded in many common risk issues and are accepted among most risk professionals, even if they over-simplify reality.[4] As assumptions, however, they match and diverge from reality to varying degrees. While risk professionals may have higher tolerances for large divergences from reality, assumptions can carry significant political risk. An assumption can trigger a reaction due to ignorance of or hostility toward the motivations and goals of trading and risk management. The worst time to be explaining the process "marking-to-market" to your board or your upper management is during a crisis! Thus, one might consider getting explicit managerial approval of these assumptions by including them in the RMPP. Some examples of possible assumptions include the following:[5]

Markets are Efficient. The marketplace in which the firm participates is assumed efficient, with adequate liquidity to exhibit meaningful price discovery; it is not subject to undue market power by an individual or block of players; and it provides enough counterparties to allow portfolio liquidation without undue penalties. These assumptions about market efficiency obviously conflict with the reality of many power markets, particularly those in illiquid regions.

No-Arbitrage. We assume that there are no arbitrage opportunities in the marketplace. For example, a person would be indifferent between buying an asset and holding it until time T versus entering into a forward contract on that asset that expires at time T. In reality, arbitrage opportunities do appear but dissipate quickly.

Term Structure of Forward Prices and Volatilities. A spot price for a future date may be valued today in terms of risk-adjusted expectations in the form of a forward price. This forward price itself would have an expected volatility. If one plotted the forward prices for all future dates, the shape of this forward price curve would have a personality over the term of forward dates (generally referred to as the "term structure of forward prices.") Likewise, there is a volatility term structure as well.

No Credit Risk. Unless otherwise noted, counterparties are assumed to always pay their obligations. This assumption directly conflicts with market reality, as evidenced by the Federal Energy Sales crisis (see Chapter 4).

Continuous Hedging. As part of its ongoing risk operations, the firm is assumed to perform continuous hedging. Continuous hedging is defined as *the process of continuously performing portfolio analysis to determine the optimum hedging strategies and immediately executing the necessary trades.*[6] This assumption implies two issues that may conflict with reality. First, we assume that a firm is indeed continuously hedging. In reality, this is rarely the case, even in liquid markets, due to the cost of the bid/ask spread and the fact that, practically speaking, it may not always be necessary. Second, we assume that the firm will always locate and be able to trade the necessary hedge contracts. It is this aspect of the continuous hedging assumption that deserves the greatest amount of discussion in the energy markets, particularly from an academic point of view.

Wilmott raises an important challenge to the continuous hedging assumption: "One of the striking features of real financial markets is that every now and then there is a sudden unexpected fall or crash... (I)t is usually not possible to hedge through the crash. One certainly cannot delta hedge as the stock market tumbles around one's ankles, and to offload all of one's positions will lead to real instead of paper losses, and may even make the fall worse."[7] This reality-meets-theory issue should resonate with most managers.

Modeling and Input Assumptions. Finally, the selection of particular models and input data itself represents an important series of assumptions that may or may not justify board-level approval. For example, the forward price assumption of "price mean reversion" versus "log-normality" can have a domino effect throughout the entire *Price-Risk Pyramid*. In another example, in the absence of good market data, assumptions about low- versus high-correlations can dramatically impact valuations. (Such model-specific assumptions will be noted in the following sections.)

Indifference Between Holding Asset vs. Forward Contract. In the derivation of financial valuation models, a bedrock assumption is that a person would be "indifferent" between a) buying the asset today and holding until some future date, versus b) signing a forward contact for the delivery of and payment for that same asset until that same future date. This assumption is guaranteed to raise the eyebrows of any power executive! Most people consider electricity a "non-storable" commodity—how can one "hold" a megawatt for future consumption? In support of this assumption, one could argue that while there are some ways of storing power directly, electricity is storable as "potential energy" in the form of the feedstock. To this way of thinking, coal or natural gas is "stored electricity" or "canned heat." Other examples would be reverse-flow reservoir/hydro-electric systems or urban chilling stations.

Each manager and company should evaluate, accept, reject, or tweak these various assumptions. While they may seem academic, making these assumptions carries a certain element of "political" risk. Imagine this scenario—your company experiences a sudden drop in profits and upper management is looking for someone to blame. Someone gets wind that your modelers made the "holding value" assumption. Next thing you know, your group is labeled and marginalized as "ivory tower" academics who don't live in reality. It can happen, as can the converse. Imagine that your company has rejected some or all of the basic risk modeling assumptions. Your firm would take on considerable modeling and operational risk since the firm is now leaving the comfort zone of the majority of thinkers and developing bold new models. Both of these examples illustrate the importance of "open disclosure" regarding assumptions with all levels of management. Energy risk is anything but easy!

Forward Price Behavior

Forward price behavior dramatically influences valuation and risk management. Due to intense seasonality and the split personality of spot-vs.-long term prices, energy price behavior is particularly difficult to understand and model. As suggested earlier, forward pricing in money markets may utilize relatively simple, single-factor models such as the lognormal distribution. A French

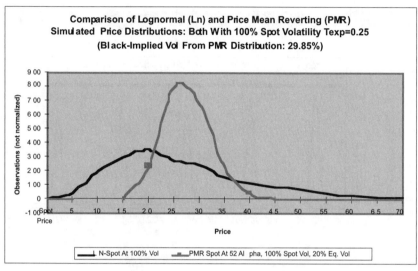

Source: Energy Risk Seminar, SAVA, 1998-2000.

Fig. 6-2: Price-Mean Reverting vs. Normal Distribution

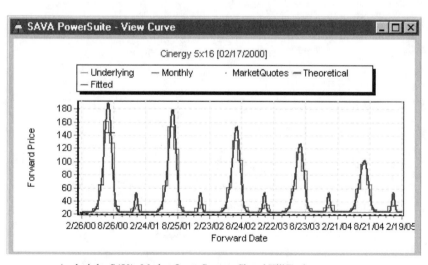

Analysis by SAVA. Market Quote Source: Chapel Hill Brokers.

Fig. 6-3: Cinergy 5X16 Daily Forward Price Curve

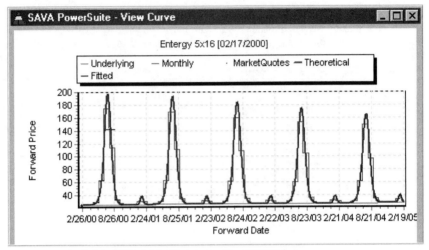

Analysis by SAVA . Market Quote Source: Chapel Hill Brokers.

Fig. 6-4: Entergy 5X16 Daily Forward Price Curve

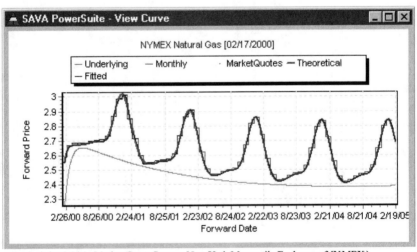

Analysis by SAV A. Market Quote Source: New York Mercantile Excha nge (NYMEX.)

Fig. 6-5: NYMEX Natural Gas Daily Forward Price Curve

professor derived this lognormal model empirically in 1900 by plotting price-return distributions at the London Stock Exchange.[8] Applying the same approach by observing power prices, the results of the distribution analysis would look very different from log-normality. As shown by Figure 6-2, power prices exhibit a price-mean reverting distribution.

Marking-to-Market Concept
Quantitative vs. Fundamental Modeling

By definition, a forward price represents the price one would contract today (also known as the Observation Date) for delivery of and payment for the asset at some future time. (See Figures 6-3 through 6-5 for sample forward price curves.) Furthermore, "(f)orward prices are risk-adjusted and net cost-adjusted expectations of spot prices at forward points in time."[9] Theoretically, there is a forward price for a MW for every second of every minute of every day in the future! Practically, however, we will limit our discussion to what we call "discrete daily" forward prices. The "forward price curve" simply plots these daily prices. In money markets, this is also known as the yield curve.

For power professionals, a common source of confusion revolves around the distinction between forward prices and expected spot prices. A forward price is a function of the expected spot price, but it also carries information regarding the cost of risk, cost of carry[10], cost of money, and other pro vs. con factors of holding the commodity in hand embedded within the concept of a convenience yield. In the wake of deregulation, this distinction also exists between quantitative and fundamental modeling, with the former focusing on non-arbitrage methods and with the latter emphasizing predictive or forecasting methods. The contemporary utility should learn to use both model approaches but use them for different purposes. As suggested by Rick Dennis of Southern Company Services, the power company should value their books using quantitative methods but strategize using fundamental models.[11] The bottom line is that manager should see to it that the fundamental and quantitative models move toward consistency.

Another source of confusion involves the important distinction between a forward price and a forward contract. A "forward price" is a very general concept, whereas a forward price contract (also known as a forward contract) locks in the forward price. In energy markets, forward contracts typically cover monthly or quarterly periods, so the discrete daily forward prices are used to calculate the value of various forward contracts. (In the *Price-Risk Pyramid*, this valuation of forward contracts occurs in the middle "valuation" layer.) Many companies plot these monthly price quotes directly as their "forward price curve."

The energy risk manager is faced with several choices when it comes to forward prices—Which forward prices are required? What market information to use?, and finally, What models should be used to describe and generate forward prices?

Which kind of forward price curves are required?

The kind of forward price analysis required is purely a function of the markets and contracts traded by the company, but power markets typically require a daily[12] forward price curve—i.e., one forward price for each date going forward until the furthest date out in one's portfolio or analysis. (This period of time between the Observation Date and the end of the analysis horizon is typically represented by the x-axis of the forward price curve graph.)

Many firms feel comfortable with monthly forward price curves, but, as will be discussed later, only daily forward price curves can be used for managing daily risk and valuing daily-settled positions.

American power companies commonly trade a combination of options and fixed-price forward contracts. These contracts can cover different time periods, or "terms," with daily periods typical in the short-term. In power markets, for example, the "spot" contract covers next day delivery and brokers commonly quote contracts for "day-after-next," "next two days," or remainder of the week. Further out in time, the market trades monthly- or quarterly-periods over which an average price is to be paid.

Even these longer periods imply daily increments since they entail daily delivery of power, which in turn will be marked against next-day spot prices at time of expiration. In this typical case, therefore, the company will need daily forward prices. While every power generation operation relies upon hourly increments for actual load balancing and short-term trading, the company will only need an hourly granularity (i.e., level of detail) in their forward price analysis if they trade and hedge hourly contracts in the forward term. Recently the Californian market moved toward 10-minute increments; companies in this market may well need such micro-granularity to fully support their books thus affected.

What market information to use?

Marking-to-Market Concept

Convergence to Market Inputs

In quantitative modeling, the best inputs for forward pricing are the kinds of market quotes one gets from brokers and exchanges. Here the focus remains on prices. (In contrast, fundamental modeling tends to build price predictions based on the "fundamental drivers" that affect price.) In a mark-to-market process, the concept is to let market price signals drive the modeling process as the primary input, much as white light is the main input into a prism. (See Figure 6-6.) The model acts like the glass prism, decomposing the price behavior by calibrating a spectrum of parameters. The optimum set of parameters is such that, when used to reconstruct the forward price curve, the model-implied forward prices best converge back to market reality.[13]

What models should be used to describe and generate forward prices? A continuing debate revolves around this question. My choice is the Pilipovic Model for the Forward Price Curve, first published by Dragana Pilipovic in 1995. The Pilipovic Model is a "two-factor price mean-reverting stochastic quantitative model".

Since this book attempts to avoid the mathematical specifics of models, and because managers will have to review all available models, it would be useful to spend a few moments understanding the components of forward price modeling. To do so, we can break the label "two-factor price mean-reverting stochastic quantitative model with seasonality functions" into its components to get a sense of the issues facing risk managers. The following are some definitions and discussion of some important terms.

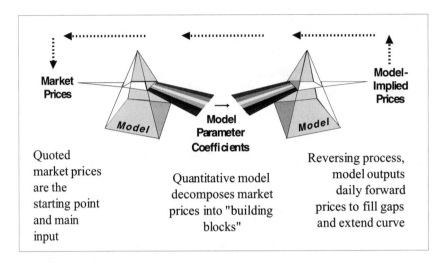

Fig. 6-6: The Model Calibration Process

Two-Factor. In mathematical terms, a "factor" is a variable that exhibits random behavior, or a process containing such a variable. The Pilipovic Model contains two such factors: the spot price and the equilibrium price. This model reflects the fact that energy forward price markets often exhibit a short-term behavior that looks very different from the behavior of the longer-dated portions of the curve. The Pilipovic Model helps us capture this "split-personality" of energies in a way that allows convergence between the short- and long-term price behaviors.

Price Mean Reversion. Models are designed to explain and define market price behavior. As suggested above, while money markets (equities, interest rates, foreign exchange, etc.) may indeed be adequately described with a single-factor lognormal model, energy markets (electricity, natural gas, oil, etc.) are better modeled by two-factor "price mean-reverting" models.[14] In simple terms, spot prices in a price-mean reverting market tend to revert to an equilibrium price over time.

The speed of this "reversion process" is a function of many market variables, two of which include the kinds of events that "shock" and dissipate in a particular market and the market's resilience to reconciling supply and demand. In power markets, the "big" events typically involve weather, including heat/cold waves or big storms. While large in terms of impact, these events tend to dissipate rapidly, allowing a spike in the spot price to generally revert to equilibrium relatively quickly. In contrast, fundamental market changes—such as a nuclear power plant being taken offline—can push spot prices off equilibrium for many months or even years. If such fundamental changes become permanent, the market replaces the "old" equilibrium price with a new one reflecting the new market conditions.

This equilibrium price is like an average or mean price to which the market will revert when supply and demand are in balance. The market itself sets this equilibrium price over time. Like all prices and market variables, the equilibrium price can and does change as the market's balance of capacity, transmission, load demand, and other fundamentals change. When looking at market prices, we see this equilibrium price in two different ways. First, the equilibrium price tends to appear—adjusted for discounting—in longer-term forward prices. Second, as mentioned before, the equilibrium price will "appear" in spot prices when supply and demand are in balance. In terms of the forward price curve, if spot prices are "out of equilibrium," one would see forward prices begin to revert back to equilibrium price behavior over the long term. We can observe mean reversion as the short-term forward prices converge to the long-term.

Stochastic. The model allows for stochastic (i.e., random) behavior in both the spot price and long-term equilibrium price behavior. This is an important issue since it helps support our objective of creating a model that realistically reflects random change in both the short-term as well as in the long-term.

Quantitative Model. While specifically designed for energy markets, the Pilipovic Model belongs to a modeling tradition that first evolved in the traditional financial markets. Quantitative models focus on the behavior of prices themselves, rather than attempting to model the fundamental microeconomic forces that drive prices. Generally speaking, quantitative models will reflect the most important fundamental drivers (although not necessarily directly), since the quantitative analysis process starts with actual prices. By comparison, fundamental modeling starts with such drivers in order to wind up with prices.

Seasonality Functions. Energies such as electricity and natural gas also show dramatic seasonality. In terms of dollars, power's seasonality dwarfs even that of natural gas. (In Figure 6-2, compare the large summer seasonality magnitude of the Cinergy 5x6 power market with the winter seasonality magnitude for NYMEX natural gas. As with all market variables, seasonality can and will change over time. The "El Nino" effect is just one example of how seasonality can vary from one year to another. Another issue impacting seasonality is overall market capacity. From the perspective of trading in the Year 2000, some traders believe that the addition of capacity in the future will start shaving off seasonal peaks in the coming years.

As yet another example, the "shape" of seasonality of early North American power markets has changed dramatically. Case in point: the seasonality functions with the Pilipovic Model have evolved with the marketplace. When first published, the Pilipovic Model employed a double-cosine function to reflect market prices, which perhaps mirrored the new market's expectations that forward prices would behave like historical temperatures. By 1997-98, however, the market matured to the point of trading the shoulder months far more narrowly.[15] In response, Pilipovic published new seasonality functions to operate with the basic underlying model.[16] In another case of market evolution, the natural gas forward price curve generally had a single winter seasonality. But as power markets increased the use of gas to fuel second-generation plants during summer peak months, the natural gas curve began exhibiting a second seasonal peak during the summer. While this summer natural gas peak was small compared to power, it does symbolize how markets can and do change.

The concept of price mean reversion will resound throughout the *Price-Risk Pyramid*. Values and risk sensitivities are based on the valuation models that in turn depend on forward price inputs. Volatility analysis is also conditioned on mean reversion. So each time a portfolio is analyzed, the effects of mean reversion appear in the valuation phase.

Volatilities: Valuing the Range of Expectations

Volatility is at the heart of risk, yet it is an elusive concept that is hard to master and model. Like forward price modeling, proper volatility analysis serves as part of the foundation of the *Price-Risk Pyramid*. Please note that the same fundamental vs. quantitative model dichotomy exists in volatility analysis. As could be expected, I will be address my comments to quantitative volatility modeling in the financial tradition

Volatility is usually expressed by the Greek symbol sigma, σ, and is defined as the following: *volatility measures the magnitude of percentage changes in prices over time, in annualized terms*. It equals the price return's standard deviation normalized by time.

As can be seen in Figure 6-7, volatility can be measured across forward time periods and expressed as a function of forward time and option strike price. (The shape of this forward volatility personality is

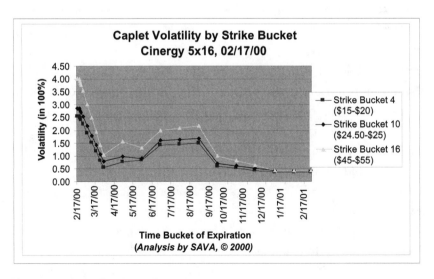

Fig. 6-7: Votality Term Structure

referred to as *volatility term structure*.) In normal price terms, energy spot price volatility tends to be very high in the short or near term, with longer-term volatility stabilizing at some equilibrium rate. This stable equilibrium volatility can have several possible explanations. One explanation is that the market tends to have a steady expectation of market behavior in the future and—in the absence of radical, fundamental changes in the marketplace—does not update these expectations on a day-by-day basis. Another idea could be that the people, at the aggregate market level, generally expected the future to be less chaotic than the present. Of course, since power markets are seasonal, it is also natural to see seasonal volatility spikes.

Another way of visualizing volatility is as a band or "confidence interval" around the forward price curve with some probability associated with that band. This concept should underscore that our measurement of volatility is a function of market expectations and that spot prices retain the possibility of jumping to any level.

Volatility models must capture the complexity of observed market behavior. It is much simpler to assume that volatility is constant or "flat" during the term of an option. This is an assumption within the Black-Scholes model. But compared to money markets, energy volatilities are anything but flat. While money market volatilities are also not flat, they are so much lower than energy volatilities. It's like comparing skiing in Wisconsin to the Colorado Rockies! (With all due respect to my home skiing resort, Wilmott Mountain, Wisconsin!)

The manager must determine (or at least approve) what kind of volatility methodology will be used on the trading and risk desks. The choices include three general methods:

Historical Volatility. Historical volatility is calculated using historical price data. This value is typically an average value for the period of time being analyzed. Since volatilities are a function of time, the analyst could calculate different values of historical volatility for different periods of time. This is due to the fact that volatility is generally not constant over time. Historical volatility values are popular among some analysts, primarily because they are easy to calculate, and because they provide historical volatility benchmarks. Unfortunately, these volatility measures only "look backward"[17] and do not capture current market expectations of forward market price behavior.

However, there are numerous volatility models that can be used to forecast volatility given its behavior from the past. Typically, these forecasting models based on past history are the fallback to volatility treatment in the absence of forward looking option quotes that make possible market-implied volatility (as described next).

Marking-to-Market Concept
Option-implied Volatilities

Market-Implied Volatility. At any given time, the market expresses its expectations of the future through different kinds of pricing information. The forward price curve contains information regarding forward pricing. Option prices, however, contain all the volatility information. A market-implied volatility would be a volatility implied by such market quotes for contracts with optionality. Calculating or approximating market-implied volatilities is a critical part of creating a "marked-to-market" valuation and risk management process. The idea is to value contracts consistent with what the general market believes, as opposed to basing the valuation and risk management on an internal or even personal view. The analyst's ability to back out meaningful market-implied volatilities is limited by the number of option quotes available. (See next section on model-implied volatilities.)

Model-Implied Volatility. Model-implied volatility is a volatility implied by market quotes with the additional help of price, volatility and/or option models and their parameters. Model-implied volatilities can be the next best thing compared to market-implied volatilities; the model parameter values are often a hybrid of market-implied and historically based data. The benefits of volatility models include:

Models can help fill in the gaps. If the analyst cannot get option quotes covering all his/her needed expiration periods, models can help fill in volatility behavior that would be theoretically consistent with whatever market quotes are available.

Models can extend volatility term structure. Models can help the analyst create theoretical volatility curves beyond the last traded contract.

Models help analyze competition. Models can help breakdown market quotes into more helpful information. For example, a model can help back-out the competition's expectations of volatility and price behavior. In addition, breaking volatility information into smaller periods of time helps the user look for pricing opportunities.

Models help "unify" volatility information. Finally, models help "unify" volatility information being implied by different yet related options. Such options are written on the same underlying forward prices but offer different optionalities, terms, strikes, etc. Certain models[18] take such different contracts and analyze them simultaneously to squeeze out as much market information as possible. In effect, this allows the user to make the most of even illiquid markets.

Marking-to-Market Concept
Mark-to-Model Approximations

As stated earlier, models can help the analyst create or approximate a marked-to-market portfolio. In effect, companies in illiquid markets develop "mark-to-model" processes as approximation for marking-to-market. If model-implied volatilities are used in such a context, it is important for the analyst, the manager, the manager's manager, the risk valuation committee, and any other concerned party to consider the degree to which the models reflect market reality.

Correlations

Correlations measure the relationship between one kind of price with another kind of price. Valuation and risk management rely upon the correlation of price returns (rather than the correlation between the prices themselves) for three reasons. First, the price of an asset is a non-negative value, hence analyzing price-to-price correlations will always give you a high positive value. (Instead, we are interested in how prices change together.) Second, the price behavior has stochastic terms that are proportional to the actual levels. And third, the risk that a holder of an asset is exposed to after the purchase is not defined by the absolute level of the purchase price, but rather by the change in that purchase price.

Symbolized by the Greek letter *rho* (ρ), correlation factors appear in many valuation equations. Often, modelers assume correlation to be either "1" or "0"—for the sake of simplicity—and so the correlation factors essentially drop from view. But the manager must be aware and insist upon the following correlations being included by their risk operations— or at least get explanations why they are not being used.

 Intra-market correlations represent the correlation within the same market of forward prices along the forward price curve. For example, one might track the correlation between spot prices and a forward price one month out. If one created a table of all such correlations, this would be the "intra-market correlation" matrix. Such a matrix is essential to linking daily-settled to monthly-settled volatilities. In this light, intra-market correlations are often the missing link in contemporary attempts to value monthly-settled caps, primarily due to the fact that there are not enough data to run correlation analysis. Here is a key place where managers must approve assumptions about the intra-market correlation matrix in the absence of mark-to-market analysis.

Cross-market correlations represent the relationship between two markets. One could simply measure a general spot-to-spot correlation between *Market A* and *Market B*, or one could analyze the intra-market correlations between the two markets. The manager would see the impact of such correlation, for example, in the portfolio analysis and risk limits. The lower the correlation between markets, the lower the portfolio risk; this is known as the *diversification effect*—losses in one market may be offset by profits in another market. (This is a gross simplification, of course.) Insurance companies exemplify diversified portfolios. A large risk exists, however, of the systematic risk suddenly growing, such as in the case of a hurricane hitting a large region covered by the insurance company.

The manager would also see the diversification effect of correlations when valuing the "spark spread" option. This is a two-commodity option in which the holder buys a certain quantity of natural gas in order to generate electricity; the value of this option depends in part on the forward price curves and volatilities of both markets—and the correlation between them. The higher the correlation of the electricity and natural gas markets, the lower the option value. Other correlations would include the correlation of volume to price as an input to swing option valuation, correlation of retail customer's load to price, etc.

The Valuation Layer

Square in the middle of the *Price-Risk Pyramid*, the valuation layer contains the financial models that price contracts and positions using the "inputs" from the bottom tier of the pyramid. The valuation layer is where we put price on both fixed-price and variable-price contracts. Fixed-price contracts depend almost exclusively on the forward price curve; fixed-price contracts include forward contracts, futures, and swaps. Variable-price contracts— also known as "options"—derive their value not only from the forward price curve but from the volatility and correlation inputs as well.

Significant attention will be given to options next. Fixed-price contracts are far easier to value than options; their simplicity makes them effective instruments. As noted earlier, a "forward contract" is different than a forward price, but there are different kinds of forward contracts as well.

In its most generic definition, a "forward contract is an agreement where one party promises to buy an asset from another party at some specific time in the future at some specified price."[19] A forward contract is "not normally traded on an exchange"[20] but instead is offered in the "over-the-counter" (OTC) market or traded bilaterally. These contracts can be standardized or customized.

A "futures contract" is a forward contract that is traded at an exchange.[21] These contracts are very standardized and typically offer the credit protection of the exchange's margin account service.

A "swap" is also a type of forward contract traded in the OTC market. Most textbooks defined a swap exclusively as a "financial contract which obligates both counter-parties to a series of cash payments for a fixed period of time"[22] with the emphasis on "cash settlement." In practice, energy markets[23] often uses the phrase "swap" to describe any position that trades a "fixed" position for a "floating" one.[24] For example, a one-month forward contract for the cash payment of physical delivery could be characterized as a swap—the buyer would be paying a fixed cash price for the delivery of electricity which will have a floating value captured by the actual spot prices that occur during each day of delivery that month.

To help set the stage for valuing a forward-type contract, imagine this totally unrealistic contract: the contract specifies that at expiration a single MWh begins delivery instantaneously and the cash payment for that MWh would be wired simultaneously. The price of that forward contract would essentially equal the forward price for that MWh.

 In energy markets, however, we typically have delivery over a longer period of time with payments lagging for a period of time after delivery. Valuing a forward price contract in energy markets is actually a relatively straightforward process. We need to come up with a single, average fixed-price by summing up the value of both the electricity delivered and cash being paid. The value of an energy swap[25] is as follows:

Equation 6-1:

$$F_{t,T}^{swap} = \frac{\sum_{x=1}^{} F_{t,x} Q_x df_x}{\sum_{y=1}^{} Q_y df_y}$$

Where:

$F_{t,T} =$ swap price for delivery period T valued at Observation Date, t
$t =$ the Observation Date
$T =$ the swap period
$N =$ the number of delivery days in swap period
$x =$ an individual delivery date (also known as a "delivery leg")
$M =$ the number of payment days for swap
$y =$ an individual payment date (also known as a "payment leg")
$F =$ discrete daily forward price
$Q_x =$ quantity delivery per delivery leg
$Q_y =$ quantity covered by payment leg
$df =$ discounting factor on date of observation (x or y)

When you look at Equation 6-1, you can see the impact of the "time value of money" in that there may be a lag when the value of the power is delivered and when the payment is being made. While this may not have a huge impact on relatively small deals, the larger the swap the bigger the impact will be.[26]

Marking-to-Market Concept

Real Prices and Role of Modeling

One final, general comment about the valuation layer. In the final analysis, the value of a contract or position will be judged by someone's willingness to pay for it, regardless of what any particular equation or methodology suggests. This fact supports the value of the mark-to-market process more than it denigrates the value of valuation models. The more liquidity in the market, the more that prices for the same contract will settle around the same price. In other words, the better the liquidity, the narrower the bid-ask. Where will these prices come from, especially in young illiquid markets? There are some traders who are simply born with the ability to put a price on things. But the rest of us will rely on valuation models.

Options and the Value of Choice

Options are all about choice. Each kind of choice that carries with it the right but not the obligation is some form of an option. In terms of the *Price-Risk Pyramid*, optionality depends heavily upon the inputs (forward price, volatility, and correlations) and can, in turn, dramatically influence the top tier of portfolio analysis and hedging. Many fine books exist to provide good introductions to options. The reader is advised to see the *Manager's Bookshelf* in Chapter 1 and the Bibliography for other references. This section will focus only on some key issues used in later chapters, with more details being introduced in Chapters 8-10.

The old adage about "buy low, sell high" applies perfectly to thinking about options. For a typical option, the buyer owns the right to buy some asset at a particular price (known as the "strike" price or "k".) When deciding to execute the option or not, the buyer compares the strike price with the going rate for the same asset. If the strike price is less than the going rate, the typical person would execute the option to buy the asset at this "lower" price. Economically, the option holder would enjoy the benefits of striking this option in one of two ways—either he/she could now own the

asset without having to pay the higher market price or he/she can resell the
asset in the open market and pocket the profit. In options parlance, a call
option is "in-the-money" if the strike price is below the going market price;
"at-the-money" if the strike price equals the market price; and "out-of-the
money" if the strike price is above the market price. (See Table 6-2).

Relative Value	Relationship of Strike Price and Market Price for a Long Call Option
At-the-Money	The strike price (K) equals the current price of the underlying asset. ($S=K$ or $F=K$). Ideally, in energy markets, this comparison should include relative discounting to delivery vs. payment dates.
In-the-Money	The strike price (K) is less than the current price of the underlying asset. ($S>K$ or $F>K$).
Out-of-the-Money	The strike price (K) is more than the current price of the underlying asset. ($S<K$ or $F<K$).
Near-the-Money (In or Out)	The strike price (K) is generally near (but not equal to) the current price of the underlying asset.
Deep-In-the-Money (alternatively Far-In-the-Money)	The strike price (K) is so much less than current price of the underlying asset with little chance of the underlying price approaching the strike price before expiration. ($S>>K$ or $F>>K$). Also applies to "Deep/Far-Out-of-the-Money."

Table 6-2: Parlance for an Option's Value

When thinking about options, the reader also should remember that the value of an option is proportional to the number of "choices" that it provides the holder of that option. In the North American power markets, the most common options are daily-settled options and monthly-settled options that cover monthly, quarterly, or other multi-day periods. A daily-settled option allows the option holder the right to exercise an option for next-day delivery for every business day during the term of the option. A monthly-settled option allows the option holder just one right per month for delivery for all business days in that month.

Since more choice means more value, a daily-settled option would have a higher premium than a monthly-settled option covering the same period. Option value also increases with the volatility of a market. In other words, as a market becomes more volatile, the value of having "choices" will increase. There are numerous other "drivers" of option value, including time to expiration (the more time, the higher the option value) and correlations (the higher the correlation, the lower the option premium).

In terms of cash-flows, unlike forward or swap contract, option buyers of an option must pay the "option premium" upfront, with this payment a "sunk cost" regardless of whether the option is ever utilized or "exercised." Alternatively, you can think of option premiums in the same way as insurance premiums. With insurance, the higher your deductible, the lower your premium. Likewise, in call options, the higher your strike price the lower your premium. You can also think about a real estate option. You see some property you might like to buy but are not ready to buy right away. For a fee, you buy an option on the property. In return for the premium you pay, you have a non-binding reservation on the property.

Understanding the naming conventions for options is a good first step toward a more complete understanding of options themselves. (Remember: fixed-price contracts without any optionality are generally called "forwards" or "swaps.") Over the years, options analysts and traders have assigned general names to several classes of execution rights. (Execution refers to the act of option holder acting on the contingent right; for example, if you have the right to buy 1 MWh of power at $500 MWh strike price, you have the right to "execute" that option by buying that power at the strike price.) Named after continents, these option classes tend to be standardized. While the following conventions use the names of continents, the traders on each continent do not necessarily use one class of contract more than the other.

- European options—execution only at expiration;
- Asian options—a European on an average price contract; and,
- American options—execution allowed any time during a pre-defined period.

In energy markets, European and Asian options are by far the most popular. (See Table 6-3 for a summary of common option contracts traded.) Many energy contracts are European-type options but with strike prices that are averages for a period. (The averaging effect is so common that most energy options can be classified as Asian. The traditional Asian, however, is not as common in power markets as it is in money markets.) Furthermore, European-type options in energy markets tend to specify multiple exercise dates within the same contract period. For example, a daily-settled option allows the buyer the right to strike the option for each individual delivery day during the term. This kind of option is also known as a "cap" or a "Bermuda" option.

American options allow the buyer to exercise any time during some pre-specified time period and up to the final expiration date. As such, these options give the holder ever more flexibility in the exercise, and thus American options will generally cost more than European and Asian options with otherwise equivalent terms. As path-dependent options, Americans are also harder to value than European-type contracts. Closed-form solutions are not possible, thus requiring the use of *tree methodologies*. Pure American options are rare in energies. Swing options are a form of American options; swing options allow the buyer to vary or "swing" the volume of energy being delivered. As such, swing options can be considered co-dependent American options.

Non-standardized contracts are often called "structured products," with the verb "structuring" used to describe the process of customizing a contract to some client's needs. A structured product is a customized derivative contract that has some unique features, often combining different kinds of swaps and/or options. Generally speaking, a structured product should carry a premium over standard products in terms of risk and reward. Energy firms should attempt to value structured products in a mark-to-market manner, while recognizing the impact of the unique client needs that inspired the need for that particular structured product. While a structured product may be used as a hedge, the fact that it is "unique" or "customized" does weaken its value as a hedge. Standardized "off-the-shelf" contracts are better hedges; structured products should be used as hedges as the "hedge of last resort" for uncommon risks.

General Family of Options	Option Types within Family
European and Asian Options	Pure European Caps (Daily-settled), Floors, Straddles
	Truncated Asian (Average Price) Caps (Monthly-settled), Floors, Straddles Into Delivery
	Asian (Average Price) Caps, Floors, Straddles Cash Settled
	European Caps, Floors, Straddles Into Daily Vs. Average
	Swaptions
American Options (rare)	American Into Spot
	American Into Forward
Swing Options (Special American) (a.k.a. full requirements contract, multiple-peaker)	Price Swing (embedded co-dependency)
	Demand Swing (valued as "European" type option)
	Forward Starting Swing
	Multiple-Peaker Swing Options
Basis Options (Boption)	Demand Swing Basis Spread Forwards, Swaps
	Boptions and Index Options
	Transpread: Transmission Demand Swing Option on a Basis Spread
	Spark or Crack Spread Options

Table 6-3: Survey of Energy Options (Source: The Energy Options Seminar, SAVA Risk Management Corporation, 1998-2000.)

Another general characteristic of options includes the "action" types of Calls, Puts, Straddles, Caps, Floors, and Collars. As stated in *Derivatives Securities*,[27] *"The names "call" and "put" come from the actions potential taken by the holders of the contracts (the long position.) Call options give the holder the option to buy, that is, to call the asset away from someone else. Put options give the holder the option to sell, or to put the asset to someone else."*

Using the call and the put as the basic building blocks, one can construct a variety of "structured products". For example, a "straddle" consists of one long call and a long put with the same exercise period and strike price. The value of a daily-settled straddle is the sum of the values of the daily-settled cap with a daily-settled floor. In energy markets, however, pure calls and puts are rare unless the contract covers a specific day or hour. Instead, it is far more common for the markets to trade structured products that cover more than one delivery date. These general products include the following:

Caps. Caps are a series of European call options that are identical in every way except for their expirations. Each of these individual options is called a "caplet."[28]

Floors. Floors are a series of European put options that are identical in every way except for their expirations.

Straddles, Strangles, and Collars. Caps and floors can be combined to make various structured products including a straddle (a long call and a long put with the same strike prices), strangle (a long call and a long put with the different strike prices), and collar (a long position in a cap and a short position in a floor).

More attention will be given to options and optionality in Chapters 8-10, particularly regarding the concept involving the basic "pay-off diagram." Options represent a fascinating topic and the reader is encouraged to look beyond this book for greater details on the subject.

Risk: The Probable Impact of Change

Risk management embodies the process and the tools used for evaluating, measuring, and managing the various risks within a company's portfolio of financial, commodity, and other assets. (See Chapter 9 for a description of these various risks.) In energy markets, proper risk management depends not only upon proper portfolio analysis tools but also upon a solid foundation of forward price, volatility, and option analysis. For this reason, risk management is placed on top of the *Price-Risk Pyramid*. The primary risk tools include the following:

- Risk sensitivity analysis (a.k.a. the "Greeks")
- Profit-and-loss (P&L) analysis
- Hedging analysis
- Value-at-Risk (VaR)

Risk Sensitivity Analysis

 Risk sensitivity analysis attempts to estimate how "sensitive" a contract, book, or portfolio is to certain set changes in the underlying marketplace. Risk sensitivity measures are commonly known as the "Greeks." (See Table 6-4.) These measures are symbolized by such Greek letters as *delta* (Δ) and *gamma* (Γ). The Greek values are expressed as positive or negative units. A positive value suggests that if the market moves one unit of a particular Greek measure, the contract and/or portfolio will gain in value. A negative value would suggest a loss if such a move occurs.

Example. Let's say that a contract had a delta expressed in one-dollar move of $20,000. This would mean that if the underlying forward prices moved up by one dollar, the contract value would increase by $20,000.

Example. If the gamma, expressed in one-dollar moves, was given by a value of negative $3,000, this would mean that if the forward prices moved up by one dollar, the delta of the contract—also expressed in terms of one-dollar moves—would decrease by a value of $3,000.

In money markets, the Greek risk measures of delta, gamma, vega, and theta are usually expressed by units in dollar terms. When looking at energy markets, it is also useful to look at delta and gamma in contractual terms. Vega is not easily expressed in contract terms, as we would need to define a standardized option contract to use in expressing the vega.

Theta is also not expressed in contract terms (as what contract would one use as the basis for its value?). The contract terms can be defined by segments of forward time. These segments may be called and organized as a "time bucket." (See Chapter 9). For example, if the time segment covers the month of June, then the contract delta of 100 would mean that you are long 100 June contracts. Contractual units can be compared across markets that share the same underlying forward contracts. One would not want to be mixing apples and oranges by mixing up 5x16 power, 7x24 power, natural gas, and other assorted contractual units.

Of the Greeks, delta and gamma will receive the most attention in this book because they are a manager's first priority to understand. If the manager can grasp these concepts, he/she may then use other more advanced books to explore other risk sensitivities. In addition, the kinds of price risk captured by delta and gamma tend to loom largest on a power company's portfolio—and thus should attract the greatest attention.

Risk sensitivity to interest rates, *rho* (ρ), certainly exists but is generally dwarfed by delta and gamma risks. There is a political risk of not including rho in a risk management process. There may be an upper-

Greek	Symbol	Sensitivity to change in:
Delta	Δ	Price
Vega	Vega	Volatility
Theta	Θ	Time (time decay)
Rho	ρ	Discount rate
Gamma	Γ	Delta (second order)

Table 6-4: Traditional Price Risk Greeks (Source: The Energy Risk Seminar, SAVA Risk Management Corporation, 1997-2000.)

level executive in the company who heralds from the money markets, where rho draws considerably more attention. He/she may either require rho out of habit or think less of any manager who is not including rho in their risk analysis.

Risk sensitivity to time decay, theta (Θ), may or may not have a dramatic impact. In the case of short-term contract, the theta risk will be dwarfed by delta and gamma. But for very long-term contracts, or in the case of valuing physical assets over 10- or 20-year periods, the impact of time can become considerable. When the manager is considering which risk sensitivities to monitor, the basic rule of thumb is to measure the potential impact and then monitor the risks that require monitoring.

Value-at-Risk (VaR): The Single Figure Estimate

Value-at-Risk (VaR) is a single-figure estimate of possible loss over some time horizon with some probability or confidence level. VaR is very popular thanks to its perceived "simplicity" (which also represents its greatest weakness.) There are several ways of expressing the level at which VaR is calculated—probability level, confidence interval, and by number of standard deviations. There are also numerous ways of calculating VaR. The typical VaR approach is to generate a single-figure estimate of potential losses for a particular time horizon.

Of the various VaR methodologies available, only two carry significance in a mark-to-market environment.

Marking-to-Market Concept
Market-driven VaR

Variance/Covariance. This methodology calculates expected change in portfolio value using statistical tools of variance, skew, and kurtosis, within the context of the valuation and portfolio analysis models and frameworks. When based on market-price inputs and market-driven models, this methodology is applicable to a marked-to-market methodology. This approach, however, should only be used as a quick analysis tool for periods of forward time, such as one of a few days, a week, or at most several weeks out. Beyond that, the method becomes less meaningful, because so many different things can happen that the number becomes a less-and-less educated guess. Furthermore, the Variance/Covariance methodology does not capture the impact options (also known as the "non-linearity" of options.) For more robust and longer-term VaR value, a meaningful Monte Carlo Simulation methodology is required.

Monte Carlo Simulations. This methodology attempts to simulate the stochastic processes resident within a valuation and risk management framework. A benefit of simulations is that one can simulate many paths of what can happen in the future, thus allowing VaR analysis of much longer time horizons such as out a month or two. The processes that should exhibit a random or stochastic behavior should be simulated using the Monte Carlo process, but the processes should be constrained by the market realities (such as market-implied forward prices and volatilities.) To be meaningful, Monte Carlo simulations should be based on a comprehensive modeling framework—one that includes proper option valuation methodologies based on a robust input layer that can be simulated. Remember the *Price-Risk Pyramid*? Here is a perfect example of how the various layers fit together. Additionally, the Monte Carlo simulations can apply the corporate hedging strategy. As a result, the company can look at VaR without hedging assumptions and VaR with hedging processes in place.

A potential danger of VaR is that some managers mistakenly equate VaR with risk management, placing all their eggs in one basket by relying on a single measure of sensitivity. VaR's virtue of simplicity becomes its greatest vice when managers rely too heavily upon the approach. We have labeled this as the "VaR Vacuum."[29] When performed in a vacuum, VaR literally drains time and resources from complete valuation modeling and risk management. The optimal solution for the manager is to understand that VaR is just one important measure within a well-balanced, integrated risk management approach, as will be outlined in Chapters 8-10.

ENDNOTES

[1] Pilipovic, Dragana, and Wengler, John, *Forward Roll*, Energy Risk magazine, August, 1995.

[2] See the *Manager's Bookshelf* in Chapter 1.

[3] See the U.S. Food and Drug Administration web site: www.fda.gov/fdac/special/foodlabel/pyramid.html.

[4] In her book, *Energy Risk*, Pilipovic notes that "(a) risk manager wants to ensure that such simplifications or at least their side effects are minimized" (p. 15).

[5] Different assumptions apply to different situations. Wilmott (p. 75-76) does a nice job of summarizing the assumptions behind the famous Black-Scholes equation: 1) The underlying follows a lognormal random walk; 2) The risk-free interest rate is a known function of time; 3) There are no dividends on the underlying; 4) Delta hedging is done continuously; 5) There are no transaction costs on the underlying; and 6) There are no arbitrage opportunities. Jarrow and Turnbull employ the following five assumptions throughout their book: 1) There are no market frictions; 2) Market participants entail no counterparty risk; 3) Markets are competitive; 4) Market participants prefer more wealth to less; and 5) Prices have adjusted so that there are no arbitrage opportunities (p. 34.)

[6] Pilipovic, 1998, p. 229.

[7] Wilmott, p. 325.

[8] Bachelier, Louis, "Theorie de la Speculation," *Annales de l'Ecole Normale Superierure* 17 (1900). Translated in A.J. Bones, *The Random Character of Stock Market Prices*, edited by Paul H. Cotner, MIT Press, Cambridge, Mass, 1967.

[9] Pilipovic, 1998, p. 80.

[10] Hull defines cost of carry as "the relationship between futures prices and spot prices... This measures the storage cost plus the interest that is paid to finance the asset less the income earned on the asset" (p. 69.)

[11] Forward Power Markets Conference, Washington, DC. Organized by Center for Business Intelligence (CBI.) October 14-16, 1998.

[12] Many firms feel comfortable with monthly forward price curves, but, as will be discussed later, only daily forward price curves can be used for managing daily risk and valuing daily-settled positions.

[13] The modeling principles of "calibration" and "implied variables" are eloquently endorsed as "ideas that work" by Emanuel Derman in his essay *The Future of Modeling* in the 10th Anniversary issue of Risk Magazine, December 1997, p. 164.

[14] Price process may revert to a price mean, yield mean, or the some other equilibrium, average, or mean. It is interesting to note that money markets do revert to an equilibrium yield; but since this reversion generally takes many years – often seen as business cycles—one generally does not see its effect appear in models (Pilipovic, 1998, p. 31.)

[15] Thanks to Parks Mitchell of Tennessee Valley Authority and Jeffrey Roark of the Southern Company for their valuable insights into early power price behavior.

[16] Pilipovic, Dragana and Wengler, John, *Debut of Two New Seasonality Functions*, The Desk, July 1, 1998.

[17] True story: During a power conference in 1998, I explained, "using historical prices is like driving with your rear view mirror." A professor actually raised his hand and said "but sometimes the road is so foggy that your only clear view is in the rear view mirror." If this is ever the case in markets it may be advisable to stay off the roads!

[18] The *Univol* model by Dragana Pilipovic is an example of such a unifying model. Pilipovic holds a pending U.S. Patent on the method.

[19] Wilmott, p. 16. Hull offers that "a forward contract is a particularly simple derivative security." (p. 2.)

[20] Hull, p. 2.

[21] Hull, p. 3; Wilmott, p. 16

[22] Jarrow and Turnbull, p. 674. Also see Hull, p. 111 where he further describes swaps as "portfolios of forward contracts."

[23] Hull specifically states that "swaps are now becoming increasingly available on commodities" and describes an oil-for-cash contract (p. 129.)

[24] I will employ this more general definition throughout the course of this book.

[25] For a discussion of how forward price and futures prices differ, see Hull (p. 56-57.)

[26] Can you imagine the following case: A CFO goes to a bank and says "how about your bank gives me $10,000 cash a day for the next thirty days and we'll pay you back all $30,000 in two months." Not likely. The bank would apply a discounting factor to compensate for the time between when the cash was being delivered and when it is repaid. The same must hold true for energy swaps, be they physically or financially settled. As with all derivatives, the "no arbitrage" principle must hold.

[27] Jarrow and Turnbull, p. 14.

[28] Hull, p. 374. Pilipovic, p. 107.

[29] Dragana Pilipovic and I first published portions of this section in *The VaR Vacuum*, Energy +Power Risk Management, November 1999.

chapter 7

THE DEAL PROCESS: FROM THE DESK TO DELIVERY

THE MANAGER'S 20,000 FOOT VIEW

RMPP   To an upper level manager, a single deal flowing through the trading desk—moving from front-to-back office—can seem like a car viewed from 20,000 feet above in an aircraft. The manager's job is to focus on the infrastructure around that deal. This chapter will explore that infrastructure from the vantage of the deal process and highlight where limits and managerial oversight might be required in the transaction flow, with special focus placed on how that flow is impacted by the *Risk Management Policies and Procedures* (RMPP). As seen in Figure 7-1, the individual transaction flows through the following steps:

- **Motivation.** Starting with why a deal is required as a function of the *Risk-Return Strategy.*
- **Approved Counterparties.** Potential deals are first filtered through the counterparty list with available trade ceiling as per the RMPP.
- **Allowed Contracts.** Potential structured products are selected from the RMPP.
- **Initiation and Negotiation.** The trader initiates and negotiates a deal, often with the support of the middle office.
- **Deal Approval, Capture and Booking.** The deal must pass through risk-limit checks when being entered into the trading system and then before being booked into the portfolio.
- **Confirmation.** The back office confirms the deal with the counterparty.
- **Settlement.** After final approval, the deal stays on the books until the delivery and payment cycles begin.

Before getting started, I should note that the words *deal, contract, asset, position, quote,* and *trade* are often used interchangeably. While each company will have its own definitions, the primary concern would be consistency. (See the Glossary for one suggestion of such distinctions.)

Starting with "Just Ask Why?"— Motivation for a Trade

Any trade starts with motivation. As suggested by Chapter 4, most transactions should be driven by one of the four *Risk-Return Strategies* and, as such, form part of a dedicated portfolio of trading:

Treasury. At the end of the portfolio analysis cycle (see Chapters 8-10), the risk manager identifies unacceptable risks at some level, be it the individual book or portfolio, either in the aggregate or for a particular time frame. The risk manager requests a hedge—either defining the hedge contract to be used or leaving it to the discretion of the trader—and the amount or type of risk to be bought or sold.

Speculation. With a profit objective in mind, the trader will be looking for potentially profitable trading opportunities.

Arbitrage. Like a radar system, the trader and analysts conduct continuous sweeps of the marketplace looking for the rare arbitrage or "good deal" opportunity.

Market Maker. The firm sets up a desk of traders and marketers through which counterparties may seek to buy or sell contracts. Once a contract is entered, the desk may also be motivated to seek trades that will offset that contract.

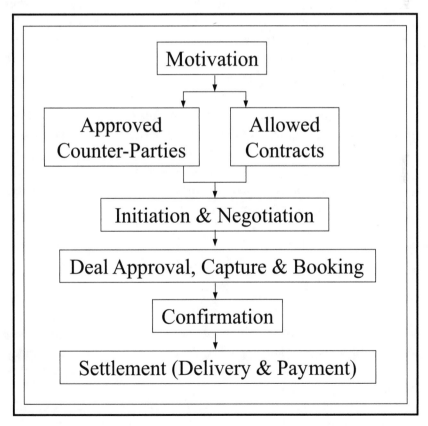

Fig. 7-1: Overview of Deal Cycle

In addition to being assigned to a particular book, each trade could be tagged in accordance to the original motivation. (Such tagging will help with trader control, auditing, and perhaps with such issues as FASB 133.) With proper approval, certain trades may be sought for reasons outside these boundaries. One such example is the "exploratory" trade. Here a small trade is entered as part of the price discovery process or as training prior to full market participation. Another example is an arbitrage opportunity that a *Treasury* book trader might see and recommend that the firm take advantage.

| Marking-to-Market Concept |
| Price Discovery Phone Calls |

Not all phone calls lead to actual deals. In the spirit of comparison-shopping, traders call multiple counterparties and brokers to search for market consensus. As a classic example of a mark-to-market activity, this process constitutes the front line of price discovery, where the trader senses the breadth of the bid/ask spread and liquidity. A special case in the price discovery phase involves analysts checking the quality of broker or exchange quotes. Suspicious quotes include: quotes for contract periods that rarely appear or for contracts that are rarely traded; contract periods that break-down traditionally combined periods such as, in the over-the-counter (OTC) power markets, seeing separate *July* and *August* quotes when the combined *July-August* typically appears; large bid/ask spreads compared to the previous or the next contract period; or other phenomenon that appear out of the ordinary.

Counterparty and Credit Risk Control

As the Federal Energy Sales story demonstrates (See Chapter 4), the risk of counterparty default represents a major managerial concern for power companies. A counterparty could default by not paying money for—or not delivering—electricity. Firms may manage their credit exposure in several general ways.

Counterparty Control. The RMPP establishes standards for the inclusion of individual firms on a list of approved trading partners. If a counterparty is not on the list, the RMPP further stipulates how to add or remove a company. At the simplest level, the RMPP could limit the total possible dollar value—known as the "notional value"—or amount of energy that may be associated with a single contract or in a book or portfolio. The RMPP should at least set notional limits per any individual counterparty; the *Procedures* could go so far as to specify specific notional limits for specific counterparties.

Simple checks against the approved trading list can be highly effective and relatively easy to implement. Joe O'Donnell of Aquila Energy tells a great story of his days with the Federal Home Loan Bank of New York (FHLB-NY) where he implemented a computerized list of approved counterparties based on their credit rating and deal volume ($). One morning, one of the traders attempted to enter a deal but his trading system rejected the deal entry. Unbeknownst to the trader, the particular counterparty's credit rating had plummeted the day before. The trader called O'Donnell to complain about his inability to enter the deal. "I just did a $100,000,000 overnight transaction with Sumitomo Trust but the deal will not go through [the system]." Fortunately for FHLB-NY, the downgraded credit rating had been entered and had prevented the trader from executing the trade!

Sometimes just asking for information from a potential counterparty—and then judging their reaction to the request—can prove useful. Prior to the crises surrounding Federal Energy Sales, "(s)ome utilities refused to deal directly with Federal because it didn't provide credit reports." As with all risk-related reporting, non-compliance can be the first clue to a problem.

Credit Enhancement. The RMPP could stipulate standards for minimizing the likelihood or impact of defaults, including the use of letters of credit, insurance policies, or other credit enhancement tools. In the Federal Energy Sales case, not all counterparties blindly traded with the entity. "In Jacksonville, FL, The Energy Authority, the trading operation for three municipal utilities, had always required Federal to pay in advance for power after Federal didn't meet its criteria."[2]

Credit Risk Control. The most advanced—and most difficult—methodology would be to adjust the value of a contract as a function of the probability of default for a particular counterparty or class of counterparty. One could also attempt to calculate a "credit delta"—the impact on the contract or portfolio given a one-unit change in payment. This kind of calculation could have two implications. First, the RMPP could specify a credit delta limit on a per-counterparty and per-book level. Second, the impact of credit risk could impact the value of a potential deal. Much like a bond trader, the power trader may be willing to pay a higher premium to a strong-credit counterparty and less for a weaker one.

Contract Types Allowed to be Traded

A list of approved contract types represents the second filter through which potential trades must pass. The RMPP should specify which common (also known as "vanilla") and uncommon ("exotic") contracts might be entered without prior approval. The RMPP should also specify how custom or "structured products" might be designed and approved. Just as importantly, the RMPP should also specify exactly which contracts may NOT be entered. The "Approved/Prohibited" list of contracts could be either general (such as by contract types like swaps and "call" options) or more specific, such as being allowed to buy (or "be long") a call option but not to sell one (or "be short.") The terms "long" and "short" refer to the resulting delta (Δ) of the underlying position. When one buys a put, the resulting position is therefore "short". (See Table 6-3 for a list of common financial contract types.) In addition, the RMPP should specify exactly how such assets as the generation plants, transmission systems, contracts, and other "real options" will be treated and integrated within the portfolio process.

As noted earlier in the book, disallowing all option trading may or may not be the most prudent path for electric utilities that fear trading losses. Approved contracts should be defined as a function of the *Risk-Return Strategy* being defined for each business unit. If the overall objective is hedging, then hedging contracts must be approved to match the kinds of risks being managed. Weather derivatives have been touted as a hedge against natural gas volume risk; if this is a concern for the firm, then the drafters of the RMPP should give serious thought to include weather derivatives on the approved list.

Contract Specifications

Contract specifications for energy derivatives can be incredibly complex—even the simplest contracts. Here are some contract specifications that directly relate to management control issues.

Market. The RMPP should require each deal to be assigned to a specific book or sub-portfolio. (See Chapter 8 for more details for a discussion of portfolio design.)

Contract Terms. Contract terms include the delivery schedule for the market. In power markets, the most common Contract Term is the "5x16" market for which delivery occurs on the 5 business days per week during the 16 peak hours. For the managerial "bang-for-the-buck," most portfolio management focuses on this peaking market behavior for the simple reason that this is where the majority of the risk resides. If the firm considers it a large enough priority, the RMPP can establish procedures for the off-peak or full-week load as well.

Trade Horizon and Hedging Horizon. The RMPP should specify two different time horizons: one for the furthest date out the trading book is allowed to go, and the other as the period acceptable in the hedge cycle. While generators possess generation assets with useful lives of 30 or more years, the manager must decide whether his/her portfolio analysis should extend its reach this far into the future. The decision should be based on liquidity and price discovery—does it make sense to analyze risk going out 30 years if there are no hedging contracts available that far out? One answer to this question is "yes" if we are modeling generation flows! But the answer should be appropriate to the objective of valuation and hedging analysis. Perhaps one rule-of-thumb would be to set the trading time horizons as a function of the firm's longest-dated existing financial contract. The RMPP might also institute special risk controls for certain periods of the year such as the peak months of summer for power and winter for natural gas. Special consideration might also be paid to spring or fall (known as the "shoulder months") due to planned outages for repairs or environmental issues such as planning for the salmon run on western rivers with hydro-electric projects. This is known as the "fish flush."

Position. As suggested earlier, the RMPP can specify the kind of position (in terms of buying and selling) that can be taken for particular contract types.

Exercise Type. The RMPP can also regulate whether certain exercise rights types may be taken as such "call" or "put" contracts. This issue relates to structured products; the RMPP should consider whether combinations of puts and calls would be allowed. These structured products can actually offer lower-price alternatives to meeting hedging objectives.[3]

Quantity. The quantity of power being sought to buy or sell directly relates to notional limits set by the RMPP.

Swing Quantity Controls. Variable volume is referred to as "swing" quantities. While the trading markets refer to options with variable volume as "swing" contracts, these contracts equate with the tradition of "full requirements" contract. Swing options can be characterized as exotic structured products with such contractual specifications as number of swing rights, maximum and minimum volume. Since most power companies trade to hedge their generation, the RMPP should anticipate how to handle swing options, as they offer a good hedge tool for volumetric risk.

Transaction Details. The RMPP should also establish rules for such contractual specifications as Transaction Price (a fixed-price for swaps or a premium for options), Strike Price (options only), and any additional fees.

Settlement. The contract settlement issues of delivery and payment are critical to the specifications for a contract. These details will appear later in this chapter, including "contract expiration," "expiration date rules," "legs," and "tenor."

We should also not forget the impact of the inputs that our market analysts create for the valuation of individual deals. The RMPP should specify approved procedures for building forward price curves, volatility matrices, correlations, discounting curves, etc.

Initiation and Negotiation

The trading desk initiates and receives countless phone calls a day. (Increasingly the exchange of information occurs on electronic or web-based exchanges.) But by the point of exchange, regardless of the medium, the RMPP has already defined many of the rules of engagement. During the negotiation process, the RMPP must specify rules of conduct for the trader as the representative of the firm. Most modern trading desks maintain telephone-recording systems as protection from within and outside the firm.

Finding the right transaction price will be a function of need; generally speaking, the party needing power to fulfill obligations will be driving up the price. Having good valuation systems will help the trader on the desk evaluate counterparty offers. The old adage of "buy low, sell high" takes on new meaning when counterparties have different abilities to value complex contracts. Of course, most counterparties will not be shopping "price" but also structure, looking for a contract that will satisfy their risk hedging requirements while minimizing their own costs. In this case a solid relationship between trading and marketing will help identify a solution. Like all things on the trading desk, this product structuring should follow the steps defined within the RMPP.

GUEST ESSAY

Negotiating the Deal

by Greg La Flame, Director of Price Forecasting
First Energy Trading Services

Power marketers are very proficient at using models to evaluate the value of any number of proposed transactions—they excel at the use of intuition and analytics. However, it is not clear that they pay attention to some of the softer issues leading to closing a deal. This essay deals with strategic considerations of the negotiation process – in other words how the negotiating process should be structured to promote positive results, long-term deal-making opportunities, and sound relationships.

153

The negotiation process should be viewed as optimizing a series of transactions and not only as independent transactions. There are four major steps to better negotiations: Vision, Preparation, Execution, and Closure.

Vision

In terms of the negotiation process, vision refers to the organization's view of the existing portfolio and how it might need to be changed to achieve some predetermined "goal" portfolio. The vision step also includes all of the fundamental analysis regarding the electric industry, structural changes, price forecasts, price volatility, etc. (in simplistic terms the "market"). Once completed, the remaining steps fall into a pattern and make sense.

Preparation

It is surprising how little emphasis is placed on preparation, and yet properly done it can lead to improved results. Items to be considered are truly understanding how each immediate proposed transaction impacts the existing portfolio, the "goal" portfolio and the other potential transactions, and the number of and types of risks associated with transaction steps to achieve the objective. One should clearly articulate and record potential "deal breakers"—predetermined terms and conditions limits for each proposed transaction. This clearly establishes the boundaries for the negotiation process and avoids emotional-related agreement to proposed terms. All the foregoing comments deal with having a road map—as the saying goes, "if you don't know where your are going, any road will get you there."

Good negotiators keep an up-to-date biography on all counterparty companies and individuals, including personal information, deals done, biases, likes and dislikes, etc. This information can be gained from publications, conferences, and during the negotiation process. It simply takes time and discipline, but it also can pay huge dividends in the long run. Such information can be useful to you as a reminder or to your associates if they are not familiar with the counterparty.

One should also "think chess" in making or responding to a proposal. If you make a proposal, consider your counterparty's likely response, and your expected reply. Modeling during the preparation phase can be very helpful in clarifying these issues.

Execution

No—we're not talking of "killing" the deal, but trying to achieve a "win-win" when possible. Key to execution is to be a good listener and note taker—listening carefully to really understand your counterparty's position and beliefs and taking good notes to remember. This will help in the counter proposal process by allowing you to communicate information and data that "will make it easy for your counterparty to agree with you". Looking at the deal from the perspective of your counterparty is critical.

If the deal is significant, a face-to-face meeting will dramatically improve chances of building trust, rapport, and understanding as compared to relying only on telephone negotiations. Finally, consider any terms and conditions offer and re-offers as they relate to your predetermined pricing and strategic portfolio goals.

Closure

Closure of one transaction should be considered as the beginning of a new transaction—be sure that you have treated your counterparty in a way that communicates that he/she has indeed been treated fairly. No one likes to feel like they have been taken to the "cleaners." Besides, if dealt with too severely, your counterparty may not be able to pay the bill or be in the mood to work with you in the future. Put simply, if the deal cannot be consummated in a reasonably equitable manner (remembering that differences in positions and forward market views may distort an equitable deal to look inequitable), then make it somewhat equitable or don't close the deal. If the deal is consummated, a class act is to attempt to give your counterparty some type of "no-cost" benefit. This type of benefit could be information, advice, or other service. This type of unsolicited goodwill builds trust, shows concern, and may lead to future opportunities.

Finally, there are two remaining suggestions and a thought. First, debrief the transaction. Note the things that worked well or items to be improved on (add this information to your counterparty biography). Secondly, track the deal until contract termination. Both debriefing and tracking provide valuable feedback to develop insight for pricing future deals. As a concluding thought, consider the concept of a "Buick for Everyone": If you end up with a Cadillac and I wind up with a Chevy (or vice versa) it was not a negotiation that promotes more deals. However if we both end up with a Buick, we'll do many more deals.

Greg La Flame is the Director of Price Forecasting, FirstEnergy Trading Services, Inc. In addition to providing price forecasting services to the organization, his operation provides analytic services for the evaluation of derivative instruments, the evaluation of various trading strategies and structures, and various business strategies. Mr. LaFlame has a BSBA from Bowling Green State University and an MBA from the University of Akron. Mr. LaFlame may be contacted via laflameg@firstenergycorp.com.

Deal Approval, Capture and Book Assignment in the Trading/Risk System

Once the trader feels confident that a particular contract should be entered, the deal must be approved and then captured into the portfolio management system. The ideal involves capturing this deal in a single system with the data populating all the requisite applications being used for trading and risk management. During this approval step, the contract receives a complete risk review to ensure that the contract does not violate any of the risk limits. Often, the middle-office plays the role of analyzing these risks. Should any risk limit be violated, the RMPP can also establish rules for managerial approval of non-compliance.

Finally, the deal should be assigned to a book or a sub-portfolio as part of the overall portfolio valuation and risk management process. Every company uses different nomenclature to distinguish the various clusters or levels of contracts. Here is a sample of such organizational language.

Portfolio. Represents the firm's total collection of contracts and assets covered by the RMPP and therefore in the trading and risk management system.

Sub-Portfolio. A sub-portfolio is any combination of deals or books that represent a sub-set of the Portfolio. A book or market would be one type of sub-portfolio. In addition, the user could organize sub-portfolios that represent a single trader or department, or even cross-market (i.e., "basis") exposures.

Book. A "book" is a subset of the total Portfolio and is the common trading-floor parlance for a sub-portfolio.

Back Office Confirmation

A final step in the transaction flow is the back office confirmation of deals. Confirmation literally involves a person from Company A calling Company B and reconfirming that each party has entered into the same deal. Conflicts definitely occur at this level and early detection helps minimize problems. The earlier the confirmation occurs, the better off are all parties concerned. The worst time to discover a counterparty discrepancy is after all the hedges have been put on or market expectations have changed.

From a budgeting point of view, the manager should be sure to adequately budget for back-office procedures such as deal confirmation. First, it frees up the trading expert to focus on what he/she does best. Deal confirmation does not require the unique skills of a trader. Second, back-office confirmation is critical for monitoring traders.

Settlement: Delivery and Payment

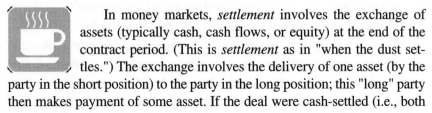 In money markets, *settlement* involves the exchange of assets (typically cash, cash flows, or equity) at the end of the contract period. (This is *settlement* as in "when the dust settles.") The exchange involves the delivery of one asset (by the party in the short position) to the party in the long position; this "long" party then makes payment of some asset. If the deal were cash-settled (i.e., both

157

assets are cash), then just one party pays the net difference to the other. If non-cash derivative contracts were involved, then the contractual ownership and cash would be exchanged. (In either case, both the delivery and the payment "legs" of the deal are transmitted electronically.)

In energy markets, on the other hand, the delivery leg can be far more complicated and differ according to market (see Table 7-1.) While there are indeed "contracts-for-difference" or indexed deals, cash-settle deals are less common than deals for delivery in the over-the-counter (OTC) power and energy markets. I remember visiting an energy risk manager at a New York money house in 1997. I had hoped to meet the vice president but she was out of the office that day—she was on a helicopter headed over New York Harbor to land on the tanker carrying the first oil shipment that the company had traded and held to delivery! (For the traditional utility, the delivery leg represents the major component of their core competence!) Contracts on the New York Mercantile Exchange (NYMEX) are designed for delivery, but traders often close out their positions prior to expiration to avoid delivery.

Contract specifications determine settlement terms relative to some "expiration" date. Expiration can mean several things. At a trading exchange, expiration means that the contract stops trading; the OTC markets do not have such last-day of trading rules, but the day of settlement is in fact the last possible day of trading OTC contracts. This does not mean that an expired contract does not have value, it's just that the original structure is no longer applicable. (Consider this analogy: a case of cola still has value if one can is removed. From a reseller's point of view, the remaining cans may be packaged as three six-packs and five singles.) More complex contracts may imply more than one expiration date. Consider the case of a monthly-settled *July-August* option. While the contract itself has a trading expiration date of, say, June 30, the contract also implies two sub-contracts expiration dates on which the buyer can decided to execute or not. (See examples in next few paragraphs.)

The expiration date is provided by some "expiration date rule" defined by a market standard or by a particular contract. (Table 7-2 suggests some common expiration rules seen in the energy markets.) In OTC power markets, for example, delivery typically occurs over some future

Settlement Leg	OTC Power	NYMEX Futures
Delivery	Most contracts traded and held through delivery	Positions commonly closed prior to expiration such that no delivery required
Payment	Payment occurs after delivery	Payment occurs continuously through margin account management with the balance due at expiration or closing

Table 7-1: Comparison of Settlements by Market

Daily [contract terms defined]	Expiration set by a number (n) of days depending on whether the market's delivery follows a business or calendar day delivery schedule
Last Business Day of Previous Month	Expiration occurs on $n\text{-}th$ last business day of the previous month
Last Calendar Day of Previous Month	Expiration occurs on $n\text{-}th$ last calendar day of the previous month
Last Business Day of Same Month	Expiration occurs on $n\text{-}th$ last business day of the same month (as would be used for a look-back contract)
Last Calendar Day of Same Month	Expiration occurs on $n\text{-}th$ last calendar day of the same month (as would be used for a look-back contract)

Table 7-2: Sample Expiration Date Rules (Source: SAVA Risk Management Corporation.)

period following this expiration date. Monthly swap contracts expire one to three trading days prior to the first delivery date. Consider the following two cases for a 5x16 power market where the standard is for expiration to occur one trading day prior to the first delivery date. For a *July 2002* swap, the expiration date would be June 28, 2002 because the first

delivery date is Monday, July 1, 2000 and the immediately prior weekend
dates are not considered trading dates.

- For an OTC *July 2002* monthly-settled option, the expiration date
  would typically also be June 28, 2002. Since this option carries
  just the one choice to execute for delivery during all of July, the
  single option expiration would also be June 28.
- For a *July-August 2002* monthly-settled option, the trading expiration date would also be June 28, but this contract contains two
  "legs"—one for the option for delivery of July power and the
  other option for delivery of August power. This type of European
  option is also known as a "cap." Each of the two embedded
  monthly-options is referred to as a "caplet." Remember, a caplet
  is to a cap as a piglet is to a pig! So, the two individual monthly
  option (or caplet) expiration dates would be June 28 and July 31.

Delivery specifications also vary by market and product; Table 7-3
offers a sampling of delivery settlement rules. In power markets, most
contracts cover delivery into some forward period. Even the "spot" contract traded on a particular day is for next-day delivery power. For
longer periods of forward time, delivery is categorized by the "tenor" of
delivery increments. For option contracts, the most common tenors are
"daily" and "monthly" settlement. For a daily-settled option, the buyer
has an option right to exercise into next-day delivery for each valid date
within the contract period. For a monthly-settled option, the choice is
reserved only for the beginning of that month. Settlement terms, in turn,
directly influence valuation. Daily-settled options, for example, are
worth far more than monthly-settled options—all other things held
equal—because they offer more choices.

- Recall that a *July-August 2002* monthly-settled option contains
  two legs with option expiration dates of June 28 and July 31. The
  buyer would have to make a decision for the entire months of
  July and of August on these two dates, respectively.
- For a *July-August 2002* daily-settled option, there would be 44
  legs, one for each business day during that two-month period.

Payment cycles also vary according to the specific market even from

Rule	Description
Day(s) Forward	Delivery on x day(s) forward after and not including expiration date
Week(s) Forward	Delivery on x week(s) forward after and not including expiration date
Month(s) Forward	Delivery on x month(s) forward after and not including expiration date
Calendar Week(s) Forward	Delivery on x calendar week(s) forward after and not including expiration date
Calendar Month(s) Forward	Delivery on x calendar month(s) forward after and not including expiration date
Calendar [2] Month(s) Forward	Delivery on x calendar month(s) forward two months after and expiration date
Remainder of Current Month	Delivery on all day(s) forward after and not including expiration date to the end of the current month
Remainder of Current Week	Delivery on all day(s) forward after and not including expiration date to the end of the current week
Day(s) Backward	Financial settlement (i.e. no delivery) based on an average price over x day(s) backward prior to and including expiration date
Week(s) Backward	Financial settlement (i.e. no delivery) based on an average price over x week(s) backward prior to and including expiration date
Month(s) Backward	Financial settlement (i.e. no delivery) based on an average price over x month(s) backward prior to and including expiration date
Calendar Week(s) Backward	Financial settlement (i.e. no delivery) based on an average price over x calendar week(s) backward prior to and including expiration date
Calendar Month(s) Backward	Financial settlement (i.e. no delivery) based on an average price over x calendar month(s) backward prior to and including expiration date

Table 7-3: Delivery Settlement Rules (Source: SAVA Risk Management Corporation.)

Rule	Description
Bus Day of Next Month (from caplet expiration)	Payment occurs on x-th business day of next month following caplet expiration
Bus Day of Next Month (from last delivery)	Payment occurs on x-th business day of next month following last delivery
Bus Days (from caplet expiration)	Payment occurs x business days after caplet expiration
Bus Days (from last delivery)	Payment occurs x business days after last delivery
Cal Day of Next Month (from caplet expiration)	Payment occurs on x-th calendar day of next month following caplet expiration
Cal Day of Next Month (from last delivery)	Payment occurs on x-th calendar day of next month following last delivery
Cal Days (from caplet expiration)	Payment occurs x calendar days after caplet expiration
Cal Days (from last delivery)	Payment occurs x calendar days after last delivery

Table 7-4: Payment Rules (Source: SAVA Risk Management Corporation.)

contract to contract. Table 7-4 lists some sample payment settlement rules. These rules may be used by a trader or risk manager to value the cash-flow(s) associated with a deal. In reality, however, counterparties do not always pay on time. Delayed payment could have a dramatic effect on the profit-loss performance of a trading desk; if counterparties are customarily allowed to pay slower than specified by contract, then the analyst should value the contract on the actual expected cash flow rather than the contracted. Or the manager should dedicate more effort into enforcing contractual obligations and exacting any and all damages for late payment proscribed by the contract. Ideally, the contracts should specify additional fees to cover the costs of delayed payments.

Contracts can also flow between the "term desk" and the "cash desk". In some organizations, there are different people with different skills on these desks. At a pre-defined point, a deal passes from the term desk to the cash desk for either unwinding or delivery. The monthly deal is traded in and out on a daily and balance-of-week or month basis, and transmission and flows are scheduled within control areas.

At Trail's End

Once an individual deal is "booked" or committed to the portfolio, that deal remains "live" until all delivery and payment are completed as per contract. During that time, the value and risk of the deal are continuously measured and managed as part of the firm's overall portfolio analysis cycle, as will be explored in the next three chapters.

ENDNOTES

[1] Kranhold and Emshwiller, 1998.

[2] Ibid.

[3] For more on the purpose and design of structured products, see Israel Nelken's "Pricing, Hedging, and Trading Exotic Options" (Irwin, 2000.) While written primarily for money markets, Nelken's approach is very handy for power managers interested in understanding the motivation behind product structuring.

chapter 8

THE PORTFOLIO PROCESS: STARTING WITH WHAT HAVE WE GOT? AND WHAT DO WE WANT?

THE HEDGING CYCLE

In the previous chapter we focused on managing an individual contract through the deal process. The next three chapters cover the process of managing all the contracts together using "portfolio analysis." Like Chapter 6, this chapter will be chock full of "Java Moments" during which technically challenging concepts will be introduced.

Portfolio analysis encompasses the valuation of portfolios of contracts or positions, and includes the processes of measuring, controlling, and hedging the risks of such portfolios. In essence, portfolio analysis covers the full hedging cycle (see Figure 8-1) necessary to answer the "Five Questions the Board Should Ask", first presented in Chapter 3.

1. What does our portfolio look like now?
2. How might our portfolio change?
3. What do we want our portfolio to look like?
4. How will we achieve and maintain our desired portfolio?
5. Have we achieved our portfolio objectives?

This chapter explores the first two questions *What does our portfolio look like now?* And *How might our portfolio change?* Valuation methods play a central role in answering these questions, hence the introduction of a useful graphing technique called the "payoff diagram." Valuation takes a snap-shot of value at the time of observation, so we will wait until Chapter 9 to cover risk measurement techniques to value how the values might change. Finally,

Term	Definition
Hedging	The process of analyzing existing risk levels and entering hedging contracts to achieve desired risk levels.
Portfolio Analysis	The process of valuing portfolios of contracts and positions. Also includes the processes of measuring, controlling, and hedging the risks of such portfolios.
Risk	The impact of unexpected change.
Risk Management	The set of skills and processes for measuring, controlling, and hedging risk.
Risk Measurement	The process of measuring the impact on the value of a contract or portfolio given a change in some variable.
Risk Sensitivity Analysis	A form of risk measurement that calculates the change in value of a position or portfolio given a one-unit change in some input. (See the "Greeks.")
Stress Testing	A form of risk measurement that calculates the change in a contract or portfolio value given a change in a variable that is assumed to replicate a highly stressful condition.
Technical Analysis	A form of trading analysis that predicts a price in the future as a function of past price levels.
Value-at-Risk (VaR)	A form of risk measurement that calculates the loss in value of a portfolio given an assumed statistical change in market prices over a time horizon.
Valuation	The determination of the value of a position or asset at the time of observation.
What If? Analysis	Similar to stress testing.

Table 8-1: Comparison of Risk Management Definitions

Chapter 10 puts valuation and risk measurement together into the practice of hedging. (See Table 8-1 for a summary of risk definitions that help break down and distinguish between the various sub-practices of risk management.)

DEFINING THE PORTFOLIO
IN THE RMPP

RMPP   Upper management should define what constitutes the portfolio within the *Risk Management Policies and Procedures* (RMPP). The document should explicitly define which exposures should be captured, measured, and managed within the trading and risk management system. This level of board decision-making might appear to be bordering on "micro-management." But would the board rather such decisions be made by the trading desk level? Perhaps the board should at least delegate responsibility for portfolio

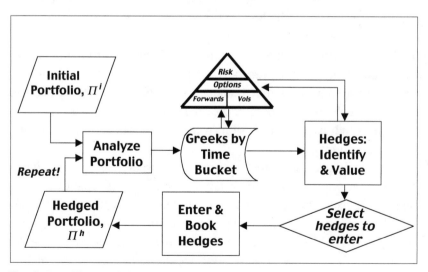

Fig. 8-1: The Hedging Cycle

design. To help control trading, the RMPP should require that all deals be assigned to a specific book to avoid trading outside the approved boundaries of the portfolio.

 For simple utility portfolios, the markets typically include its single service region's electricity market (often times a NERC coordinating council.) More typical and complex portfolios will include contingent markets or basis markets between which power is traded. Most utilities also will have books on other energies, especially those who have full-fledged natural gas marketing and/or trading operations. Electric companies with feedstock-only exposure (to fuels such as natural gas or coal) have a more difficult decision as to whether to include these energies as books. Inclusion of feedstock fuels in the portfolio should be a managerial decision based on the inherent risk. For many utilities, there's a fine line between procurement and feedstock fuel trading. If an electric firm has a large natural gas exposure, for example, it would be a logical decision to manage a natural gas book. In that case, however, there is also risk that the firm dedicates too much attention to becoming a gas-trading house as well. Power and gas trading are different and do require special skills. Being good at one market does not guarantee being good at the other, as many utilities discovered in the late 1990s. (It should also be said that a poor gas trader will probably be a poor power trader as well!) Coal presents a good example of a large exposure that may not immediately qualify for the top priority list for inclusion—coal contracts remain illiquid with limited price discovery, but are fortunately fairly stable price behavior to date. (Of course, management should still monitor the coal market exposures.)

Other candidates for inclusion in the RMPP portfolio specification include the following:

Generation Assets. Most utilities begin trading in order to hedge their generation assets and the retail commitments (see below.) Logic suggests that such utilities must include generation within their portfolio valuation process. This issue may become increasingly important due to FASB 133. Measuring the risks of the wholesale trading desk's positions in the absence of generation would be like the sound of "one hand clapping."

Marking-to-Market Concept
Treating Assets as Options

While logic dictates inclusion, traded portfolios rarely include generation assets. Why not? Because it is very difficult to do so! As Chapter 2 suggests, generation assets may be articulated and valued as "real options", but this is easier said than done. The decision to dedicate the proper resources to value "assets as options" must come from the management level. Management must also be responsible for requiring its staff to create proper real options methodologies based on the mark-to-market approach. A risk exists that the traditional fundamental modeling will be used for valuing assets instead of using market-sensitive, forward-looking, quantitative option modeling. Again, upper management must set this standard in order to provide clear guidance to staff and to minimize internal conflicts.

Retail Positions. The same arguments about including generation in the portfolio apply to retail positions. One should consider industrial load and other retail contracts as "structured products." Including retail contracts in the RMPP process allows more realistic position measurement, but also raises the problem of valuation. In addition, the ability to value the optionality of retail contracts could prove to be a competitive advantage to a company.

Transmission. Transmission assets and the transmission aspects of contracts represent another complexity for a portfolio. (This directly relates to basis risk.) Utilities focusing on congestion management concerns might find it helpful to approach the problem using the portfolio approach. Congestion could be valued and managed with what amounts to basis hedging contracts. As these would reduce the basis risk in any power movement deal, they are a natural component of the package of hedges that go with any power business.

Other Traded Markets. Any other existing trading activities involving such markets as weather derivatives or bandwidth trading should also be included in the portfolio.

The RMPP can specify inclusion or exclusion of particular markets. It might be worthwhile for the board to additionally explain the exclusion of particular exposures. The RMPP could also state the process for evaluating whether or not excluded exposures could qualify for inclusion. This would entail periodic risk analysis of the excluded exposures in order to determine if full-blown risk analysis would be justified.

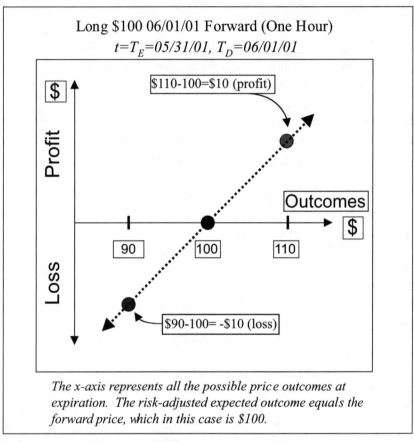

Fig. 8-2: Simple Payoff Diagram

TODAY'S VALUE AND THE PAYOFF DIAGRAM

To a large degree, power trading deals with future needs and risks—trading contracts today for electricity delivered at some later dates. Spot trading and risk management are critical, to be sure, but the exclusion of forward trading is like standing on a ship's deck in a squall, responding only to the wave crashing across the bow. When looking forward, by contrast, we also scan the horizon and judge the weather. We consider all the possible outcomes and then attempt to assign probabilities of each possible outcome. Using the *Price-Risk Pyramid*, we see that today's forward price represents the risk-adjusted expected outcome, whereas volatility measures the range of all possible outcomes. We combine this information using valuation models for calculating value. More on this later.

Marking-to-Market Concept
Markets Can and Do Change

In this nautical analogy, the "shore" symbolizes the *Time of Observation*; we stand on the shore looking out to the horizon (which, completing the analogy, is the forward term.) Typically, the Time of Observation equates to "today" or the date of valuation. The Time of Observation can be a different date, however, as would be the case during an audit of some past date. The key issue is determining the value of a position relative to that date's market's expectations. Markets can and do change! Look at the stock markets; companies constantly report expected earnings and then later the market corrects itself based on actual earnings. The same applies to power pricing. One major benefit of "marking-to-market" is that existing contracts are continuously revalued relative to "today's" expectations (or those relative to the Time of Observation.) A manager would be unfair to criticize a deal that went sour if it were a good mark-to-market deal the day it was analyzed and entered. But once "booked" into the portfolio, the risk management process would continuously revalue the contract, a process that could either reveal a bad trade or good trade going bad due to changes in the marketplace. Potential causes for bad trades include but are not limited to unacknowledged illiquidity risk, incomplete hedging processes, poor analysis support, unskilled trading, and last but not least, a poorly defined (or worse, an undefined) trading strategy. Unfortunately, responsibility for addressing these problems falls squarely on the manager's shoulders!

 A graphical technique called the "payoff diagram"[2] helps us visualize the value of a contract relative to all the possible outcomes of the spot market at the time of that contract's expiration (also known as "expiry.") As seen in Figure

8-2[3] , the x-axis represents all the possible "outcomes" or spot prices that might actually occur at expiration. The y-axis represents the profit or loss for the position given the possible outcomes. A payoff diagram does not represent what will *actually* happen at expiration; instead, the diagram offers a snapshot—taken at the *Time of Observation (t)*—of all possible spot prices that might occur in the future at the *Time of Expiration (T_E)*—the time at which the contract actually settles.

In this case represented by Figure 8-2, we analyze owning a very simple fixed-price firm-quantity on-peak forward contract at expiration: a \$100 *June 01, 2001 Hour 1* forward for a single megawatt of power, 1 MWh. The one-hour contract in this example is so simple that our sample contract does not exist in standard traded energy markets! But we must use such simplifications to demonstrate our principles. In real markets, forward contracts cover multiple hours, days, and/or months of delivery and payment dates (also known as "legs.") These multi-period forward contracts may be characterized as "swaps" because we are swapping the fixed forward price for the floating spot price on the days of delivery. Our *Time of Observation (t)* is May 31, 2001 and is the same date as the *Time of Expiration (T_E)*. This means that we are contracting to pay \$100 for the first peak hour on the *Time of Delivery (T_D)* June 1 2001. Since this forward is a contract, we must ultimately pay the \$100 and we must take delivery, regardless of what the hourly spot market price will be on that date.

Our example bases the \$100 forward price on an assumed broker quote; as noted above, this \$100 marked-to-market price can and will change as each day passes between the current *Time of Observation Date* and as the contract nears expiration. As long as the forward price value of that hour of power equals \$100, the marked-to-market value of the contract is zero! When a forward contract is entered into at the *Time of Observation*, no cash is exchanged. The contract is marked-to-market, so it represents the fair-market exchange. The contract picks up non-zero value if the underlying market forward price diverges from \$100!

If on May 31, 2001, the actual spot price (for next day delivery) winds up being \$110, the value of the contract would be \$10. (The value of the contract moves around as markets do!) Ignoring the impact of discounting (for simplicity, the examples in Chapters 8-10 will ignore the impact of discounting by assuming a zero-discount curve), we expressed this relationship generally as follows.

Equation 8-1

Forward Position = New Observed Price – Contracted Price

To be more specific, on any given day of observation between the time of contracting for a forward contract, T_C, and prior to the last day of trading or contract expiration, T_E, the value of the long forward position is given by the next equation.

Equation 8-2

Forward Position $= F_{t,TD} - F_{t=TC,TD}$

Where:

$F_{t,TD}$ = forward price for delivery on *TD* valued at observation *t*

t = Time of Observation

TD = Time of Delivery

TC = date on which the forward contract was contracted

On the day of contract expiration, T_E, the value is given by the next equation.

Equation 8-3

Forward Position $= F_{t=TE,TD} - F_{t=TC,TD}$

This value may be positive (profit) or negative (loss) depending on whether the price on the day of expiration is greater or lesser than the contracted price, $F_{t=TC,TD}$.

As seen in Figure 8-3, the profit-loss (P&L) profile follows a 45% angle. Since, in our example, we own the forward (i.e., we are "long" the 1 MWh contract), our profit-and-loss has a 1-to-1 slope where a one-dollar increase in price creates a one-dollar increase in contract value. This slope also equals the *delta* (Δ) of the contract, but we will explore this particular concept later in Chapter 9. For a swap contract, this slope is constant regardless of the potential outcome. The diagonal value line crosses the *x*-axis at the forward price quoted for that particular *Time of Observation*; in Figures 8-2 and 8-3, the line therefore crosses at the $100 mark. If we had sold the forward (i.e. we were "short"), the diagonal line would have a negative 45% angle and still cross the *x*-axis at $100. (See Figure 8-4.) In the latter case, the profit-loss scenarios are inverted; if we are short the forward, we must deliver the power regardless of spot prices and accept the fixed $100 price. So, if prices do jump to $110, our short position would experience a $10 loss because we would be missing the opportunity to sell at $110 because we contracted to sell at $100.

In our simple example, we can use Equations 8-1 and 8-3 to calculate contract value; we could also look at the payoff diagram. But for purposes of real life calculations for both swaps and options, we require a more complex mathematical treatment. The overall forward price is the risk-adjusted value of each possible outcome multiplied by the probability of each possible outcome.

Equation 8-4

$F_{t,T}$= sum of (the P&L of outcome x times the probability of outcome x)
=...($90-$100)*$p^{\$90}$ + ... ($100-$100)**$p^{\$100}$+ ... ($110-$100)*$p^{\$110}$...
= $\sum_{x=0}^{\infty} S\, F^x_{TE,TD}\, {}^*p^x$

Where:

$F_{t,T}$ = forward price for delivery on T_D valued at observation t

t = Time of Observation

T_E = Time of Expiration

T_D = Time of Delivery

$F^x_{TE,TD}$ = forward price at expiration T_E corresponding to outcome x

p^x = probability of outcome x occurring

x = a particular outcome in prices. Number of potential outcomes assumed to be infinite

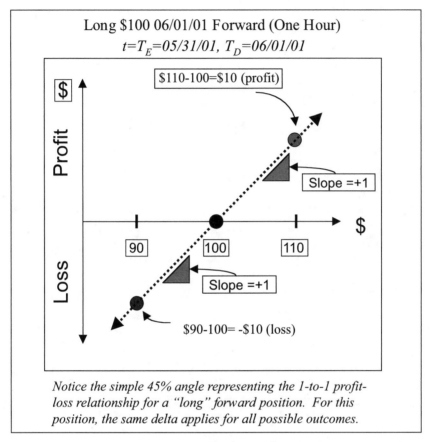

Fig. 8-3: Delta on Payoff Diagram

Figure 8-5 overlays a probability distribution on the payoff diagram from Figures 8-2 and 8-3. As suggested in Chapter 6, the forward price is the risk-adjusted expected spot price—the average of the market expectations on that given *Time of Observation (t)*. (Also recall from Chapter 6 that volatility relates to the width of the distribution.) Pricing behavior models such as price-mean reversion or log-normality express these distributions; Figure 8-5 plots a simulation of price-mean reversion.

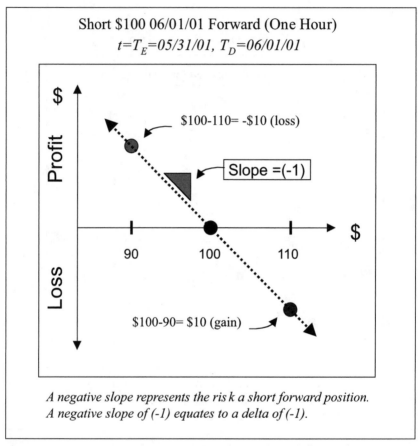

Fig. 8-4: Short Forward Position

The manager should pay very close attention to the kind of distributions being used to express the probabilities of outcomes. The correct distribution assumptions can provide better valuation and risk management. They also can help understand the market. For example, consider the following two cases of implying the expectations of a price spike from a swap price:

Suppose that the 5x16 *July-August* swap contract is trading at $150/MWh. There are a total of 43 of such business days during the con-

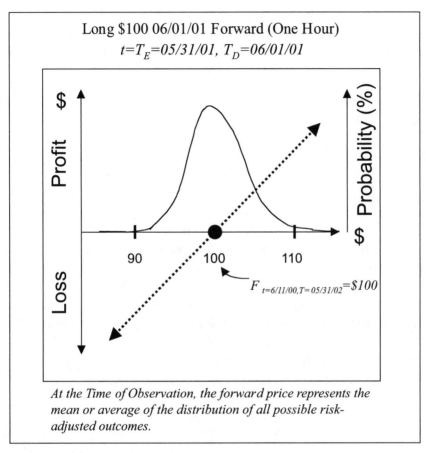

Fig. 8-5: Probabilities of Outcomes

tract period. Consider two different market participants who imply different types of information from the $150/MWh price.

Brad, the market speculator, believes that this price is too low, and is going long on this contract. Frankly put, Brad believes that the "market is wrong." (These words alone are a major "red flag" for any manager. When you hear these words, really listen to the reasoning and demand proof that the individual is truly better informed than the market.) This is Brad's reasoning: Brad believes that the prices will spike to $1,250 level on five out of 43 days. (Hence, the probability of $1,250 price is 5/43 = 11.63%.) To confirm his suspicions, Brad uses the following equation to back out a flat forward price for the 38 non-spiking days of July and August.

Equation 8-5

$$F_{t,T} = \textit{Peak Price} * p^{\textit{Peak Price}} + \textit{Non-Peak Price} * p^{\textit{Non-Peak}}$$
$$\$150 = \$1,250 * (5/43) + F(\text{rest of time}) * (38/43)$$
$$F(\text{rest of time}) = (\$150 - \$1,250 * (5/43)) / (38/43)$$
$$= \$5.26$$

He concludes that this $5.26 price is much too low a level for the price the rest of the time, and hence he confirms his belief that the $150 price is too low.

The second participant, Janet, believes that markets are efficient and that the $150 price is relevant. She too believes that prices will spike to some higher level on five out of 43 days, but she wants to imply or back-out the price of the spike given the market price. She begins with assuming that the rest of the time the prices will be in the $50 range, and she uses this information to calculate the price spike level.

$$\$150 = F(\text{spike}) * (5/43) + \$50 * (38/43)$$
$$F(\text{spike}) = (\$150 - \$50 * (38/43)) / (5/43)$$
$$= \$910$$

Janet concludes that the market is implying a $910 price spike level roughly 12% of the time. Thus, though Brad and Janet both agree that prices will spike five out of 23 days, their different assumptions lead to very different interpretations of market data. A manager must be on constant lookout for such divergences among his/her staff.

Options: Incorporating Choice into the Payoff Diagram

Up to now, the payoff diagrams in this chapter have plotted fixed-price contracts. We started with forwards for their simplicity, but the real benefit of payoff diagrams appears when we try to capture the "element of choice" provided by options (and assets which have embedded optionality). With the forward contract, the holder is obliged to take delivery and pay even when the deal poses a loss. Unlike a forward contract, an option gives the holder the right but not the obligation to exercise.

In looking back at Figure 8-2, we can think of an option as being able to capture all the "upside" of a forward contract (i.e., the right side of the payoff diagram) and yet avoiding all the "downside" (the left side of the diagram.) As an example, let's imagine we bought a call option for the exact same single peak hour for which we could reserve the right to pay a "strike price" of $100 per MWh. This would be an "at-the-money" option since the strike price equals the forward price (the "underlying") at that expiration. Since there is no such thing as a free lunch, we paid a $10 premium for this option. At expiration, we would execute if the spot price exceeds the $100 level. If spot prices on that day drop below $100, we have no obligation to execute and can simply pay the lower spot prices in order to get energy delivery.

Figure 8-6 plots the classic "hockey stick" payoff diagram for a call option at expiration.[4] Note that at expiration the option is worth zero ($0) for all possible outcomes of $100 or less. For outcomes greater than $100, the payoff diagram takes off with a slope of +1, just like a forward contract. Mathematically, this payoff silhouette can be expressed as the "call parity value". The call parity value ($C^x_{t,TE}$) at expiration for a particular outcome, x, of the stochastic underlying market price ($F_{t=TE,TD}$) equals the maximum of zero (0) or the underlying price minus the strike price (K), whichever is greater. In other words, parity value of an option at expiration cannot be negative. The assumption is that one would not execute an option and buy the asset for a higher strike price than the underlying market price; we assume the option holder would simply ignore the worthless right to execute the option and buy the underlying directly at the cheaper price. In power, it is possible that an option holder might execute "non-economically" because he/she needs the power and is not market savvy, but this scenario typically means a supply crunch that usually causes a price spike rather than a price drop.

The call parity value can be expressed by the following equation.

Equation 8-6

$$C^x_{t,TE} = max(0, F_{t=TE,TD} - K)$$

Where:

$C^x_{t,TE} =$	the parity value for particular outcome x
$t =$	Time of Observation
$TE =$	Time of Expiration
$TD =$	Time of Delivery
$max =$	the maximum function
$x =$	outcome
$F_{t=TE,TD} =$	forward price stochastic for expiration TE valued at observation t
$K =$	strike price

Whereas Figure 8-6 plots the payoff diagram for a call option, Figure 8-7 graphs what is known as a "profit diagram", since it adjusts the possible payoff outcomes by any premiums paid for the contract. (In other words, a profit diagram is like a payoff diagram adjusted for premiums paid.) Recall that we paid a $10 premium for this option. In our call option example, the profit diagram looks just like the payoff diagram shifted downward by $10. (The payoff diagram for a forward contract looks just like a profit diagram, since one does not pay an upfront premium for a forward contract.) On the profit diagram, we see that we don't start seeing a profit until the underlying market moves above $110 because we had to recoup the $10 premium paid to buy the option. That said, we at least start recouping the premium at the $100 point and the delta does become positive.

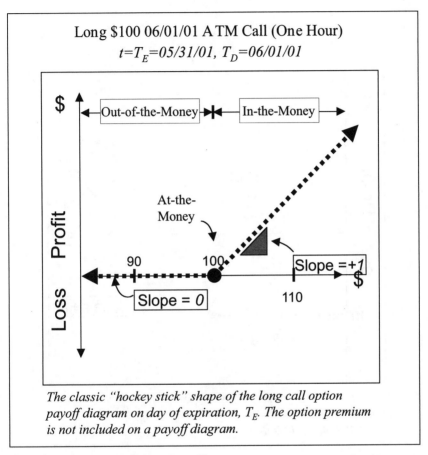

Fig. 8-6: Long Call Option Payoff

Note: To value the option, in the most general sense (ignoring such factors as discounting), we simply sum up all of the possible outcomes of parity value, adjusted for the probability of the outcomes. Graphically, we can overlay the payoff diagram for a call option with the probability distribution (as we see in Figure 8-8.) Note that we are not graphing the impact of the premium). Put in simplistic terms, the overall option value equals the sum of each probable outcome multiplied by its probability of occurring, which can be expressed mathematically as the next equation.

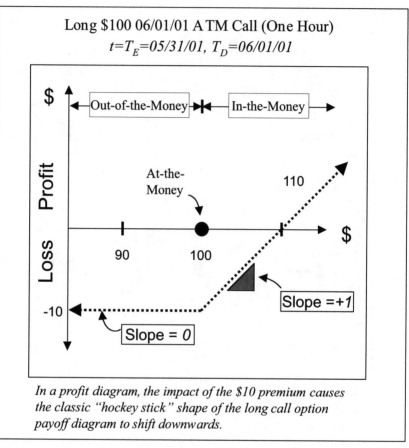

Long $100 06/01/01 A TM Call (One Hour)
$t=T_E=05/31/01,\ T_D=06/01/01$

In a profit diagram, the impact of the $10 premium causes the classic "hockey stick" shape of the long call option payoff diagram to shift downwards.

Fig. 8-7:   Profit Diagram for Call

Equation 8-7

$$C_{t,TD}=\ _{x=1}\infty\Sigma C^x_{t=TE,TD}*p^x$$

Where:

$C_{t,TD}=$ European call option premium

$C^x_{t=TE,TD}=$ the call parity value for particular outcome x on TE

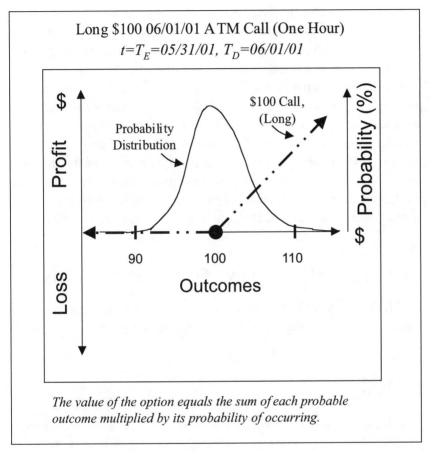

Fig. 8-8: Parity Value of a Call Option

$t =$	Time of Observation
$TE =$	Time of Expiration
$TD =$	Time of Delivery
$x =$	variable denoting a particular outcome
$p^x =$	probability of outcome x

The "hockey stick" profit diagram may be rotated into four basic positions, each representing a unique combination of a "call versus a put" and a "long versus short" position. Figure 8-9 graphs the four positions for the same strike price. (A rough rule of thumb: the difference between the call premium and the put premium should be equal to the difference between the forward price and the strike price. The relationship is referred to as the parity value and is precise when discounting effects are included. So, ignoring effects of discount, the call and put premiums should be equivalent for an at-the-money strike price.) To help the power executive relate to this basic profit diagrams in Figure 8-9, Table 8-2 provides examples of these four basic option positions in terms of real assets or traditional retail positions.

Profit Diagrams for Portfolios

Profit and payoff diagrams also help us visualize how portfolios behave. Figure 8-10 depicts a simple two-contract portfolio: we buy the

	Synthetic Put	Sythetic Call
Long (Bought) Contract	The utility sells a "load curtailment contract" which embeds the right to withhold (or "buy back") power from a base-load swap contract. (Graph A)	Owning a gas-peaker plant that can be easily switched on if prices exceed $100. (Graph B)
Short (Sold) Contract	Under regulation, a utility is forced to buy any output from an independent power producer at $100 at producer's request. (Graph C)	The utility enters a full-requirements contract to a large, fixed price sophisticated industrial end user that plans its load as a function of power prices. (Graph D)

Table 8-2: Basic Option Positions in Traditional Utility Terms

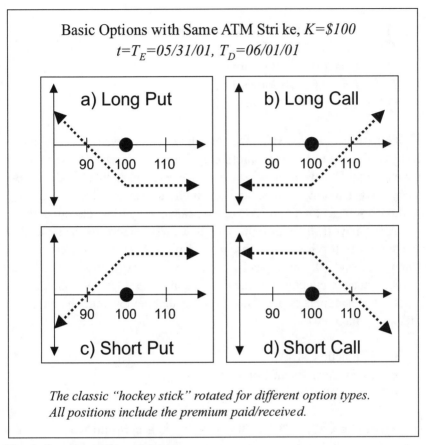

Fig. 8-9: Four Mirror Images

same $100 forward from Figure 8-2 and we also sell identical contract, but for $110. Mathematically, while still ignoring discounting effects, the value of the portfolio (π) is represented by the next equation.

Equation 8-8

$$\Pi = (F^{\$100})*(Q^{\$100}) + (F^{\$110})*(Q^{\$110})$$
$$= (\$100/\text{MWh})*(-1 \text{ MWh}) + (\$110/\text{MWh})*(+1 \text{ MWh}) = \$10$$

Where:

Π_t = Overall portfolio value at observation t

$F^{\$100}$ = Price of $100 forward

$Q^{\$100}$ = Quantity of $100 forward

$F^{\$110}$ = Price of $110 forward

$Q^{\$110}$ = Quantity of $110 forward

Graphically, we can value the portfolio (π) on a given observation date (t) by adding the two contract profit diagram values together for each possible outcome. The two negative slopes cancel each other out ($1+(-1)=0$). But since we bought low (at $100) and sold high (at $110), we lock in a guaranteed profit of $10 for all possible outcomes while ignoring discounting.

A flat payoff diagram represents that rare instance of guaranteed or fixed returns (or losses, as the case may be.) As will be covered in Chapters 9 and 10, the slopes in a payoff diagrams represent risk. Much of risk management concerns the analysis of these slopes. We should consider three examples of portfolio diagrams that demonstrate the impact of offsetting diagonals:

- Synthetic Call
- Load Curtailment Contract
- Two Call Portfolio

Synthetic Call. A "synthetic" position is a portfolio whose payoffs replicate that of a standard contract. As an example, a portfolio that contains a long forward and a long put option represents a "synthetic call option." We should be indifferent between a synthetic call option and a direct purchase of call options. The profit diagram for this portfolio appears in Figure 8-11. To help us "read" the diagram, we divide it into a "Left Zone" for all possible outcomes between $0 and $100—we are assuming that all prices will be non-negative—and a "Right Zone" for all possible outcomes greater than $100. In the left zone, the slopes of the put and the forward cancel each other out to leave a flat curve representing the $10 paid for the premium. To the right, the diagonal portion of the forward is only offset by the put's premium. In total, the portfolio's profit diagram replicates that for the long call option shown in Figure 8-6.

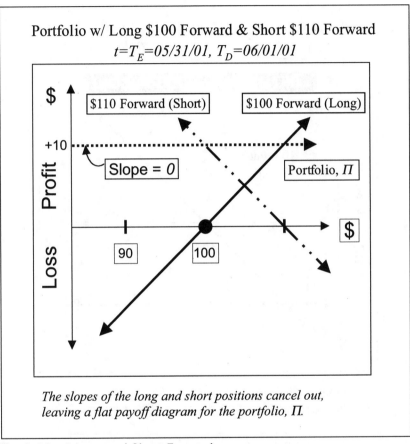

Portfolio w/ Long $100 Forward & Short $110 Forward
$t=T_E=05/31/01, T_D=06/01/01$

The slopes of the long and short positions cancel out, leaving a flat payoff diagram for the portfolio, Π.

Fig. 8-10: A Long and Short Forward

Load Curtailment Contract. A Load Curtailment Contract is a structured product that allows the supplier to curtail or not deliver all or a portion of power contracted for delivery. (This resembles the traditional concept of non-firm power.) As a synthetic long put (with a profit diagram similar to Figure 8-8a), the portfolio includes a short forward and a long call. In practice, the utility simultaneously sells an industrial customer a fixed-price, fixed-volume swap, but simultaneously "buys" a

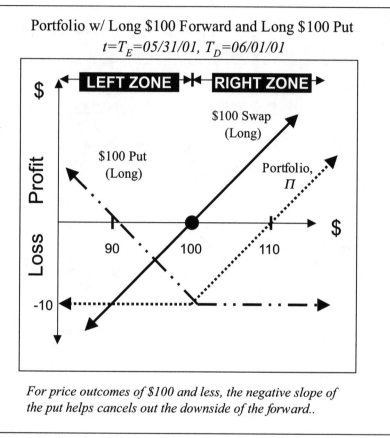

Fig. 8-11: Synthetic Call Option

"zero-premium" call option. A "zero-premium" option does indeed carry a premium; the premium is embedded within a fixed-price cash flow. So the structure is also known as a "pay-as-you-go" contract. During the term of this contract, the utility would deliver the fixed-volume of power at the lower but fixed price. But if spot prices spike, or if the spot market experiences capacity constraints, the utility would have the right to curtail load from the end user. This is the type of "load shaving" that many

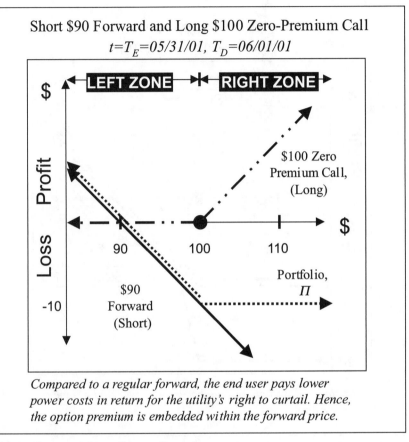

Short $90 Forward and Long $100 Zero-Premium Call
$t=T_E=05/31/01$, $T_D=06/01/01$

*Compared to a regular forward, the end user pays lower
power costs in return for the utility's right to curtail. Hence,
the option premium is embedded within the forward price.*

Fig. 8-12: Load Curtailment Contract

thinkers propose as ways of coping with an energy crisis or to promote
conservation. Could it be possible that the availability of structured products like load-curtailment options will resurrect the ghost of demand side
management (DSM)?

Figure 8-12 demonstrates the portfolio pay-offs; the "Left Zone"
reflects the negative slope of the forward exposure that is then cancelled
out in the "Right Zone" by the zero-premium call. Compared to a marked-

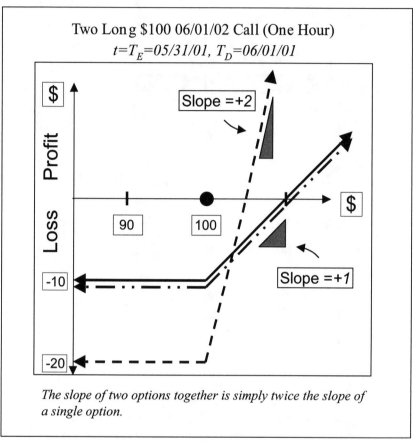

Fig. 8-13: Two Long Call Options

to-market forward price for the same period, the base-load swap price for the load curtailment contract would be reduced, in effect amortizing the value of the call premium.

Two Call Portfolio. Finally, consider a simple portfolio with two long call options as shown in Figure 8-13. Note how the "Left Zone" remains flat but is now "twice" as negative since two option premiums are being paid. In the "Right Zone" we see a new phenomenon, a diagonal with a slope of +2, representing the impact of the two call options: for

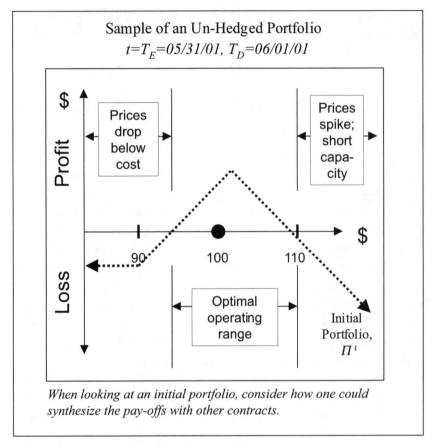

Sample of an Un-Hedged Portfolio
$t=T_E=05/31/01, T_D=06/01/01$

Prices drop below cost

Prices spike; short capacity

Profit

$

Loss

90   100   110

Optimal operating range

Initial Portfolio, Π^t

When looking at an initial portfolio, consider how one could synthesize the pay-offs with other contracts.

Fig. 8-14: Generator's Initial Portfolio

every one dollar increase in expected outcome, two dollars gain is realized. In effect, the risk impact of different contracts in the same portfolio is additive. In this example, the slope of a portion of the payoff diagram represents the risk sensitivity at that particular underlying price. So, if the portfolio contains two option contracts, the slope at any given point will be based adding the slopes of two individual options. Likewise, we see the additive relationship in the total premium being paid: when you buy two options with a premium of $10, you wind up starting $20 in the hole.

GUEST ESSAY

How to Explain Profits and Losses: P&L Decomposition

by Kevin Kremke, Director of Risk Assessment, Reliant Energy

The manager arrives at the office early Monday morning to begin poring over the weekly profit-and-loss (P&L) reports. In the back of her head the thoughts begin to appear: *"There it is! I can see the P&L numbers on my report, but how did the system derive it? How do I know if the numbers are correct? What caused any changes?"*

Decomposing P&L into its rudimentary components is a critical task of the risk management process. Internal and external auditors, executive risk committee members, and even front office personnel should look for the risk manager to demonstrate a comprehension of the structure and risks of a portfolio; explaining P&L by its respective risk components is essential in doing so. A risk manager must possess some level of confidence in the risk system and its output, but there are three primary reasons why independent P&L verification is important.

1. *Model validation:* If the model parameters are inaccurate, the model may systematically mis-price all instruments—decomposing P&L with the risk components may elucidate the problem.
2. *Market validation:* Independent P&L breakdown is a secondary level of ensuring that market prices and volatilities are input correctly.
3. *Executive reporting:* Demonstrating an analytic understanding of P&L conveys a message of professionalism and expertise that the risk of the portfolio is well understood.

Risk managers have been plagued with the "Black Box" problem of accepting model output prima facie from the advent of even the most sophisticated trading systems. The P&L of many linear portfolios are easily explainable: take the position (quantity – long or short) times the net change in prices from one day to the next. This simple procedure is analogous to a stock portfolio. If your portfolio is long 100 shares of a particular stock—and that stock rises by $2.25—your total daily profit is $225. Even in an irreducible futures portfolio, many risk managers subjectively analyze system output for P&L reasonableness. If the portfolio is short some December NYMEX Natural Gas contracts and long some January contracts, analyzing P&L is as simple as looking at the respective settlement prices and positions—no system should have difficulty determining this P&L.

Most energy commodity portfolios, however, are not this linear due to the presence of options. Once options are introduced into a portfolio, analyzing the P&L becomes less one-dimensional. Unlike typical futures, forwards, and equity contracts, option prices display a nonlinear relation to the value of the underlying instrument. For example, the value of a July $3 call option on NYMEX Natural Gas is tied to the value of the July futures contract. However, a $0.50 move in the underlying futures contract does not necessarily equate to a $.50 move in the option contract—the relation is not one-to-one and is not constant—this is a perfect example of non-linearity of options.

Predicting the P&L

Fortunately, however, accurately predicting the P&L of an options portfolio is fairly straightforward once the risks are measured accurately. The option Greeks explain changes in the value of an option with respect to changes in different market factors.

- **Delta, Δ** - change in the option value with respect to changes in the underlying
- **Gamma, Γ** - change in the delta with respect to changes in the underlying
- **Vega** - change in the value of the option with respect to changes in the volatility
- **Theta, Θ** - change in the value of the option with respect to the passage of time

In a portfolio of options, decomposing P&L is as "simple" as taking the portfolio's Greeks and applying them to the respective changes in market factors. "Simple" in that the concept is not immensely onerous, but the mechanics of extracting the data from the risk system are often not as easy as explaining the concept. There is a fairly simple formula that looks intimidating, but is in reality quite simple yet powerful. The Taylor Series Expansion is as follows:

$$d\pi = \Delta \cdot d\widetilde{F} + \frac{1}{2}\Gamma \cdot d\widetilde{F}^2 + \Theta \cdot dt + v \cdot d\sigma$$

...which to most managers really is "all Greek." The notation and the derivation are the complex ingredients to this concept, but the theory is easily articulated as the sum of the impact of the "Greeks":

	(Delta) x (Change in underlying)
	(Gamma) x ½(Change in underlying)^2
	(Theta) x (Change in days)
+	(Vega) x (Change in volatility)
	Total Portfolio Change

The Taylor Series Expansion formula should explain almost all the P&L changes of a portfolio, but other higher order Greek letters may correspond to further changes, such as interest rates (rho or ρ) or additional statistical measures. These other measures, however, are typically inconsequential to a portfolio of commodity derivatives and their analysis may provide more nuisance than value.

Additionally, the risk manager must segregate the P&L effect of new trades that were not included in the calculation of the original Greeks. One important technical note is that this procedure must be completed separately for each group of common risks (unless the system accounts for intramarket correlations.). The July option Greeks must be applied to changes in the July contract and July implied volatility separate from the changes in the November contract.

Checking the Accuracy of P&L Predictions

If the risk system and corresponding models are working accurately, the predicted or theoretical P&L change should be close to the actual

Portfolio	Theoretic P&L	Delta	Gamma	Vega	Theta	New Trades	Actual P&L	Error Term	Explained P&L
Book 1	(93,646)	(110,509)	12,456	5,698	(11,770)	10,479	(105,417)	(11,771)	88.83%
Book 2	23,220	28,943	1,478	2,417	(8,549)	(1,069)	20,803	(2,417)	111.62%
Book 3	110,061	137,403	8,906	1,305	(37,552)	0	102,558	(7,503)	107.32%
Book 4	402,456	276,522	(45,697)	(19,641)	185,059	6,213	470,621	68,165	85.52%
Total	442,091	332,358	(22,857)	(10,221)	127,188	15,623	488,565	46,474	90.49%

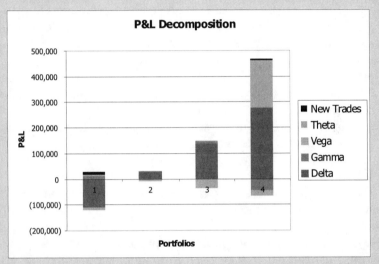

P&L generated from the risk system. Very rarely will the two numbers be exactly the same, but the *Risk Management Policies and Procedures* (RMPP) must establish some bands of tolerance in which the predicted P&L may deviate from the actual system-generated P&L, resourcefully known as the "error-term."

For example, the RMPP may dictate that further investigation is necessary if the theoretical P&L can only explain the actual P&L outside of 90-110%. *Table 1* shows the P&L decomposition of four books in a portfolio. While the overall P&L can be explained within the bands of tolerance, some of the individual portfolios may warrant further investigation. *Chart 1* presents a graphic display of the P&L sensitivity to each respective risk factor.

The system has calculated actual P&L and your theoretical Taylor series expansion model doesn't fully explain the daily changes. *What next?*

Where do you begin looking for an explanation for the error? A deviation from theoretical P&L can be caused by many factors, and experience with the idiosyncrasies of your risk system may lead you to the answer. The solution, however, is typically not very transparent. What are some of the commonplace problems causing an out-of-compliance error term?

- *Model assumptions:* Perhaps some of the parameters of the valuation model are not reflective of reality. For example, significant shifts in the slope of the forward curve can have an effect on the actual P&L that will not be captured by the theoretical model.
- *Operational risk:* Input error is a very universal and pervasive issue that is difficult to quantify, but proper procedures and policies can minimize exposure.
- *Additional risk:* Such practical issues as counterparty default are not captured by the theoretic model.

Conclusion

No system can capture every risk to which an organization is exposed, and reality dictates that those risks that are measured will occasionally be reported incorrectly. However, letting these errors go unexplained indefinitely may present systematic problems that could lead to significant losses or even unexpected and unexplained profits, neither of which reflects favorably on the professional risk manager or the manager in charge of the trading and risk operation. Decomposing one's P&L helps build confidence in the risk management process and identify any systematic problems in that process. The relatively simple technique of comparing the theoretical to actual P&L should become a part of a daily routine in order to infuse more discipline necessary to a risk management function.

Kevin L. Kremke is the Director of Risk Assessment at Reliant Energy in Houston, where he is ultimately responsible for managing all market risk related to retail energy. His primary work entails modeling energy derivatives and structured contracts, facilitating product development, and refining the risk system to incorporate changes in the dynamic energy market. Kevin has a bachelor's degree from Ball State University and an MBA in finance from the University of Chicago. In his spare time, Kevin is a competitive cyclist. He may be reached at Kevin_L_Kremke@reliantenergy.com.

THE GENERATOR'S INITIAL PORTFOLIO

A power generator's exposure to spot prices can be graphed as a function of cost and market conditions. In this example, we assume that the generator has a retail swing commitment, but with a possible risk of shortage. Relative to the hedging cycle, we will call this "the generator's initial portfolio" (π^i) or its un-hedged portfolio. This initial portfolio may (or may not) already contain hedge contracts entered previously; we only call it "un-hedged" because we intend to revalue its currently risk levels in order to determine what (if any) new hedge contracts must be entered. The initial portfolio answers the first of our "Five Questions"—*What Do We Have?* Figure 8-14 provides a simple example with three general groupings of potential outcomes, reading from left to right:

Prices Drop Below Cost. When market prices drop below operating costs, the portfolio shows a loss. The flat portion of the payoff diagram portrays the fixed-cost of maintaining the generating plant even if no power is being generated for sale, or uneconomic use of generation when it would have been cheaper to go out into the market for power.

Optimal Operating Range. In response to market pressures, optimal operation occurs between the cost of production (on the lower extreme) to the market conditions that maximize production output (on the high extreme.) In Figure 8-13, the spot price of $100 represents an inflection point, the optimal marginal cost of production. All possible spot price outcomes between $100 and $110 would show a profit but would have decreasing rates of return. Here we are assuming a supply-demand correlation between market price and overall market volume. We can see this correlation during summer temperature spikes when prices jump as demand begins to swell.

Prices Spike, Short Capacity. Price spikes typically appear as the market responds to a combination of increased demand and insufficient supply. Within the optimal operating range, the generator may be "long" capacity with enough power to supply their retail commitments. But during price spikes, the same generator may find themselves "short"—due either to increased demand or diminished internal capacity—and must buy open-market power at high, sometimes incredibly high spot prices.

197

Capturing the Initial Portfolio in the RMPP

RMPP Management should design the *Risk Management Policies and Procedures* (RMPP) to properly capture the "initial" portfolio. The word "initial" can carry literal meaning for the company that is first writing its RMPP or just starting a trading program. More realistically, every morning, before the start of the trading day, the portfolio of all positions represents the "initial portfolio."

When designing the RMPP, the manager should answer the following issues as part of answering the larger question of *What Have We Got?*:

Market definition. What markets should be analyzed and traded upon?

Deal Capture. Are all exposures and trades captured, valued, and reported in a single system? Are physical assets to be integrated in the portfolio?

Proper Valuation. Are the portfolio and the individual contracts being marked-to-market on a regular basis? Are the valuation techniques being used appropriate and meaningful?

Consistency. Is there portfolio-wide, and therefore, company-wide consistency across these issues of market definition, deal capture, and valuation?

Sample Profit Objectives by Risk-Return Strategy

In the previous section on the initial portfolio, we discussed how a generator's unhedged position might be plotted on a payoff diagram. The point of trading and risk management, however, is to mold the "initial" portfolio (π^i) into the "objective" portfolio (π^o). The payoff diagram of our objective portfolio answers the second of our "Five Questions," *What Do We Want to Have?*

Ideally, we desire guaranteed profits. Better yet, we seek unlimited upside! Figure 8-15 expresses this unlikely dream. In reality, however, utilities should map their objectives as a direct function of the *Risk Return*

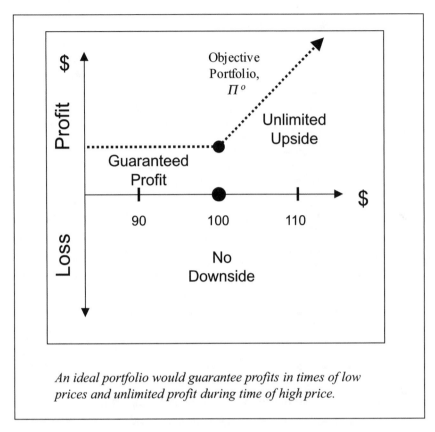

An ideal portfolio would guarantee profits in times of low prices and unlimited profit during time of high price.

Fig. 8-15: A Dream Profit Diagram

Strategies defined in their RMPP (see Chapter 4.) Figure 8-16 provides samples of payoff diagrams for each of the four strategies.

Treasury. Like a corporate treasurer interested in stabilizing cash flows, one energy strategy is to assume a "reliability first" strategy, and our top priority is to have power available to meet load. The basic strategy attempts to place a "floor" on potential losses when prices are below $100. For higher prices, accompanied by capacity constraints, we attempt

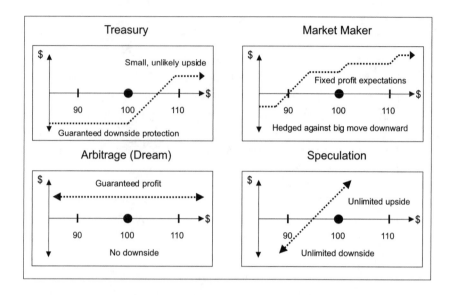

Fig. 8-16: A Profit Diagram by Risk-Return Strategies

to guarantee supply in the future by purchasing insurance in the form of options, with the effect being a lid on forward profits.

Market Maker. Here we try to create back-to-back trades and capture the bid/ask spread between them. We try to keep potential losses to a minimum, with hedges entered here to avoid losses due to either a big downward or upward price move.

Arbitrage. Here we see another "dream" portfolio similar to Figure 8-15. We receive a guaranteed profit regardless of how prices actually turn out.

Speculation. The speculative portfolio remains unbounded, with no hedges against large price moves up or down.

We will see in Chapter 10 how one can hedge or adjust the initial portfolio to meet these objectives.

Articulating Objectives in the RMPP

RMPP

As Figure 8-16 suggests, setting objectives is the manager's top priority since they directly express expectations regarding potential profits and losses. Issues that must be considered in the RMPP include:

Motivation. Effective control of trading begins with a clear vision statement about which of the four *Risk-Return Strategies* should be followed to meet corporate objectives.

Portfolio Organization. If more than one strategy is desired, does the company wish to organize strategic trading into separate books? What firewalls will be designed to prevent cross-book trading that is counter to the objectives?

Profit and Loss Objectives. What potential profits and losses does the company specifically seek to achieve and/or to avoid? Does the company wish to establish lower or upper boundaries to potential gains/losses? What is the company's budget for achieving these pay-off objectives?

Authority. Who will have the authority to monitor how well portfolios are meeting their objectives?

ENDNOTES

[1] SAVA first used this phrase for a November 1999 seminar of the same name.

[2] Payoff diagrams are staples in most books on derivatives and risk management. See Hull (p. 6-10); Turnbull and Wakeman (pp 15-19); and Wilmott (pp 27-37). For an incredible array of exotic payoff diagrams, see Nelken (2000).

[3] I first presented these payoff diagrams at *IIR's Energy Price Risk Forum,* London, U.K., in May 2000.

[4] Note: When an option is far from expiration, the option value as a function of the underlying price is curved. Please see Hull, 1989, pages 298-307 for more details.

[5] This is an example of a "synthetic" put that is comprised of selling a swap and buying a call. See Chapter 8.

[6] Very generally, a linear portfolio is one that contains no options. The P&L of the portfolio exhibits a linear relationship with movements in the underlying instrument price.

chapter 9

Measuring Risk: How Might Our Portfolio Change?

The Gamma Criterion

In the hedging cycle, "measuring risk" plays the central role of answering the manager's question of *How Might Our Portfolio Change?* Risk can be defined as the impact of unexpected change.[1] Whereas valuation attempts to calculate a single value amidst all possible outcomes, risk measurement attempts to revalue a contract or portfolio given assumptions about potential change. As in Chapter 8, we rely heavily on payoff and profit diagrams to explore how we measure risk so that we might manage it.

As with the rest of the book, this chapter is written for the manager or generalist.[2] That said, we must core down to a certain level of technical detail. A manager sitting on top of nuclear plants should posses some basic knowledge of uranium, its behavior, and what it can do to people! So I submit the "Gamma Criterion"—all managers should at least understand what "gamma" risk represents. If he/she grasps gamma, he/she'll definitely understand "delta" and most other risk measurement basics. With understanding comes the ability to measure risk. If we can measure risk, we can set limits. If we can set limits, we can manage risk. That's the focus of this chapter.

Risk Category	Specific Risk	Measurement
Market	Illiquidity	Bid/Ask Spread
	Price Discovery	Traded Volume and "Churn" Ratio
	Re-regulation	What If? Scenarios
Price	Change in market (forward and/or spot) prices	Delta, Δ, the impact on value given a one-unit change in underlying price
	The rate of change in market prices measures the acceleration, deceleration, or stability of change.	Gamma, Γ, the impact on delta given a one-unit change in underlying price
	Volatility	Option prices
		Vega, a one-unit change in volatility
	Interest Rates (Inflation)	Rho, ρ, a one-unit change in discounting rate
	Time (Time Decay)	Theta, θ, a one-unit change in time
	Basis	Cross-market risks given a one unit change in cross-market correlation
	Correlation	Risks given a one-unit change in correlations
	Foreign Exchange	Cross-currency risks
Profit & Loss	Worst Case Losses	Value-at-Risk (VaR)
		Stress Testing
	Earnings	Earning-at-Risk
Credit	Counterparty Exposure	Notional limits by counterparty
	Payment Default	Credit Delta, Credit VaR
Volumetric	Change in quantity	Volume-adjusted "Greeks"
Modeling	Change in value due to modeling errors	Change in value given changes in models or model variables
Marketing	Reliability – or the ability to deliver	Strong relationship between RMPP and actual marketing efforts
	Credibility & Trust	Presence on approved counterparty lists at other companies
Human	Trader (illegal)	Non-compliance with RMPP
	Human error	Any other measurements that cannot be explained.
	Political	Public attempts to re-regulate the markets.
	Managerial	Incomplete or ineffectual RMPP
	Modeling	Fluctuating P&L, VaR or other number
	Modeling	Convergence to Market; Estimating errors
Operational	Valuation errors	How well answers respond to redundant systems

Table 9-1: Litany of Risks

The Litany of Risks

Many variables impact the value of a contract or portfolio. A potential change in any one of these variables represents a unique risk and risk measurement. Table 9-1 attempts to summarize the variables that impact value. The source of the risks include the following:

- **Market Risk**. The impact of general market conditions such as illiquidity, inadequate price discovery, and the threat of re-regulation.
- **Price Risk**. The impact of change in market prices on the value of the contracts in the portfolio. This risk class covers numerous aspects of price behavior including volatility, correlations, interest rates, etc.
- **Profit &Loss (P&L) Risk**. Really a sub-set of price risk, P&L risk deserves special mention since it is near and dear to the hearts of management.[3]
- **Credit Risk**. The risk of a counterparty defaulting on its commitment to either pay or make delivery on a contract.
- **Volumetric Risk**. The risk of change in the volume or load of power. This could be due to physical demand, plant outages, or swing-like optionality contracts.
- **Transmission Risk**. The risk of transmission constraints or congestion affecting volume or transmission costs impacting price risk.
- **Modeling Risk**. The risk that the models used for valuation and risk measurement produce results that are less accurate or relevant than originally believed to be.
- **Marketing Risk**. The risk to the company's market positioning due to market-driven decision-making. Some traditional companies continue to emphasize "reliability" or the ability to deliver power; making economic decisions to curtail delivery could put this positioning at risk. In another case, high losses or the impression of rogue trading can lead to bad press that can directly erode the "goodwill" value of the company's reputation or cause counterparties to either eliminate it from its trading list or require more expansive credit-enhancements for all trading.
- **Human Risk**. Risk management remains a human enterprise, fertile ground for the good, the bad, and the ugly. People can

cause risk due to ignorance, hubris, or criminal intent. Human risk is not limited to the "rogue trader" but includes quantitative analysts who fail to include all the necessary risks in their models (or make mistakes in their models), as well as managers who might encourage inappropriate trading strategies in hopes of greater profits. Community factors outside the traded markets can equally impact risk. Throughout 1999 and 2000, market analysts discussed how new gas peaker plants will shave volatility by expanding capacity during price spikes; opposition from the communities targeted for these plants could delay or even prevent their construction.[4]

- **Operational Risk**. Even the "best laid plans" can go awry. Operational risk represents the change in value due to systems failures.

Typically, price risk attracts the greatest attention and will be the primary focus of this chapter. Price risk represents a dramatic threat following deregulation, and there are plenty of ways of measuring it! As the market learned during the Federal Energy Sales crisis, credit risk can command equal attention with pure price risk. Whereas the energy markets can directly borrow ideas like the "Greeks" from the money markets, we may need to create new measures such as "volumetric Greeks" to account for risks unique (or especially dramatic) in our market. The key for the manager is to be aware of whatever variable represents the greatest risk to the value of the company—whether it is listed in Table 9-1 or not!

INTERVIEW

Managing Human Risk: Money, Confidence, and Trust

An Interview with Dunham Cobb, Director of Risk Strategies, FPL Energy

Trust serves as bedrock for trading and risk management. If a trading operation loses the trust of upper management, that trust can rarely be regained without a radical change in the structure of and personnel within the trading operation.

Dunham Cobb of FPL Energy offers an intriguing approach to managing human risk by viewing trust as an "account" to be managed just like a money account. He has developed his ideas over a diverse career.

Question: *When senior management sets up a trading operation, what kind of "accounts" does it create for that business unit?*

Cobb: Senior management sets up three accounts for its trading operation. The company gives the traders a certain amount of money, confidence, and trust.

Question: *Does upper management manage these three accounts differently?*

Cobb: Absolutely. If the money account is drawn down, management will refill it quickly as long as performance is reasonably near budget. When something occurs to lessen management's confidence, they will refill the account slowly if they see an exercise of better judgement. But if the trust capital is ever severely diminished, that account will be rarely replenished, and in fact can lead to all three being closed.

Question: *What can be the biggest reasons for a dramatic loss of trust and how can a risk management hedge against such problems?*

Cobb: Anything that leads senior management to think you are hiding something. Specifically, if there ever is a significant "event" (rogue trading, etc.) it is *critical* that they hear it from you *immediately*! This can often turn a lemon into lemonade. Senior Management does not like such events, but it also knows that they happen in even the best run organizations. By communicating so forthrightly, you are making a strong statement, "You can trust me to deliver good *and* bad news, regardless of the consequence to me personally." They may be left with questions as to your judgment (the event happened on your watch, after all), but not as to trust.

Question: *"Rogue trading", or any other act of moral hazard, can certainly impact all three of these accounts—money, confidence, and trust—not to mention make management fearful. Are there common misconceptions about moral hazard, and if so what are they?*

Cobb: Yes there are, and this could be the topic of an entire article. The strongest mandate I ever received from upper management was, "Don't let me ever wake up on Sunday morning and see the company's name in the same headline as a trading scandal!" Management is afraid of being the next Barings Bank, and fear can obfuscate the truth.

With few exceptions, "rogue traders" are not people driven by visions of Ferraris and Caribbean villas, nor are they typically villainous. The most common act of *moral hazard* is committed by an average person motivated by the fear of losing his/her job and/or reputation. Why? Because most improper activity starts with covering up an error that, if discovered, could lead to its perpetrator's dismissal. Since they perceive their job already at risk, they have "nothing to lose" by trying to hide the event.

Management must recognize that, if someone wants to do something improper, you cannot prevent him or her from doing so. The best courses of preventative action are to (a) minimize the most common cause—errors—by instilling better habits, and (b) put adequate IT systems and thoughtful procedures in place that ensure numerous sets of eyes are involved as a deal passes from cradle to grave.

Question: *I once saw a documentary on airline safety that described the problem of pilots focusing too much on their instruments and failing to see from their windshield that they were about to crash. Have you seen a parallel phenomenon in risk management?*

Cobb: Yes. Risk management has been described as having two sides... the hard (quantitative) side, and the soft (behavioral) side. The "instruments" of risk management tend to fall on the hard side, i.e., VaR, MtM, position reports, etc. Such tools are very objective. But if a trading organization ignores the soft side, i.e., has not instilled and does not demand appropriate behavior, then "garbage" data will be captured and the information reflected in the reports—the instruments—is just "garbage out."

Question: *If trust is lost, can an individual risk manager do anything to help upper management restore its faith in the trading operation?*

Cobb: Maybe... but I doubt the risk manager will ever get the opportunity. With few exceptions, the trading operation's walls do not contain the ripple effect of an "event". The Board will, in turn, begin to question upper management's judgement, and I have yet to see the risk manager's head that will not be offered up to stay in the Board's good graces.

Question: *How do you think people outside of trading and risk management think about our part of the industry?*

Cobb: The further removed the audience is from trading, the less they understand—and the more they fear trading and risk management. Likewise, the less someone understands trading and risk, the more they fear it, and the bigger their reaction will be to an incident. This is especially true with shareholders, who can lose trust in a company very quickly after some trading embarrassment.

Question: *What are the top priorities for any company to manage human error so as to retain the confidence and trust of the market?*

Cobb: The simple answer is that a trading operation's management must unequivocally endorse and enforce trading procedures! This is a complex question, so the answer I give here risks making unfair generalizations... but here goes.

First, errors are the greatest danger to a trading organization... PERIOD! For one thing, some of the greatest disasters in commodity history started with an error that was subsequently covered up. No one wants to commit an error, but if they are large enough, people can be incented to cover them up. But meltdowns are very rare. How errors really kill you is the infamous "death by a thousand cuts"... the aggregations of many small errors that add up to millions and millions of dollars lost, a couple of thousand bucks at a time. And what causes most errors? Bad habits!

From my experience, the two "key logs" in this issue are: the nature of traders and the nature of VPs of Trading. Let's face it, traders want to trade. Anything which gets in the way of the next deal is a major annoyance... little things such as accurate and timely deal capture. Traders (as do all of us) also have bad habits that manifest as errors. Strict enforcement of procedures, including negative consequences of non-compliance, can change a bad habit into a good one.

Now comes the "VP of Trading" issue. Most people in this position were once traders who also were annoyed by procedures. It is uncanny (and unfortunate) how often they will side with the trader over the procedure, effectively undermining any chance of creating new and better habits. I have seen organizations literally crippled by this.

In conclusion, agree to procedures, track non-compliance (errors) of those procedures, apply consequences to non-compliance, and have management demonstrate seamless solidarity with the procedures. Bad habits and most errors will disappear quickly.

Dunham Cobb is a graduate of Yale University with a BA in Economics. He was a registered securities broker for 13 years, the final 11 concentrated on futures trading. FERC Order 636 led to his entry into the natural gas business, when he joined Heath Petra Resources, which was later acquired by Eastex Energy, Inc. After serving Eastex as Vice President of Risk Management for a year, he joined Columbia Energy Services. From 1995 through 1997, Mr. Cobb served as director of risk management at CES as it grew from a small regional player to a top-10 national wholesaler. After CES' acquisition of Penn Union, he accepted the position in Florida with FPL.

Dunham Cobb may be reached via Dunham_Cobb@fpl.com.

MEASURING PRICE RISK

RMPP
When drafting the *Risk Management Policies and Procedures* (RMPP), the manager must decide which elements of price risk to include and exclude. A simple rule-of-thumb suggests that if a variable significantly impacts value, then it ought to be included. Interest rate risks, for example, may impact value, but may not justify being included as a top-priority hedging issue. Another rule-of-thumb is measurement. Measurement means enforcement. If one cannot measure, one cannot enforce, and managing that particular risk exercise becomes an exercise in futility.

Like a control panel of an airplane cockpit, risk management incorporates many different (and complimentary) ways to measure risk. Extending our flying analogy, the risk manager controls his/her craft in two ways, *Looking Out the Windshield* and *Looking at Controls and Simulations:*

Marking-to-Market Concept

Volatility Measures Risk

Looking Out the Windshield. Looking at actual conditions provides the primary information to the pilot. To the risk manager, marking-to-market measures risk conditions in the form of prices and market-implied volatility. In today's world of the "day trader," many investors want to see streams of stock prices floating across their favorite web sites. Water-cooler conversations ponder, *"How's the Dow?"* The same should hold true for the power executive. He/she might ask that broker sheets be delivered every morning or that current power prices be posted on his/her machine.

Looking at Controls and Simulations: Risk measurements allow the manager to gauge and sift through the multiple variables affecting portfolio value. In conjunction with looking "out the windshield," these measurements help detect potential and emerging situations. Consider this analogy from physics. Location, velocity, and acceleration are like value, delta, and gamma.

The more volatility, the greater the risk and the smaller guarantee of outcome. (This explains why higher volatilities create higher option prices.) Market-implied volatility directly feeds into the valuation models used in risk calculations; good mark-to-market risk measurement depends on market-expectations of risk rather than just assumptions. Market-based readings also measure illiquidity. Consider the case of a manager approving Value-at-Risk (VaR) methodologies. A common approach, the Variance-Covariance method, fails to capture the non-linearity of options. This may be perfectly adequate for firms with little or no optionality in their portfolios; but the manager overseeing portfolios with significant optionality should also require VaR methods that do capture option behavior (such as Monte Carlo simulations) or other risk measures to develop the big picture. While other books have greater detail on this topic, here's a great question for a manager to ask his/her risk manager: *Does our VaR methodology capture the non-linearity of options?*

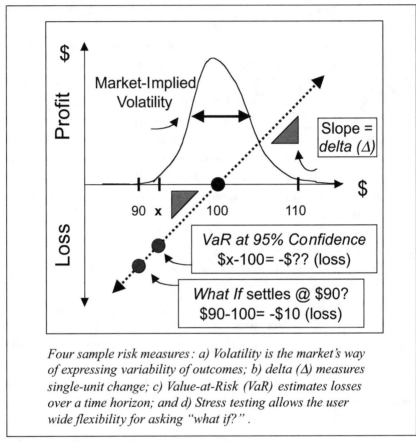

*Four sample risk measures: a) Volatility is the market's way
of expressing variability of outcomes; b) delta (Δ) measures
single-unit change; c) Value-at-Risk (VaR) estimates losses
over a time horizon; and d) Stress testing allows the user
wide flexibility for asking "what if?".*

Fig. 9-1:   Different Risk Measures

Figure 9-1 attempts to show how select price risk measures cover different aspects of the payoff diagram. Volatility
helps describe the distribution of possible outcomes.[5] The risk
sensitivity delta (Δ) is represented by the slope of the payoff
diagram. Whereas delta (Δ) looks at just a single-unit change in outcome,
measures like Value-at-Risk (VaR) and stress testing (*What If?*) analysis
attempt to calculate worst-case scenarios.

Completing our aviation analogy, the VP in charge of trading and risk may not necessarily know all the details that his/her "pilots" would need to know. His/her role, however, could be characterized as the "air traffic controller," managing flight paths and conflicts from the tower.

VIEWING PRICE RISK ON THE PAYOFF DIAGRAM

As suggested in Chapter 8, the payoff diagram provides a snapshot of all possible outcomes when a forward position expires into spot. The forward price as of the *Time of Observation* represents the mean of the probability distribution of these possible outcomes. The shape of the payoff diagram suggests the risk of the position given a change in the underlying price. Figure 9-2 offers several abstracts of delta risk profiles that offer four general categorizations, which are not mutually exclusive!

Zero Risk. A flat payoff diagram indicates fixed or guaranteed outcome. Regardless if a profit (Diagram A) or loss (B) is locked in, the contract or portfolio carries no risk.

Simple Risk. Certain contracts carry simple risk in the sense that the impact of change is consistent for all outcomes. Diagram C charts a long swap position. No matter if prices end up being high or low, the impact of a one-dollar change in price always causes a one-dollar change in P&L. The same holds for a short swap position (Diagram D.)

Composite Risk. A composite risk profile shows the potential for the risk itself to change. A simple call option at expiration (Diagram E) shows a flat payoff diagram when it is out-of-the-money (to the left), but shows a swap-like exposure when it is in-the-money (to the right.) This is the kind of exposure offered by complex operating environments such as that suggested by the "Generator's Initial Portfolio" (in Figure 8-12). Composite payoff diagrams also occur for exotic structured products; Diagram F displays a "bear spread" comprised of "buying a call with one strike price and selling a call with another strike price."[6]

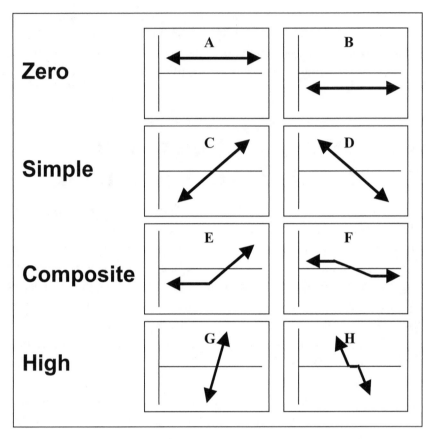

Fig. 9-2:   Sample Risk Profiles

High Risk. A high-risk position implies very rapid change in contract or portfolio value given a relatively small change in the underlying variable. Diagram G depicts a portfolio with multiple swap contracts. While we could characterize the risk as "simple" in the sense that it is easily calculated, the payoff diagram slopes so severely that every dollar change in the underlying price dramatically alters the profit-loss scenario. Diagram H simply tries to map a similar high risk for a structured product.

DELTA AND GAMMA ON THE PAYOFF AND PROFIT DIAGRAMS

Strictly defined, the delta (Δ) equals the change in contract or portfolio value given a one-unit change in the underlying price. Delta is commonly measured as the "dollar delta" if the one-unit of change is equal to a dollar. A manager with an electricity portfolio might challenge the meaningfulness of a dollar delta during summer peak months when power price can move by 10s if not 100s of dollars. If multi- or non-dollar units are used, be sure to distinguish between the measures.

Alternatively, "the delta of a derivative security, Δ, is defined as the rate of change of its price with respect to the price of the underlying asset."[7] (At expiration, this underlying price might converge to the spot price; prior to expiration, the underlying price equals the forward price.) Intuitively, calculating delta can involve valuing a position (Π) using the current marked-to-market underlying price (F), simply revaluing the position (Π^*) with one dollar added to the underlying price ($F+\$1$), and then taking the difference between the values as demonstrated by the following equation.

Equation 9-1

$$\Delta\$ = \Pi^*(F+\$1) - \Pi(F)$$

Where:
$\Delta\$$ = dollar delta
Π = value of position given F
Π^* = value of position given (F+$1)
F = underlying price

Marking-to-Market Concept
Deltas Can and Do Change

For simple cases, the delta of a contract or portfolio equals to the slope of the payoff diagram. As seen in Figure 9-

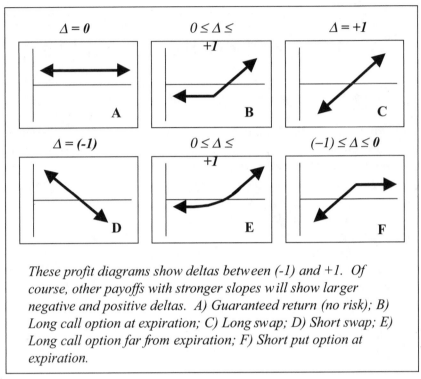

$\Delta = 0$ $0 \le \Delta \le +1$ $\Delta = +1$

A   B   C

$\Delta = (-1)$ $0 \le \Delta \le +1$ $(-1) \le \Delta \le 0$

D   E   F

These profit diagrams show deltas between (-1) and +1. Of course, other payoffs with stronger slopes will show larger negative and positive deltas. A) Guaranteed return (no risk); B) Long call option at expiration; C) Long swap; D) Short swap; E) Long call option far from expiration; F) Short put option at expiration.

Fig. 9-3: Sample Delta Values

3, delta may be positive, zero, or negative. If the payoff diagram is curved, the delta equals the slope of the tangent of the curve at the point of the underlying price. For composite risks (i.e., not a simple or flat straight line), delta is a measure of the slope at the point where the payoff diagram intersects with the current underlying price.

Just like prices, deltas (and gammas) can and do change. Gamma (Γ) measures this sensitivity to change, the impact on delta given a one-unit change in the underlying price. (Don't forget our location, velocity, and acceleration analogy.) In the language of calculus, gamma is the second-order derivative of price (and the first-order derivative of delta). In a mark-to-market process, the manager not only must ensure delta's proper calculation, but also be prepared to hedge a moving delta. Also, we will discuss the importance of continuous delta hedging in Chapter 10.

 Consider the case of a long call option approaching or at expiration. (See profit diagram in Figure 9-4.) The underlying price can have a full range of potential outcomes that directly influences the delta of the position. Each potential spot price outcome will impact the overall position delta, with each degree of influence proportional to the probability of that particular outcome. To get a sense of how different potential outcomes have different deltas, consider Figure 9-4. Reading Figure 9-4 from left to right, we can isolate six general (and approximate)[8] risk sensitivities:

❶ **Deep-Out-of-the-Money.** The underlying price will not likely jump up to the strike price. Even if the underlying price moves a bit, the delta is zero and will probably remain so. Here the gamma reads zero as well.

❷ **Out-of-the-Money.** The underlying price remains unlikely to reach the strike price but with less certainty compared to being deep out-of-the-money. Delta remains close to zero, but gamma picks up a bit.

❸ **Near-the-Money.** When the option is near-the-money, even small market moves can dramatically impact the value of the option. In one instant, the delta can be zero or one ($+1$) and typically measures somewhere in between. (Of course this over-simplifies reality, but we're working with basics here.) Gamma starts growing from very small to very large. How can we surmise this? For the out-of-the-money outcomes, delta generally equals zero. This is generally true for outcomes up to one dollar less than the at-the-money value. But consider the case where the outcome is $0.50 less than the at-the-money value. While the value of the position is still zero, increasing the underlying price by $1.00 using the manual method to calculate delta would actually change the value to +$0.50. We see here that the position is more likely to change. Delta starts growing, and gamma measures this rate of change.

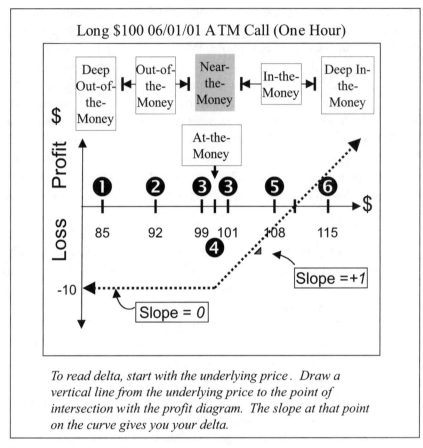

Fig. 9-4: Delta by Underlying Price

④ **At-the-Money.** Close to expiration, an at-the-money option experiences great risk. Sitting on the bubble, a one-dollar move upward brings profit, but a one-dollar move downward makes the option worthless. Here the delta also measures somewhere between zero and one and can swing wildly. Gamma reaches its peak value for an at-the-money option!

⑤ **In-the-Money**. Here the delta equals one or is very close to one. Gamma also drops off slightly from the at-the-money peak.

⑥ **Deep In-the-Money.** When deep in-the-money, the option begins to act like a swap. The underlying price is unlikely to drop all the way to the strike price. The delta definitely equals one. Even though delta remains near one, gamma trails off back to zero.

Our figures demonstrate an over-simplified case of a "super spot" contract for one hour of power. Power companies, however, trade bulkier swap contracts that cover many hours over many weeks. Sometimes risk analysts will report "overall dollar delta." Consider a *September 2000 5x16* swap for 25 MWh observed from May 23, 2000. The swap is valued at $43.25/MWh. The total quantity to be delivered is 8,000 MWh (based on 25 MWh per 16 peak hours per day for 20 business days. Using the NERC holiday schedule, we delivery for all business days in September 2000. We exclude all weekends and the Labor Day holiday.) The overall delta equals *$7,823.48*. To properly calculate the overall delta, consider the following must be calculated.

Equation 9-2

$$_{Overall\$}\Delta^{Sept01\ Swap} = {}_{\$}\Delta * Q * df$$
$$= \$1/MWh * 8,000\ MWh * df = \$8,000 * df \approx \$7,823.48$$

Where:

$_{Overall\$}\Delta^{Sept01\ Swap}$ = overall dollar delta

$_{\$}\Delta$ = one dollar change

Q = quantity for entire swap

df = discounting factor (averaged for all delivery days)

By comparison, when calculating the value of the swap, the discounting factor, *df*, is applied to both the value of the delivered power on each successive day, but also to the payment.

In Times of Crisis: Price Risk During a Price Spike

Stockholders dread price crashes, but price spikes cause nightmares for power executives because of volumetric risk. Prices surge with load; for the utility with reliability concerns and contracts for delivery, being caught "short" without capacity forces the utility to go to "open spot market" at the worst possible time—bidding increasingly higher prices for a dwindling supply.

Risk measurements help us gauge how our portfolio would respond to a price spike. The "Greeks" delta and gamma indicate how value and first-order risk would change for the first dollar of movement, whereas the "doomsday" measures like Value-at-Risk (VaR) suggest total losses given some confidence interval. (Just like the airplane cockpit, we want to make sure we monitor these different controls!) Table 9-2 suggests how a portfolio with certain risk profiles will respond to a price spike. The bottom line suggests that one does not want to be "short" for any of the risk measures given a price-spike market.

PLOTTING PRICE RISK BY TIME BUCKETS

The activist manager needs an effective framework for viewing value and risk over the full time horizon of his/her portfolio. Payoff diagrams alone do not supply this information. This section will introduce the *time buckets* framework to help organize risk across time.

For complex portfolios with contracts of ranging expirations, payoff and profit diagrams become much more complicated. In portfolio analysis, each profit diagram represents a snapshot given a particular *Time of Observation* and a particular *Time of Expiration*. Conceivably, a manager would like to see a profit diagram for each period of time covered by a portfolio, i.e., for each month in which the firm has exposure.

Risk	Initial Portfolio, Π^i	Portfolio Response to Price Spike
Delta, Δ	Long, $+ \Delta$	• Value increases • Ideally capacity is hedged too
	Short, $- \Delta$	• Trouble, especially if short gamma too
Gamma, Γ	Long, $+\Gamma$	• Value increases • Delta increases
	Short, $- \Gamma$	• Trouble • Decrease accelerates
Vega	Long, $+Vega$	• More volatility adds value
	Short, $- Vega$	• Trouble

Table 9-2: Portfolio Sensitivity to Price Spikes

To help aggregate all the forward exposures together, managers should request seeing value and risk to be reported by time buckets or some similar framework. A *time bucket* is a period of forward time; the full time period covered by the portfolio's contracts is divided into discrete time buckets. Time buckets allow the manager to break down overall values (and risks) into more specific periods of time. The alternatives to time buckets are to either generate a single overall value (which does not provide necessary details) or generate per-day values (which is impractical due to an excess of detail.) Table 9-3 provides a sample of a time bucket framework; each manager and RMPP should specify the framework that would be appropriate. Some issues to consider during the design of time buckets include the following:

- If the portfolio covers exposures going out about 10 years forward, for example, the firm could organize their analysis into 60 monthly time buckets.

- Alternatively, the firm might desire more detail or "granularity"; the extreme case would be to divide the five years into 1,780 calendar day buckets. (The obsessed manager would request 42,720 hourly buckets!)

- The sample time bucket framework in Table 9-3 provides a general idea of how near-term periods are divided into relatively short buckets (such as daily or weekly) but how longer-dated periods cover broader periods (such as monthly, quarterly, even yearly). The first three time buckets are daily periods. The fourth time bucket is set to "To End of Week" as organizational convenience, as is the fifth time bucket. Beginning in the month of May, the buckets broaden to cover weekly periods. Monthly time buckets begin in June; quarterly periods begin in October. Thereafter, semi-annual and annual time buckets would be appropriate.

Time Bucket #	Rule	Start Date	End Date
0	Today (Spot)	4/16/99	4/16/99
1	Next Weekday	4/17/99	4/19/99
2	Next Weekday	4/20/99	4/20/99
3	Next Weekday	4/21/99	4/21/99
4	To End of Week	4/22/99	4/25/99
5	To End of Month	4/26/99	4/30/99
6	Next Week	5/1/99	5/8/99
7	Next Week	5/9/99	5/15/99
8	Next Week	5/16/99	5/22/99
9	To End of Month	5/23/99	5/31/99
10	Next Month	6/1/99	6/30/99
11	Next Month	7/1/99	7/31/99
12	Next Month	8/1/99	8/31/99
13	Next Month	9/1/99	9/30/99
14	Next Quarter	10/1/99	12/31/99
Define remaining time buckets to cover full horizon of portfolio			

Table 9-3: Sample Time Bucket Format

More practically, we define time buckets to cover different lengths of time, starting with our most detailed periods in the near term and relaxing the detail in the long-term. As the *Time of Observation* changes day-to-day, the actual begin-end of the time buckets will change but the framework remains the same. A manager should expect granularity commensurate with the firm's exposure, and hedging policies.

With a time bucket framework and hedging policies, a manager can isolate value and risk according to period of exposure. Rather than just seeing the overall value of a portfolio, for example, the manager can see which time buckets post a profit or a loss; in addition, analysts may also plot risk measurements like delta and gamma (see Figure 9-5.) We can also analyze time-bucket detail for an individual contract. As we will see in Chapter 10, analyzing risks on time-bucket basis provides critical direction for identifying unwanted risk and hedging them.

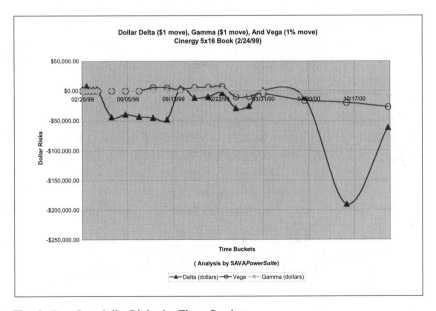

Fig. 9-5: Portfolio Risks by Time Bucket

CREDIT RISK

Credit risk causes nightmares for managers. On the one hand, we easily understand how default impacts our bottom line. On the other hand, we struggle to accurately measure the potential for non-payment, particularly if the risk of default correlates with prices. Absence of credit data further complicates the problem. Corporate credit ratings may over-generalize the counterparty's business units, possibly over- or understating the credit quality of the trading operation.

As suggested in Chapter 7, a firm may control credit risk via counterparty controls such as listing approved trading partners and per-partner notional limits. Measuring credit risk can supplement this process. One concept compares with the "real options" approach: we express the likelihood of default as a "payment volatility." A contract with a very solid counterparty with credit enhancement would have zero or very small payment volatility. For this contract there would be very little optionality in payment. A contract with an unreliable partner, on the other hand, would be more volatile due to the risk of non-payment. The value of this weaker contract would be less than the stronger one.

The firm could use credit risk measurements in one of two ways. First, the credit risk could be compared to overall credit risk limits. Second, the firm may choose to charge an extra credit-premium to the weaker counterparty, with the premium equal to the optionality value of non-payment. A more sophisticated approach includes the correlation between default and price. As seen with the Federal Energy Sales case, the price spike precipitated the credit crisis.

VOLUMETRIC AND TRANSMISSION RISK

In addition to price deltas, power companies should also calculate and graph quantity deltas. Just as a portfolio can be either "long" or "short" in terms of value, the same holds true to being "long" or "short" volume (often referred to as "capacity.") We can calculate volumetric risks the same way we calculate the Greeks for dollar risk. Like the price Greeks, we simply change an input quantity by a single unit and check the impact on value. Table 9-4 suggests some volumetric risk measures to join the fraternity of Greeks.[9] Transmission can be categorized along with volumetric risk with a strong basis factor.

SETTING RISK LIMITS

Risk limits articulate the corporate objectives for trading and risk management. While traditionally associated with prevention—limiting "worst case" scenarios—risk limits also stake out the range of flexibility in which profits may be sought. Companies following a "Speculation" strategy of seeking greater profits will need to define limits far greater than a more conservative "Treasury" approach.

To set risk limits, the manager follows a four-step process (summarized in Table 9-5):

Deciding Which Risks to Limit. As with most business decisions, selecting risks to be monitored and limited requires "bang for

Greek	Symbol	Sensitivity to change in:
Omega	Ω	Quantity (Swing); alternatively could be called "quantity delta"
Nu	ν	Omega; alternatively could be called "quantity gamma"
Phi	Φ	Quantity Vega (Swing)
Chi	X	Quantity-Price Correlation (Swing)
Psi	Ψ	Cross-Market Correlation Sensitivity (Boption)

Table 9-4: Volumetric Risk Measures (Source: Pilipovic and Wengler, "The Power Greeks," The Desk, November, 1998)

| Deciding which limits to include |
| Committing to enforcing the limits |
| Determining granularity and methods |
| Quantifying limits |
| Monitoring and updating limits |

Table 9-5: Steps for Setting Risk Limits

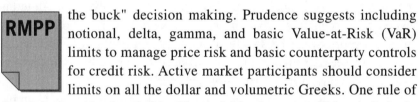

the buck" decision making. Prudence suggests including notional, delta, gamma, and basic Value-at-Risk (VaR) limits to manage price risk and basic counterparty controls for credit risk. Active market participants should consider limits on all the dollar and volumetric Greeks. One rule of thumb is the pain threshold—if a variable changes within a relatively common range, can the company cope with the impact or will the impact cause significant economic or political pain? The manager may wish to assign an analyst the task of testing the impact of various risks, even those not included in the RMPP.

How to Enforce: Inclusion of a risk limit should also depend on enforceability. Why include a limit that cannot be enforced? One motivation for including a non-enforceable limit is to provide the illusion of thoroughness. Such inclusion itself could be a signal to the Board of Directors or to shareholders of ineffective risk management practices.

Enforcement can be reactive in response to quantified limits or reporting. (See Table 9-6.) A computer trading or portfolio management system tracks the quantified limits; each time a deal is considered, the limits should be checked and any potentially non-compliant contracts should be prevented from being booked. I once heard of a system that checked limits well after the trader signaled to a counterparty that the deal was done! While the trader's company may have felt comfortable with the delayed checking, the counterparty has no legal reason to agree to "undoing" the deal.

Risk Type	Reactive		Proactive	
	Quantified Limits	Reporting	Personnel Policies	Education
Price	☑	☑	☑	
Credit	☑	☑	☑	
Reliability	☑	☑		
Human	☑	☑	☑	☑

Table 9-6: Enforcement Techniques

RMPP   Reports should be designed to be read. In turn, it is the responsibility of the managers to read the reports—and then react to what is being reported! While positions may be technically within the RMPP limits, the manager is ultimately responsible if something unexpected occurs or the assumptions behind the RMPP are no longer realistic. Another benefit of managers reading reports involves ensuring that he/she receives said reports. Delayed or incomplete reporting should register as an immediate "red flag" of potential problems on the trading desk.

Perhaps as important as its punitive role, enforcement should also be proactive. The RMPP should clearly specify the steps that all individuals should follow on the trading desk and support offices. Generally speaking, people like to know the rules of the game they are playing. In terms of prevention, education cannot be stressed enough. The new world of power trading and risk management includes only a few veterans. Trade publications and books help distribute market information.

Professional seminars provide invaluable knowledge and experiences, especially when the participants have a chance to talk with each other. Some traditional managers fear that employees will give away valuable trade secrets at these events. I believe this fear might be unjustified. I have never heard a valuable trade secret from anyone at a conference—maybe because some manager didn't let any valuable employees attend! Risk remains a people business, and people like to meet people of similar professional interests. So be sure to budget for seminars and travel expenses. Seminars allow companies to grow from within, nourishing existing employees, especially engineers and analysts who may understand the "juice" side of the business but not the market or risk side.

What Detail to Measure: The manager should set "granularity" or level of measurement detail in accordance to the risks involved. For example, the "Greek" risk limit should be set for both the overall portfolio and individual time buckets as well. The firm might also wish to set special seasonal limits, with special emphasis on the summer months of July and August. For Value-at-Risk (VaR), the manager is responsible for selecting (or at least approving) the methodology, confidence intervals, and time horizon. These issues interplay, to be sure. The Variance-Covariance methodology, for example, works well only for only short time horizons, up to a week or so. The confidence intervals must also be chosen with care. The 99% confidence interval is more conservative than the 95% confidence interval, but represents a statistically far-less likely "worst case scenario," one that might be more scary than useful.

How to Quantify the Limits. In setting the limits, the manager should focus on the "big picture" issues; but at the end of the day, a number has to be recorded! The manager could set a single set of limits or could create progressive risk limits analogous to a flood channel designed for regular and unusual water levels (see Figure 9-6). The concept involves setting standard limits under which traders may operate without extra approval. Should traders recommend a trade that would violate these standard limits, the RMPP would articulate a process in which a manager could sign-off on the deal. A second set of maximum standards would be in place as the ultimate boundary that may not be crossed. Several methodologies are available for calculating risk limits; the next part of this chapter will detail them.

Monitoring and Updating the Limits. Finally, risk limits play a vibrant role in making the RMPP a living document. The manager should design a process for evaluating the limits themselves. Continuous bumping up against a limit dramatically signals that something is wrong, perhaps a mismatch between the objectives of the firm, the strategy of the

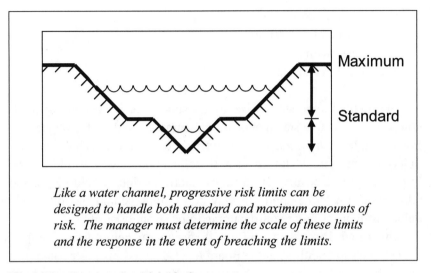

*Like a water channel, progressive risk limits can be
designed to handle both standard and maximum amounts of
risk. The manager must determine the scale of these limits
and the response in the event of breaching the limits.*

Fig. 9-6: Progressive Risk Limits

trading desk, and the limits themselves. The manager must be aware of
this kind of situation, root out the cause, and fix it. Either the trading desk
is too aggressive or the risk limits are too oppressive. This is the classic
"trader vs. risk manager" conflict that must be resolved at the managerial
level. If you really believe in your risk limits, be sure to lend your political support to the risk manager publicly. If the manager does not publicly
back the "local sheriff", it could be a signal to the Board and the shareholders that there is a problem with the trading and risk operations.

QUANTIFYING RISK LIMITS

Risk limits may be quantified using one or more of the following methods:

- Strategic Expression
- Informed Discussion
- Stress Testing
- Actual Performance

Strategic Expression. Risk limits should be set according to the company's objective statements, trading strategy, and P&L expectations. For example, if a company proclaims a conservative "reliability first" objective, the "Greek" limits for both dollars and volume would be easily required to be positive at all times; short positions would be precluded. A more moderate approach may be to allow certain flexibility with delta, but more firmly require gamma to be strongly positive.

Informed Discussion. Informed discussion helps define people's expectations, particularly at the Board level. The risk manager could present to the Board the company's current risk profile plotted by time buckets. Imagine if Figure 9-5 were displayed. Perhaps a Board member might speak up and state "I don't mind the short delta during the summer of 1999, but I really think that the delta dip in the fall of 2000 looks dangerous." Perhaps working groups could be formed that mix upper managers with line-level traders; again, portfolio positions could be displayed and discussed. As always, the manager must remember that derivatives is a people business regardless of the technical sophistication of our tools.

Stress Testing. Stress testing techniques like Value-at-Risk (VaR) and other "What If?" methods help quantify worst-case scenarios. Upper managers often think that they understand them more readily than the more challenging "Greeks," so this might be a good place to start for the "informed discussion."

Actual Performance. Setting up limits the first time can be the hardest job, even when using the most educated of guesses. Equally important will be the manager's monitoring of actual performance. Limits being continuously reached or violated might prompt revisiting the limits. Limits rarely reached provide a very different signal; either the limits were set too high for effective monitoring or the trading desk is not being as aggressive as the company expects.

One final rule of thumb: risk limits should be consistent with each other. Delta limits, for example, should be consistent with VaR limits. In fact, the firm might wish to first set VaR limits with direction from the board and then roll-out delta limits that are mathematically consistently with the larger VaR rules.

ENDNOTES

[1] Pilipovic defines risk as "an uncertainty; anything that cannot be predicted with 100% certainty is risky.

[2] See the *Manager's Bookshelf* in Section 1.8, the Bibliography, and other fine books for greater detail.

[3] One issue that a manager new to trading should be aware of is how option premiums can impact P&L reports. While such option premiums are indeed "cash in hand," the manager should be sure that traders do not report such premiums in isolation of the potential liabilities of the options that they sold to collect such premiums.

[4] Mendell, David and Bukro, Casey, *"Peakers" generate new power struggle*, Chicago Tribune, July 16, 2000.

[5] Distributions should also be described in terms of "higher moments" of skew and especially kurtosis. See Pilipovic, 1998, p. 43-45.

[6] Hull, p. 178.

[7] Hull, p. 298.

[8] For the sake of the generalist, this chapter utilizes straight lines, few equations, and no closed-form solutions. For more quantitative details, see Hull's section on delta (298-307) and gamma (310-314.)

[9] Dragana Pilipovic and I introduced these labels in 1998. Regardless of the name used, the manager might consider either including these risk measures or document why they are not.

chapter 10

HEDGING: NAVIGATING TOWARD OUR PORTFOLIO OBJECTIVES

HOW WILL WE ACHIEVE AND MAINTAIN OUR DESIRED PORTFOLIO?

Our aviation analogy compares valuation (Chapter 8) to determining location and risk measurement (Chapter 9) to gauging velocity, acceleration, etc. To complete this analogy, hedging equates to navigating, the multi-disciplined task of plotting a map between where we are and where we're going— and getting us there. Hedging provides the fourth question of the *Hedging Cycle—How Will We Achieve and Maintain Our Desired Portfolio?*

By definition, hedging is the process of analyzing existing risk levels and entering into hedging contracts to achieve desired risk levels. We are assuming continuous hedging, even if this is not the case in reality. The assumption of continuous hedging is bedrock in risk theory. Very real costs prevent continuous hedging from becoming reality—the bid/ask spread, the cost of premiums, the cost of analysis, etc. In market experience, however, the practical violation of the theoretical assumption has not caused significant problems.

Hedging should reduce potential risk and therefore potential profit as well. The phrase "hedge fund" is an oxymoron unless the company promises returns well below market average! Special care should be taken to find "high quality" hedging contracts. Proper hedging requires proper valuation and risk measuring skills; in fact, it employs the full *Price-Risk Pyramid* much as opera brings together the performing arts of music, singing, writing, and design. In his/her role, the manager must become a "hedging aficionado" capable of digesting the boring parts as well as appreciating the exciting parts of the dramatic work of hedging.

HOW STRATEGY DEFINES
HEDGING OBJECTIVES

RMPP Hedging implies a purpose, navigating toward some objective. The strategy defined in the *Risk Management Policies and Procedures* (RMPP) should dictate this direction exclusively—otherwise non-managerial staff determines hedging policies. Managerial vision can take a full spectrum of hedging attitudes. Figure 10-1[1] suggests the full gamut starting with the "unhedged" extreme. Here the management proclaims that it will not perform any hedging, accepting the impact of market price moves. The reluctant utility that resists trading and risk management technology represents a special case of this unhedged strategy, subjecting their firm and shareholders to spot price behavior. This may be a valid strategy—don't get me wrong—but this particular management had better understand what their recalcitrance truly represents.

On the other extreme, a conservative utility may wish to follow the "fully hedged" extreme, ordering their trading desk to hedge away as

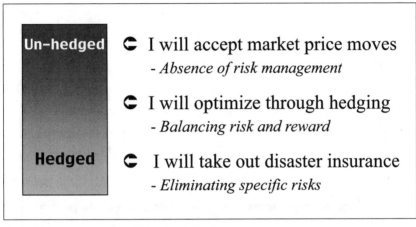

Un-hedged ⟳ I will accept market price moves
- *Absence of risk management*

⟳ I will optimize through hedging
- *Balancing risk and reward*

Hedged ⟳ I will take out disaster insurance
- *Eliminating specific risks*

Fig. 10-1: Strategy Defines Hedging

many risks as possible for as far out as feasible. We liken this to paying for "disaster insurance" because hedging contracts can cost premiums upfront and/or reduce potential profit in the future. While an extreme, this strategy is valid if that is what the company truly wants. A firm committed to "reliability first" might find this hedging approach appealing. Like all things in business, however, most utilities will follow a hedging strategy somewhere between the extremes, optimizing their generation and traded assets, balancing risk and reward through hedging.

 As we did in Chapters 8 and 9, we can visualize hedging using payoff and profit diagrams. Imagine a company with an initial portfolio of a single long swap. (See Figure 10-2.) Assume that the firm's RMPP states that the portfolio should always be delta neutral. As the figure suggests, we see a conflict between profit diagram of the initial portfolio (Π^i) and the objective portfolio (Π^o). The initial portfolio (Π^i) carries a delta risk of $+1$, whereas the objective portfolio (Π^o) desires a delta risk of 0. (This zero or flat risk position is also referred to as a "delta neutral" position.)

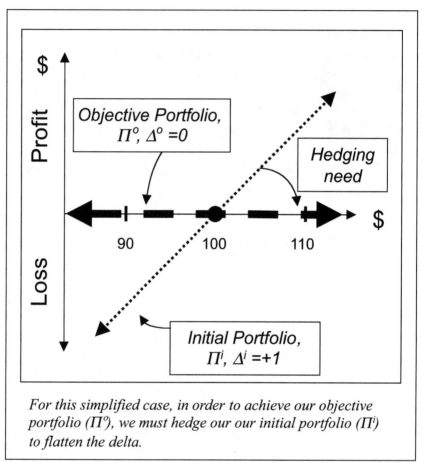

*For this simplified case, in order to achieve our objective
portfolio (Π^o), we must hedge our our initial portfolio (Π^i)
to flatten the delta.*

Fig. 10-2: Comparing Initial & Objective Portfolios

Applied to this situation, the hedging cycle poses this question: *How
do we modify our portfolio with the long delta to become a portfolio with
zero delta?* Graphically speaking, we must rotate the slope of the payoff
diagram from +*1* down to *0* or flat position. We need a hedge position that
offsets the positive delta; for this simple case, we need a hedge with a

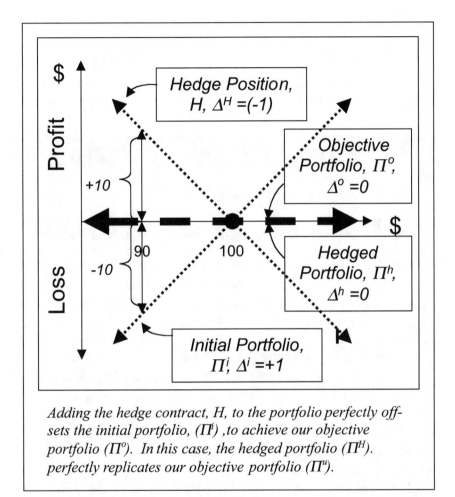

Adding the hedge contract, H, to the portfolio perfectly off-sets the initial portfolio, (Π^i) ,to achieve our objective portfolio (Π^o). In this case, the hedged portfolio (Π^H). perfectly replicates our objective portfolio (Π^u).

Fig. 10-3: Achieving the Desired Portfolio

negative delta of *–1*. We need to sell a swap to offset our initial long swap position. On a payoff diagram (see Figure 10-3), we can see how a short swap can be added to the long swap, with the payoffs canceling each other to achieve the delta neutral objective. Note that in this simple case we perfectly achieve our hedging objective; there is no "residual risk." In reality, complex portfolios can rarely be perfectly hedged due to a variety of factors, including lack of available hedging contracts, mismatches in trading lots (e.g. one needs to hedge 53 megawatts but only 50 MWh contracts are traded), etc. The RMPP might wish to specify how much residual risk would be tolerated given the hedging objectives and risk limits.

INTERVIEW

Hedging on the Sea of Liquidity

An Interview with Tom Hahn, APB Energy/Chapel Hill Division

Tom Hahn navigates the sea of trading liquidity every day as a broker. In bringing together buyers and sellers, Hahn has seen trading volumes increase and hedging strategies evolve through the late 1990s and predicts greater market expansion in the first decade of the new century.

Question: *How would you define "hedging"?*

Hahn: Hedging is using derivative instruments to reduce your risk in a given market without significantly reducing your return, or hedging is trying to increase your return without increasing your risk. Everything is about risk and reward. If something looks cheap it's cheap for a reason! In this market you really do get what you pay for.

Question: *Does market liquidity—as defined by the volume of trading occurring—impact the ability of a company to hedge or the effectiveness of those hedges?*

Hahn: Good question. In terms of ability, illiquidity might force you to look at option strike prices that you otherwise would not. If you had a peaking unit with a marginal cost of production at $72/MWh, for example, the owner might say that they are willing to sell a call option at twice this cost—a $144 call option. Because of the illiquidity in this market, there is not a call option being quoted at the $144 strike. You probably have only a few choices, a $100 call, a $200 call, maybe even a $500 call.

The company is going to have to go into the market and choose the best strike that works for them.

The other factor with illiquidity is location. There are only about seven or eight really actively traded regions and hubs like PJM, Entergy, and Cinergy. If you are located outside a liquid region or hub, the hedging tools may not be available in your area, but you can look to the next best thing—a hedge in a more liquid market. But this brings in basis risk too. When you look at natural gas, this is how everything started, with trading in places like New England using the NYMEX Henry Hub (Louisiana) contract as a "good enough" hedge.

Question: *Do you see this NYMEX Henry Hub basis phenomenon recurring in power markets?*

Hahn: I do. There is no single contract for all national markets, but there are several major hubs. Many of the prices are being influenced by these big hubs. ComEd has lately started growing; Entergy and TVA are growing more. ERCOT in Texas has started to trade quite a bit more. NYPOOL and NEPOOL are also relatively new locations that are trading more actively in the last 18 months. I also expect Florida-Georgia will grow too. It's just going to take some traders and some brokers to start making markets and encouraging other people to trade. A big role of the broker is to encourage liquidity.

Question: *What makes a good broker?*

Hahn: A good broker should be able to do more than quote where the market is. A good broker should help their client value the option, chart the risks, and analyze P&L. I view my job as helping people do what they need to do at a fair price with greater confidence.

Question: *What benefit would a small utility gain from talking to a broker?*

Hahn: A small utility might be talking to one or two large marketers. But brokers talk to in excess of 100 different counterparties every day. If you are only talking to one or two counterparties, you may not be getting the best price or best information. Broker information can be verified using models; a good broker uses reliable, widely accepted models. In contrast to a regular counterparty, brokers are neutral parties, and they only get paid commissions when trades are completed. Brokers have no incentive to allow a client to deal on an off-market price: we actually have a disincentive because we can lose a client relationship if someone is unhappy with any particular deal.

Question: *How did liquidity change through the late 1990s? I presume there was growth, but was it linear or exponential?*

Hahn: I would say that the growth was exponential. It certainly feels that volume has been doubling year to year. This power market is still much smaller than the natural gas market. The bona fide hedgers ultimately like to hedge 30% to 40% of their output or input price exposure; airline companies, for example, generally hedge 30-40% of their jet fuel exposure. I am seeing most electric utilities only hedging 5% to 10% of their price exposure. I have started to notice certain traders coming out with larger volumes. There is still huge hedging potential in power.

Question: *Many electric utilities face price risk in markets with little or no traded markets. How can these companies still hedge?*

Hahn: If you are a new entrant in this market, that is where calling a broker can really be of value. What has been the historical trading behavior? What should options cost? You might have to use non-standard products for hedging. At that point you may be better off going to a large power marketer, who can sell you non-standard products, which can then be put into their portfolio.

Question: *If a client called with a hedging issue, how would you advise them differently if he/she were trying to hedge a physical obligation versus a purely financial position?*

Hahn: We don't see too many purely financial contracts in the power markets. Most of our options settle into delivery. So, the credit and counterparty risk is already there in our market contracts and prices. There are differences, though, when we compare physical and financial settlement. If I said I could buy a $200 physical option versus a $200 financial option for a term several years out, the prices would be fairly similar. Longer-term physical and financial positions move hand in hand. If you don't plan on holding either position to delivery, the difference is not that important. But as those positions get close to prompt or expiration, suddenly the differences become very important. In the short-term, people start paying more for hedges with physical delivery. This speaks to the need for continuous hedging or at least monitoring your positions on a continuous basis.

Question: *The new FASB 133 accounting rules encourage companies to distinguish between hedges and speculative positions. Have you on the brokerage desk seen any impact of this new rule?*

Hahn: Not yet. I've seen articles on it and people talking about it. But we have not seen any change in trading volume due to it. A lot of the firms doing trading have always been thinking about these issues anyway.

Question: *I know that you really enjoy thinking of different hedging strategies, combining calls and puts to solve problems and create opportunity. Have you seen the market begin to share your enthusiasm or do you believe the market prefers sticking to vanilla contracts?*

Hahn: Absolutely. The majority of the options that we are trading now are as part of a spread. Two or three years ago it was a lot more outright individual options—a call or a put. Now we are seeing much more spreading. If somebody is buying an option, they usually are simultaneously selling another option or the underlying power.

Question: *Many utilities are far more comfortable with fixed-rate contracts like swaps and forwards. Any tips for companies beginning to think about hedging with options?*

Hahn: Combined thought: Options are a very important hedging tool instead of just selling or buying forwards. But before trading options, it is critical to understand how to properly price them and properly manage them. You can't just use the standard Black model. You have also to think intelligently about liquidity and the ability to get out of positions. I might be able to sell a contract but not necessarily buy it back. Options are very valuable tools for hedging, but they are still illiquid. You can't think about these options as a tradable commodity like you would forwards. You should be prepared to hold the options until expiration.

Question: *How does this expectation of holding an option until expiration affect its value?*

Hahn: The bulk of the premium that you pay for an electricity option is going to be related to liquidation expectations. Due to the large minimum volumes that trade in power (25MWh to 50MWh), it is difficult to trade on the change in your option's delta, as you can in most commodity markets. Furthermore, there can be liquidity constraints, so traders don't usually buy these options with the hopes of making money from the changes in premium prices of the option contract. You generally expect to hold an option to expiration and capture the value then and there based on where the underlying power is trading If you buy a $40 call option and pay $2, you really think that power is going above $42 at expiration.

Question: *Brokers play a key role in the evolution of any market, helping to bring buyers and sellers together. How would you characterize major e-commerce innovations: web-based brokerage and online trading? Is the former a minor adaptation while the later is a whole new species?*

Hahn: First of all, beginning in 1998 and 1999 there was a lot of interest in online platforms, primarily driven by vendors trying to take advantage of the stock market and IPOs. Now with the NASDAQ falling we are seeing a different approach. Many brokers are becoming affiliated with an online exchange or actually launching their own exchange. Smaller utilities may not need to be in constant contact with a broker, and an online exchange is great. You can't beat the ability to look at a screen to see where the market is now. But when you need to execute an option trade, or trade a more complicated spread, a broker can actually help look over a client's shoulder and increase one's confidence, maybe discuss bidding strategies.

Question: *Looking forward from our vantage in the Year 2001, what factors do you think will play roles in increasing liquidity in the power market?*

Hahn: As deregulation continues, a lot of smaller utilities, cooperatives, and large industrials will start to come into the market to trade. Another factor is that during the late 1990s a lot of companies put together three-or-four-year deals with power marketers that are now beginning to come off the books. We've had a lot of calls from companies who had locked in multi-year deals that are starting to come off the books in 2001 and 2002, and now need to start planing for the years beyond.

Finally, four years ago nobody really knew where summer or winter could go. By 2002 or 2003 we will have a lot more experience and historical data—and that helps liquidity a lot. That has been the trend in many other markets. After 10 years any market has a good idea of where things can go. As the power markets become increasingly deregulated, and as more and more player enter the market, volatility should start to decrease and people will have greater confidence to trade larger positions. Innovations like credit enhancement or a clearinghouse approach might also have an impact. I am very enthusiastic about the increase in liquidity over the past few years and expect it to continue going forward.

Tom Hahn co-founded Chapel Hill Brokers in 1998 and is now Executive Vice President of APB Energy's Chapel Hill Division. Between 1991 and 1998, he traded oil derivatives for Morgan Stanley, Lehman Brothers, and the George E. Warren Corporation. Mr. Hahn holds a finance degree from the University of Delaware.

Tom Hahn may be contacted via tom.hahn@apbenergy.com.

HEDGING REQUIRES
GOOD HEDGE CONTRACTS

Marking-to-Market Concept

The Need for Quality Hedges

First things first—identify good hedge contracts to hedge price risk. The ideal hedge contracts are liquid and provide good price discovery, providing a true mark-to-market standard. They should be standardized rather than one-off custom deals. That said, creative structured products can be effective, but should be first approved by a manager according to the RMPP process. These contracts should not be adding risk to the portfolio due to illiquidity or credit risk problems. If a risk manager wishes to identify a good hedge contract, he/she should contact the trading desk first to seek their opinion.

The RMPP should state which hedging contracts are allowed or define an approval process for them. As usual, the RMPP must give traders and risk manager's approval to use the tools necessary to achieve the corporate objectives. A blanket forbiddance of options trading, for example, might hamper the desk's ability to hedge delta or gamma risks in the most cost-effective manner. As with most things in business, you get what you pay for and you pay for what you get.

In the greater context, price risk is the primary but not the only risk to be hedged. The manager must keep an eye on all risks and hedge them using a combination between people management and risk tools. (See Table 10-1).

HEDGING ANALYSIS

Given our initial and objective portfolios, hedging analysis attempts to determine how many hedge contracts should be bought (or sold) to achieve

Risk Type	Hedging Technique
Market Risk	• Managerial "go/no-go" decision to trade in the marketplace. • Assumptions made about market
Price Risk	• Hedge contracts • Continuous monitoring of limits
Profit Loss (P&L) Risk	• Continuous marking-to-market of positions to ascertain current P&L • Continuous monitoring of current P&L to objectives
Credit Risk	• Counterparty control • Credit-adjusted valuation and risk measurement • Credit enhancement tools such as letters of credit
Volumetric & Transmission Risk	• Counterparty control • Hedge contracts • Building capacity
Modeling Risk	• Managerial understanding and approval of models • Continuous monitoring of limits
Marketing Risk	• Definition of corporate strategy by upper management • Effective integration of "Concentric Ring" of functional duties • Good day-to-day management
Human Risk	• Managerial receipt of reporting from all levels • Good day-to-day management
Operational Risk	• Managerial perseverance

Table 10-1: Hedging Technique by Risk Type

the risk objectives. The first step, of course, involves identifying which risks must be hedged. Ideally this is performed on a time-bucket level; we might identify too much risk in the *July-August* time buckets, for example; we can then look for *July-August* contracts with which to hedge.

Hedging analysis is relatively straightforward if and only if the rest of the *Price-Risk Pyramid* is in place. The lower levels of input analysis must first be built, with hedging processes put on top of a solid market analysis and contract valuation process. The RMPP should assign the duty of hedging analysis; this job could be performed by an analyst, risk manager or dedicated trader. If the firm relies heavily on Value-at-Risk (VaR) for risk management, the analyst would re-run the VaR analysis for each assumed set of hedge contracts. There are three general methodologies for determining the number of hedge contracts to be traded.

Plug and Chug. Given the initial portfolio, the analyst manually enters a certain number of hedge contracts into the portfolio systems and determines how well the modified portfolio resembles the desired risk profile.

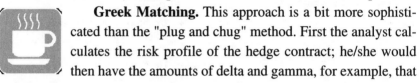 **Greek Matching.** This approach is a bit more sophisticated than the "plug and chug" method. First the analyst calculates the risk profile of the hedge contract; he/she would then have the amounts of delta and gamma, for example, that could be provided by each hedge contract. Then he/she may simply calculate the number of hedge contracts needed to buy (or sell) to match the amount of risk desired to be "shaved off" from the portfolio.

The calculation would be as follows for the case of delta hedging— divide the total amount of portfolio delta to be hedged by the per-contract delta of the hedge contract. This ratio equates to the optimum number of hedge contracts to enter. This said, however, the exact number of hedge contracts is rarely available. For example, one may calculate the need for 48 MWh of hedge contracts, but counterparties will only want to trade a rounded 50 MWh contract. (See Chapter 10 on "residual risk.) This same approach can be used for calculating gamma and other hedges as well. Another way of thinking about this is to mix-and-match the "hockey sticks" in the payoff diagrams. In Figures 10-2 and 10-3, we see that we need to sell one swap to hedge the initial portfolio. If our initial portfolio had a delta of +2, then we would calculate the number of swaps to sell to be two.

Minimum Variance Analysis. Minimum Variance Analysis (MVA) is a mathematical procedure of calculating the number of given hedge contracts to be bought (or sold) that would minimize the variance of a portfolio. The manager sitting on top of a sophisticated, complex portfolio should require his/her desk to implement MVA.[2]

Note that assumptions about intra-market correlations will greatly impact the results of MVA. If we assume 100% intra-market correlation, then MVA could recommend hedging July risk with August contracts, since the 100% correlation implies that all boats rise (and fall) with the tide. Assuming 0% intra-market correlation would be the other extreme, requiring only contracts covering the same time buckets to hedge risk in those time periods. This would be the most conservative hedging policy; it would also be appropriate for doing volumetric hedging analysis. The RMPP should anticipate this issue—it is conceivable that the firm performs valuation with a textured intra-market correlation set but uses a 0% correlation set for hedging analysis. The manager should take special care to require valuation of the hedge contracts using the market-appropriate intra-market correlation set and only use the 0% correlation set for MVA.

In addition to stating which method should be used, the RMPP should also specify how frequently hedging should occur, perhaps on a per-time-bucket level. Short-term time buckets could be analyzed and hedged several times a day, for example, while longer-term periods could be analyzed and hedged once every few days or weekly. In addition, the company might try to budget for hedging (either in terms of premiums to be paid or profits to be lost) or perhaps design a special hedging book with dedicated traders following a "Treasury" function.

A SIMPLE CASE STUDY IN ACHIEVING PORTFOLIO OBJECTIVE

 Let's use profit diagrams[3] to consider a simple case study of hedging the "Generator's Initial Portfolio" first suggested in Figure 8-12. Consider the case shown in Figure 10-4; the "x" at $15 represents the fixed cost of maintaining an idle generation unit. The "y" at $115 marks the optimal point of produc-

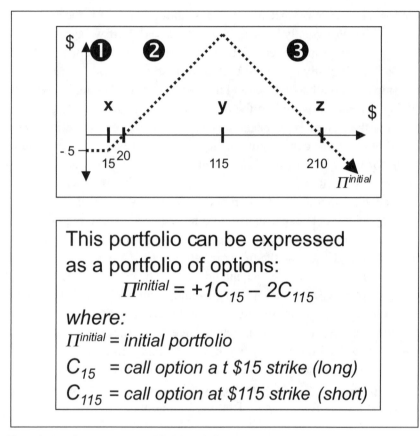

This portfolio can be expressed
as a portfolio of options:
$$\Pi^{initial} = +1C_{15} - 2C_{115}$$
where:
$\Pi^{initial}$ = initial portfolio
C_{15} = call option a t $15 strike (long)
C_{115} = call option at $115 strike (short)

Fig. 10-4: Generator's Initial Portfolio

tion, with increasing demand decreasing the marginal rates of return. At point "z" we surpass the generator's capacity; since the firm has full-requirements contracts, the company may need to go to the open market to buy increasing expensive spot power in the event of a load or price spike. We can synthesize this portfolio as one long call option with a strike of $15 and two short call options with a strike of $115.

We will assume that the corporate policy dictates guaranteed P&L and delta neutrality. In the end, our objective will be to create a flat or zero-delta payoff diagram. We will not concern ourselves here with the cost of achieving delta neutrality. To hedge the initial portfolio, we will move from left to right on the payoff diagram in Figure 10-4.

❶ Up to point "x", we see a flat delta and don't need to hedge this zone.

❷ After "x" however, the payoff diagram assumes a $+1$ delta slope. If we hedged by selling a swap with a -1 delta, we would level off the zone between x and y but would introduce negative delta for the zone before x. Selling a $15 call would satisfy our needs. In Figure 10-5, we see a "temporary" or interim portfolio (Π^H) of the initial portfolio with the short $15 call. The sloped portion of the $15 call cancels out the positive delta slope of the initial portfolio between points x and y.

❸ In initial portfolio shown in Figure 10-4, the payoff diagram after point y follows a (-1) slope. But with the addition of the short $15 call option, we can see in the temporary or interim portfolio (Figure 10-5) that the zone after point y now shows a delta of (-2); when hedging, we must remember to account for hedging the hedge! Our answer is to seek a hedge that offers a zero delta for outcomes less than y but positive delta above y. A long $115 call option fits the bill; but since it has only $+1$ delta above y, we will need to buy two of them. Figure 10-6 shows the full "transit map" of the various positions offsetting to generate the fixed payoff of the Π^H. (This P&L could be positive or negative.)

A "LOWER COST" CASE STUDY

Using the same initial portfolio, let's relax our RMPP objectives to allow a range of profits and losses with deltas required to be positive. The firm wishes to achieve profits during both the optimal production range and the higher

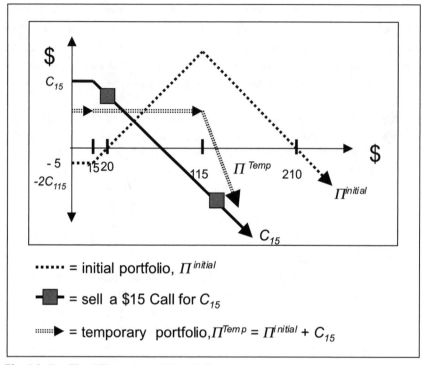

Fig. 10-5: The "Temporary" Portfolio

price zones. In return, the firm is willing to take on the risk of losses given low-price scenarios. Figure 10-7 portrays this payoff diagram; traders would refer to this payoff as a "collar." A collar is a combination of a long position in a cap and a short position in a floor. To achieve this portfolio, we still buy the two $115 calls as we did in the earlier example. But rather than selling the $15 call, we sell a more valuable $85 call. (See Figure 10-8.) This makes the aggregate hedging strategy less expensive but leaves some risk of losses.

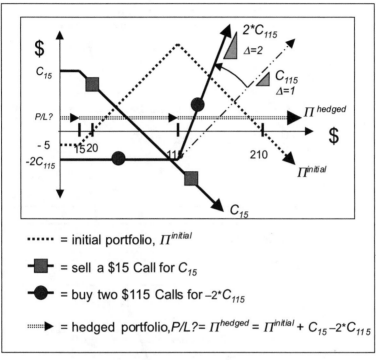

Fig. 10-6: The Hedged Portfolio

HAVE WE ACHIEVED OUR PORTFOLIO OBJECTIVES?

The fifth and final question of the *Hedging Cycle* involves checking how well we met our portfolio objectives. Measuring residual risk is one answer. Figure 10-9 depicts the special case where one wants zero risk

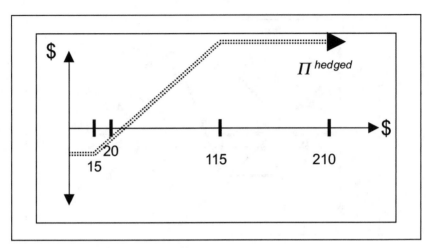

Fig. 10-7: The "Collar" Portfolio

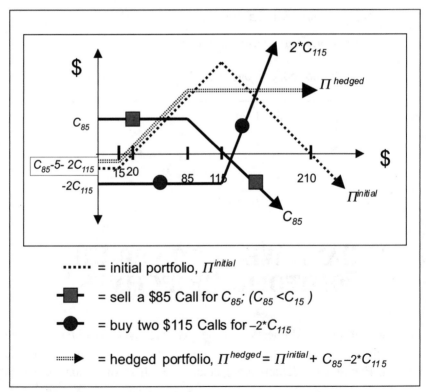

$\cdots\cdots$ = initial portfolio, $\Pi^{initial}$

▬ = sell a \$85 Call for C_{85}; ($C_{85} < C_{15}$)

⬤ = buy two \$115 Calls for $-2*C_{115}$

$\cdots\cdots\blacktriangleright$ = hedged portfolio, $\Pi^{hedged} = \Pi^{initial} + C_{85} - 2*C_{115}$

Fig. 10-8: Collar Hedging Strategy

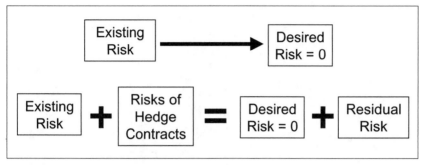

Fig. 10-9: Residual Risk

RMPP but the risks of the hedges do not perfectly offset the initial risk. The RMPP could specify acceptable remaining risks by forward time bucket. Meeting *P&L* objectives also measures how well the firm implements the RMPP. Failure to meet profit objectives begs the question of causation: is someone not doing their job? Are the RMPP reflective of company objectives or market reality? Can the market sustain our objectives? Self-reflection itself measures the firm's ability to manage risk. Achieving corporate objectives will be a natural by product of the full-hedging cycle and effective implementation of the RMPP.

ENDNOTES

[1] Thanks to Jacki Billimore of the International Petroleum Exchange (IPE) for idea for figure.

[2] For more details, see Pilipovic, 1998, p. 179-189.

[3] See Hull's chapter "Trading Strategies Involving Options" (p. 173-188) for more examples of using profit diagrams for describing strategy.

chapter 11

CRITICAL PATH IT ISSUES

THE INESCAPABLE NEED FOR COMPUTER SYSTEMS

RMPP Computers make risk management possible. The inescapable need for systems to solve our problems creates a dependency, which in turn creates more problems. The secret to understanding the critical information technology (IT) issues lies with the manager first understanding his/her *Risk Management Policies and Procedures* (RMPP) and the principles embedded within them. The RMPP is the ultimate specification for the computer system. In the ideal world, the manager could plop the RMPP document in the lap of a computer vendor and simply say, "Give me that."

A large part of this chapter focuses on system selection (or building one). In the spirit of full disclosure, I worked on the software marketing side for several years and definitely formed some strong opinions. This chapter is written as a fair assessment of IT issues and assumes that the manager will ultimately rely on prudence and business sense.

Systems are like cities, constantly changing under the dynamic needs of the citizenry. New needs arise; old functionalities fail or become outdated. In money markets, for example, major banks have overhauled or replaced their computer systems several times in the past two decades. As another example, simply consider the cascading versions of Microsoft Office products and managerial problems associated with upgrading and resolving release conflicts. The manager's responsibility in IT management is to make sure the systems are maintained and modified in anticipation of the business unit's changing needs.

DEFINING THE TRADING AND PORTFOLIO MANAGEMENT SYSTEM

Marking-to-Market Concept

Market Price Signals to System

Figure 11-1 provides an abstract of a trading and portfolio management system. I define this system to include both people and technology; the system typically comprises multiple solutions from multiple vendors, operated by a blend of employees and consultants. The system must conform to the RMPP in terms of design requirements, processes, and risk limits; the system must also accept market signals to ensure mark-to-market authenticity. Much hand wringing involves "real time market feeds" for systems. If the firm performs real-time market analysis and pricing, real-time feeds are a must. If the analysis and hedging cycle is performed on a daily cycle, however, the relative bang-for-the-buck value of real-time data might be diminished. In such a case, an overemphasis on real-time data could cause problems if it prevents or obfuscates the group's ability to understand what price signals are available.

We see three inter-related circles at the center of Figure 11-1. They represent the three primary functional areas of a trading and portfolio management system.

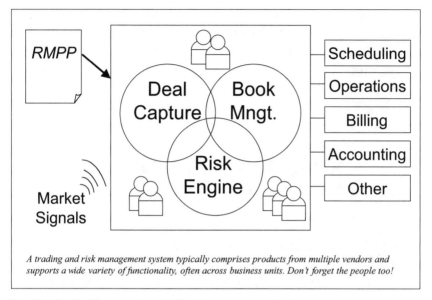

A trading and risk management system typically comprises products from multiple vendors and supports a wide variety of functionality, often across business units. Don't forget the people too!

Fig. 11-1: Trading and Portfolio Management System

Deal Capture. Supports the traders and ensures that their activities are recorded in the system.

Risk Engine. Provides the models for valuation and risk analysis. Provides consistent processes for both trading desk and risk management operations.

Book Management. Approves new deals and manages existing books of deals in portfolio. Includes risk-reporting functions. "Book Management" not only receives new deals, but first checks potential deals against limits prior to booking and confirmation. Even existing deals are marked-to-market using market price signals on an ongoing basis.

In addition to these three primary functions, the trading and portfolio management system might incorporate or integrate with such functionalities as scheduling, operations, billing, accounting, and other business activities. Incorporating these functions represents an important aspect of managing one's operational risk. The secret to integrating these components is good database design; something as simple as inconsistent deal identification "ID" numbers can create major intra-system communication glitches. Another common concern involves consistency in the deal capture process; the ideal requires a deal to be entered once and then the information populates the necessary portions of the system.

SPECIFY YOUR NEEDS IN THE RMPP

RMPP Building a system without a good RMPP is like building a house without blueprints. System quality begins with the kinds of strategic decisions that only upper management should be making. Portfolio definition, reporting requirements, risk measures to be included, risk limits to be checked—we should have decided these! Now we can focus on the problem of selecting or building the related system components and building our staff.

Consider the matter of portfolio design. A utility will naturally want to support electricity, but what about natural gas markets as well? Most utilities will require this; does the system support the differences between these two markets, in terms of contract specifications, energy units, market conventions, etc.? Perhaps a tougher call involves coal, weather derivatives, bandwidth, and other related markets. If the price risk of coal represents a significant potential impact on the portfolio value, then be sure to account for the commodity in the system design. If the priority is longer dated, however, the ability to support coal could be delayed from the immediate system needs and put on a "to do" list.

During the system selection or building process, any major question not resolvable by the RMPP could suggest that the RMPP failed to cover the necessary range of managerial objectives. True, this places a great deal of responsibility on the drafters of the RMPP, but that's their job!

HIRING AND MANAGING THE RIGHT IT STAFF

While we covered some of this topic in Chapter 5, it bears repeating that the manager must properly understand the importance of hiring and managing a good IT staff. For the most part, IT folks provide support and problem solving rather than just hardware or programming services. The manager should seek a blend of cables and communication. The manager should also not seek to cut costs in the area of IT, both in terms of computer technology and the people who run them. Continuing our aviation analogy, the mechanics and ground crew that keep the airline flying symbolize the IT staff.

One pet issue— relational databases form the storage pool for information in trading and risk management systems. In the late 1990s, energy trading system vendors began shifting from proprietary data storage design to the practice of laying their applications on top of such database management systems as Microsoft Access, SQL Server (also commonly known by its legacy name, Sybase), and Oracle. The manager should hire a decent database administrator (DBA) and treat him/her like Eric Clapton. A good DBA helps keep information consistent, debugs any problems, and relates with the outside vendors. Database management is a fast growing field, with dramatic new roles in such areas as web page design. Local colleges and technical schools teach many classes on the subject, so the utility will not have to look far for new hires.

MATCHING YOUR BUDGET TO YOUR EXPOSURE AND HEDGING STRATEGY

A few years back I met with a large air carrier. The firm wanted a worldwide risk system to hedge their massive jet fuel exposure. At meeting's end I inquired about their budget. Their response—$25,000, all inclusive! First of all this amount pales in comparison to actual costs for trading and risk software. Secondly, the firm's jet fuel exposure dwarfed this amount. The point here is that firms should budget for systems in accordance to their exposures and their total needs. Consider IT spending a hedging premium to protect against all the risks covered by the RMPP—the least of which is human error. If nothing else, compare the costs of a good system with the potential costs of a bad system.

The total cost of a trading and portfolio management system can seem huge. Initial license fees can range anywhere between $250,000 and $2 million. Some simpler systems might charge less; more complex systems charge more. Most software companies pro-rate their fees by the number of users on the system.

It is difficult to break out of the turnkey system fee the price of the risk-specific engine. Here the manager will face some of the following dilemmas.

Few Niche Specialists. Very few companies specialize in valuation and risk analytics for the power industry. A number of vendors do so for money markets, but their applicability to unique energy behavior should be thoroughly tested. Beware of money-market vendors selling energy-risk software with little or no specific adaptation from money market applications. Energy risk requires the full *Price-Risk Pyramid* being supported. The trading and portfolio management vendors may or may not have a quantitative research and development team. Thus, the energy manager enjoys limited opportunities to comparison shop.

High School Kids on the Web. I once met a gas trader who used a $10 option valuation program that he bought on the Internet from a high school kid. He definitely got what he paid for; I am curious how his firm's shareholders would feel about the situation.

Build vs. Buy. Perhaps the greatest dilemma—and greatest risk—involves deciding between building versus buying a risk engine. (See next section for a broader discussion of the Build vs. Buy Dilemma.) Many risk managers enjoy designing and implementing new models; creating customized solutions is certainly part of the job. The manager, however, should monitor how much effort is put into research and development, and then determine if this is an appropriate usage of time. People tend to confuse inventing new software with effectively using software. By analogy, one would not expect a virtuoso violinist to spend his/her time building a violin to surpass a Stradivarius! His/her job is to play—not build—the instrument. Likewise, the manager should ensure that his/her staff is making their tools "sing" rather than reinventing the proverbial wheel.

THE BUILD VS. BUY DILEMMA

If anyone can build a good computer system, I would imagine that an electric utility could. These people run huge, complicated technologies! Software vendors often do not understand power as well as utilities do, so their systems often do not adequately reflect reality. Off-the-shelf products can carry bugs, delivery times can be severely delayed, and a host of problems always seem to nip at the manager's heels. Building in-house offers the sense of focus, control, and independence. A well-crafted in-house customization can provide true competitive advantage. Having said this, you must ask yourself and answer it honestly—what makes me think that your company would do a better job at building a system than the available vendors?

I have seen several good in-house systems. The secret to good system development is—you guessed it—good design and management. Unfortunately, with the few notable exceptions, I encounter poor in-house systems more often. "Do-it-yourself" software can be risky. The problem revolves around the difficulty of the software business; does the utility really want to enter the software business? If the utility decides to build in-house, the manager must be convinced that the firm's in-house resources somehow know something that software companies do not and have some core competence that justifies the risk. In-house programming means in-house design, in-house specifications, in-house project management, in-house testing, in-house documentation, and in-house support. The irony is

that many of the same companies who attempt to build their own computer systems have business units that outsource fleet management of their
service vehicles. Go figure. To be honest, individual self-interest can be a
prime motivator for in-house development. Some employees fantasize that
they will build a fabulous system, which could then be spun off as the basis
of a subsidiary with the employee being in charge. This motivation can be
excellent as long as the manager understands, accepts, and controls it.

Some final concerns about in-house development.

No Third Party Credibility. Auditors traditionally prefer third-party
solutions that are well documented. There's safety in numbers, particularly if the manager can cite similar utilities using the same systems.

Recouping Costs. Some utilities initiated in-house development
projects expecting to recoup costs by licensing the software to other utilities. The manager should not make this decision lightly; in fact, only the
board should make this decision as it impacts the company's business
plan. Remember, to recoup your costs you will have to "beat the market",
becoming a better software vendor than the best software vendor in the
market. And in the end, if you compete against other utilities in the marketplace, what in the world would motivate your competitors to trust your
system enough to license it?

Value of Source Code. Source code consists of the actual lines of code
that are then compiled to create a software application. To a software vendor, source code represents pure intellectual property to be protected; com-
piling the source code into applications helps protect the developer from
software piracy. Some utilities, however, prefer and even require access to
source code. These end users wish to avoid the "black box syndrome" by
confirming what lies beneath the hood; the firm might also want the flexibility of customizing the application. The manager should simply be aware
of the true cost of source code. Any vendor with true competitive value will
charge much more for source code. In addition, with access to source code
comes responsibility for support. It's like those warning stickers on the bottom of your radios; the vendor will charge more to support or fix any problems created by customization. Worse still, new releases of the vendor's
application may not be compatible with any customization, boosting the
real costs of source code access considerably.

Ultimately, for most companies, the entire system will be a mixture; a hybrid of "buys" from best-of-breed vendors and "builds" from in-house crews. In this sense, the ability to integrate and perform internal support becomes a key factor to success. Ultimately, the responsibility for this system should fall on the manager's shoulders.

IDENTIFY VENDORS THAT MATCH YOUR CORE COMPETENCE

Figure 11-2 provides a perceptual map for system selection. Your company's need and the abilities of potential vendors can be plotted side-by-side on this map. The map identifies the optimal selection according to a particular vendor's proximity to your own location.

In the figure, the *x*-axis represents the comprehensiveness of a vendor's offering, with modular or limited-purpose products on the left extreme and complete, turnkey systems on the right. The right-hand extreme equates to the "Whole Product" concept described by Moore, Chapter 5.The *y*-axis represents the sophistication of potential solutions. High quality products usually cost more, so the vertical axis also correlates with price.

 Prior to evaluating vendor offerings, the manager must first figure out where his/her needs lie on the map and use these needs as his/her target. From the manager's perspective, a RMPP that calls for integrating best-of-breed components into an in-house system would place his/her needs on the left portion of the map. If the RMPP calls for a large, single-source trading and risk management system, the target falls in the right hand portion (as it is in the Figure 11-2.) With cost being the other dimension, the manager works within the budget accorded by the RMPP.

With the target defined, the manager may now invite the vendors to demonstrate their wares. In the ideal world, the manager would simply need to photocopy the RMPP. In reality, the manager should compile a

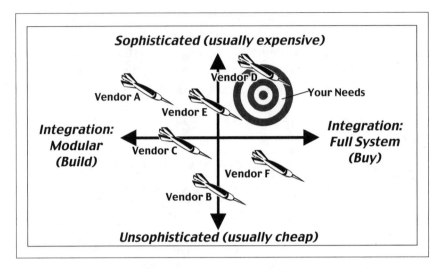

Fig. 11-2: Perceptual Map for System Selection

system-specific version. (Perhaps this could become an appendix to the RMPP.) Some firms retain consulting firms to create specifications sheets or *Requests for Proposals* (RFP). The effectiveness of these search processes depends entirely on the manager's ability to state the firm's objectives for the system. The ability of each vendor appears on the perceptual map. With any luck, one or more vendors will hit the target and become a final candidate.

UNDERSTAND THE HERITAGE OF VENDORS

A final tip for managers—understand the heritage of your vendor. Where did the vendor come from? What were they doing before deregulation? For example, some system vendors come from a fundamental analysis background, whereas other emerged from the natural gas pipeline optimization market. Still others come from money market backgrounds. Regardless of the images they place on the brochures and web pages, the origins of their systems may be hard-coded to their original core competence, which might not be power trading and risk management. Old priorities might represent weak spots as they relate to new market needs. A pedigree outside the world of energy risk may not be a bad thing: perhaps this firm brings a core competence that your firm requires. As with all things managerial, the manager can make better decisions by asking the vendor where he/she has been for the past few years.

chapter 12

LOOKING FORWARD: THE NEXT TEN MANAGEMENT ISSUES

NEXT YEAR'S "TOP TEN CHECKLIST" OF ISSUES TO WORRY ABOUT

This book focuses on the "top priority" risk issues facing power executives and their companies. Starting with the "Top Ten Checklist" presented in Chapter 1, each chapter focused on basic energy risk problems and solutions, the kinds of "entry level" topics that a new manager must understand. Likewise, a company would encounter these issues if it were new to trading or perhaps going through the birth pains of deregulation.

In this final chapter, however, I will suggest 10 issues that I believe will confront the power industry in the future. (See summary in Table 12-1.) While I refer to them as "Next Year's" checklist of things to do, I do not mean to predict that these issues will definitely rock the market in the Year of 2001, or perhaps even in the year after one reads this book! Some

Issue	Summary
The Big One: FASB 133	Understanding, satisfying, and influencing major new accounting standards will require significant managerial attention.
Building Liquidity	The industry must actively build trading volumes by improving market efficiency, increasing internal appetite for risk tools, and building demand.
The Risk of Reregulation	Following the years of liberalization, the industry must demonstrate its maturity as a market of consenting adults to avoid reregulation by government.
The Risk of an S&L-Type Crisis	Strong parallels exist between the regulated American power markets and the savings-and-loan (S&L) industry prior to the infamous S&L crisis. The power industry and general community alike must take efforts to avoid a similar exploitation and its disastrous outcome.
Power as Wall Street Darling	Well-managed power companies will increasingly attract investors looking either to diversify their portfolios or take advantage of the market's volatility.
The Big Tent Approach to Portfolio Management	Utilities will gradually expand their approach to portfolio management to include physical assets, retail positions, and all relevant exposures.
A Market in the Hand is Worth Two in the Bush	Unless their corporate strategy dictates, managers must focus on their company's core markets and resist the temptation to enter peripheral markets.
Finishing Old Business	Managers will continuously need to ensure that the firm maintains and complies with a decent *Risk Management Policies and Procedures* (RMPP).
Gosh Darn IT!	A manager's effectiveness will be highly dependent upon his/her information technology's (IT) quality of integration, accuracy, and reliability.
Keeping the Faith, Spreading the Gospel	Managers must keep their operation "marked-to-market" and spread this type of awareness within the organization and the general industry.

Table 12-1: Next Year's "Top Ten Checklist" of Issues to Worry About

of these issues may be like the perennial "car of the future" that one sees at every auto show. What I do mean is that these are the kinds of issues that can emerge in the future and warrant the manager's attention. These are also the kinds of issues that a newcomer to the world of energy risk will confront after getting the basics under control.

The Big One: FASB 133

No single issue will grab more attention from management than FASB 133. FASB 133 is the relatively new accounting standard from the Federal Accounting Standards Board (FASB) that specifies different treatment for hedges versus speculative trading. In terms of accounting, a position that can be defined as a hedge will have a preferential treatment compared with a speculative one. To be defined as a hedge, the firm will need to specifically identify the underlying position that is being hedged with the subject contract.

Managers will need to dedicate significant time—both their departments' and their own personal time—to understanding and satisfying the new rules. This holds true for all companies involved with derivatives—but the problem will be exacerbated for power executives due to the complexity of the typical electricity portfolio. Most electric utilities perform trading in order to hedge some or all of their physical generation assets—so these physical positions will need to be articulated as the underlying positions that are being hedged. In this regard, many managers will also need to find time for influencing how FASB 133 is implemented and adjusted for the specific needs of the power and energy markets.

Building Liquidity

The power industry must actively increase liquidity and enhance price discovery. Market efficiency will depend on the continued evolution of standardized contracts both at exchanges as well as over-the-counter. Likewise, the industry must avoid market inefficiencies like price controls or market caps. Each individual company must acknowledge its own internal appetite for risk tools. Enlightened middle managers could play a leadership role in educating upper management on the value of risk technology, all the while keeping a watchful eye on trading operations to avoid embarrassing losses that could reinforce the negative stereotypes of "derivatives."

Electricity companies must also "build market demand" for trading, with industrial end users showing the greatest potential of joining the market. End users are "naturally short"—the perfect complement to the power companies being naturally "long" positions. The presence of both sides of the marketplace could not only invigorate trading volumes but also attract new market makers and speculators that are necessary to make markets truly efficient.

The Risk of Reregulation

Following the years of liberalization, the industry must demonstrate its maturity as a market of consenting adults to avoid reregulation by government. Public backlash to price spikes, rolling blackouts, or larger utility bills typically involves calls to the government to take action.

Some end users will resist complete deregulation if it means the removal of tariffs or pricing policies that guaranteed lower prices. Threats from within the power industry also exist—recalcitrant utilities that are unwilling or incapable of becoming market driven could lobby to squelch competition from newer, nimbler energy competitors. A special kind of internal reregulation could occur if the industry ignores mark-to-market principles when designing central market clearing mechanisms.

The progressive manager has several solutions to hedging the political risk of reregulation. The best solution is to build greater liquidity and hence better price discovery. Market efficiency builds a momentum of its own that resists the influence of single players. Politically, regulation is typically acceptable only for weak, not vibrant markets. Another solution is to learn from the banking industry, which proactively attempted to self-regulate with standardized agreements and international standards for risk management.

GUEST ESSAY

"Reliability—the Ultimate Risk"

by Robert Smock
Vice President and Publishing Director
Energy and Utility Group
PennWell Corp.

Managing price risk in a competitive U.S. electricity market would be tough enough with a healthy electrical generation and delivery system.

Unfortunately, the U.S . electric infrastructure is sick and getting sicker. It is getting old. The average age of a power plant in the U.S. is approaching 30, and that's old for a power plant. Outage rates climb, maintenance needs skyrocket. Same for transmission and distribution systems. But few utilities are investing in these assets. They are deteriorating, and we're starting to see the results in increased and more widespread failures of the electrical system. In other words, the industry is facing growing operation and political risk due to a decaying infrastructure.

It's been estimated that electrical outages cost U.S. business almost $30 billion a year. Historically, most of those outages are due to weather-related failures of the power delivery system. However, a disturbing trend has developed in recent years. Electrical systems are increasingly failing due to aging equipment, lack of maintenance, and inadequate control systems. We've seen large-scale, dramatic failures of the electrical low-voltage distribution systems, of the high-voltage transmission systems, and even of generating capacity, which has been insufficient in several regions.

Neglect of electrical infrastructure in the 1990s is most probably due to uncertainty about the outcome of the deregulation trend in the U.S. Existing utilities want to reduce costs and electricity prices to fend off deregulation or, if that fails, to fend off the resulting new competitors. In addition, utilities are not sure what assets they will be left holding. There has already been a massive sell-off of generating assets by regulated utilities in deregulation hotbed regions (California, New England, Pennsylvania, etc.) A similar trend is developing for transmission assets. Independent System Operators (ISO) are taking over operation of utilities' transmission systems. Will ownership be next?

As of late in the year 2000, the industry was still waiting for the retail deregulation shoe to drop. Wholesale competition is growing, but it can't fully develop without a more competitive, open retail market. Wholesale electrical ratemaking and transactions are controlled by the federal government, which has introduced some degree of openness. Retail electricity, however, is controlled by the states, each bearing its own political risk.

About half the states have moved in some fashion toward a competitive retail electricity system, but it won't fully take effect in most of those states until after the year 2002. After the public relations catastrophe in

San Diego[1] during summer 2000 when people were hit with higher summer peak prices—a natural result of market pricing—many states are rethinking their policies. California's statewide crisis in January 2001 only amplified public concern. The new cry is, "America ain't ready for electrical system reform." This adds to the uncertainty and the reluctance of utilities to invest in their systems. And...there's a reluctance of investors to support the privately owned utilities. Average investor-owned utility stock price during the past five years was only 12 times earnings compared with double that for the S&P 500. During that biggest five-year bull market in history, the DJ utilities index rose a paltry 50%.

Another dramatic example of electrical reliability problems is the Commonwealth Edison distribution system in Chicago. In the summer of 1998 a large downtown outage caused by failures of aging equipment in downtown substations hit the headlines. The utility promised to fix things. An even worse downtown failure in the summer of 1999 really angered Mayor Richard Daley: "We are sick and tired and they (outages) had better change."[2] There were changes in utility management and more promises, backed up by a $1.5 billion improvement program. A U.S. Deptartment of Energy investigation[3] of the Chicago outages reported:

- "Load forecasting and distribution planning tools failed"
- "Real-time information and historical records on distribution system conditions were limited"

During the summer of 2000, embarrassingly, yet another failure blacked out downtown Chicago.

Chicago isn't the only victim. There were outages in New York City, Long Island, New Jersey, and the Delmarva Peninsula. In June 2000 a heat wave in San Francisco caused widespread voltage reductions, brownouts, and even rolling blackouts to keep the electrical system from collapsing. The winter of 2000-2001 brought two California utilities to their knees.

During the summer of 2000, the California Independent System Operator (CalISO), which runs the high-voltage electric grid in the state, issued 31 power shortage "emergency alerts" including a "stage 2" alert, meaning that generating capacity reserves over demand were less than 5%. In the old regulated days, the reserve margin minimum was 15% to avoid brownouts and blackouts. CalISO predicts the state will be 5GW short for summer, 2001. The CEO of Pacific Gas & Electric, the largest utility in the state, says California faces rolling blackouts in the summer of 2001[4] In October 2000, CalISO announced a plan to buy $250 million worth of "emergency" generating capacity—totaling about 2 GW—to get it through summer peak demand periods.

The peak price problem in San Diego in the summer of 2000 was not caused by unprecedented high demand. Peak demand for San Diego Gas & Electric Co. in the summer of 2000 was 5% lower than the year before. It was the lowest in five years, obviously retarded by market prices double the regulated prices of the previous summer. The problem was caused by a shortage of generation capacity, certainly not enough for a truly competitive market.

Writing in the Spring 2000 issue of EPRI Journal, Karl Stahlkopf, vice president for power delivery of the Electric Power Research Institute (EPRI), said, "The near-term threat is one of considerable urgency. Interregional bulk power transfers have been increasing exponentially, with some major transmission operators now participating in as many transactions in a day as they used to handle in a week. The limitations of the current power delivery system has already been dramatically revealed by some highly visible outages, such as those in New York and Chicago last summer, and by unexpected wholesale price instabilities." EPRI, the utility industry's technology development arm, has launched a "Power Delivery Reliability Initiative" to attack the problem.

The utility industry's reliability watchdog, the North American Electric Reliability Council (NERC), says, "The industry is facing a real and immediate crisis."

In June of 2000 the U.S. Senate passed a bill that would create a reliability regulatory body with the power to enforce compliance with mandatory rules. NERC, the existing agency, is a voluntary industry group with no enforcement power. The federal bill stalled in the House of Representatives, but another disastrous summer—sure to happen sooner than later—will result in a federal electrical reliability organization (already known in Washington as the ERO).

A cost crisis is also coming. In response to the dwindling generating reserves, power producers have started construction on 50 GW of new capacity and announced 200 GW more (total capacity of the US is about 700 GW). The problem is that 90% of this new capacity will be fueled by natural gas. In the past two years the non-contract price of natural gas has more than doubled to an all time high of more than $5 per million Btu. What will it climb to with all this new gas-fired power plant construction? What effect will that have on electricity prices?

It all adds up to a growing reliability problem—and a growing risk management problem.

Robert Smock is Vice President and Group Publishing Director, Global Energy Group, PennWell. Bob grew up near Pittsburgh and graduated from Carnegie Institute of Technology in 1964 with a B.S. in Chemical Engineering. After working as an engineer for General Motors' Packard Electric Div. for several years, he moved to the magazine publishing industry as midwest editor of Steel *magazine. He then became an editor for a series of engineering books published by Barnes & Noble Publishing Co. He moved to the power industry in 1971, when he became an associate editor of* Electric Light & Power *(EL&P) magazine. He became editor of* Power Engineering *magazine in 1986 and editorial director of* EL&P, Power Engineering, *and* Power Engineering International *magazines in 1991. He became publisher of PennWell publishing company's power industry magazines in 1995 and Vice President and Publishing Director of the Global Energy Group in 1998. The GEG includes all of PennWell's power and water magazines and conferences.*

The Risk of an S&L-Type Crisis

Strong parallels exist between the regulated American power markets and the savings-and-loan industry prior to the infamous savings & loan (S&L) Crisis. Both industries had unique regulatory environments that combined financial incentives to private ownership in return for providing certain local economic development benefits. Individual firms in both industries tended to be very locally oriented, with strong presence at the board level of local or regional economic, political and social leadership. Both industries faced radical change in the form of deregulation, the intent of which was "for the public good" on the surface but often driven by very private economic gain.

Exploitation during the S&L deregulation process proved disastrous.[5] The power industry currently carries a very similar political risk associated with individuals or individual companies controlling deregulation in a way that destabilizes the overall marketplace. Obviously, the power industry does not have an equivalent to the S&L's deposit insurance, and hence the public financial exposure could never reach the astronomical proportions of the S&L crisis. But the public could pay the price in the form of outages, cost inefficiencies, or loss of local political control.

Power as Wall Street Darling

Well-managed power companies will increasingly attract investors looking to either diversify their portfolios or take advantage of the electricity market's volatility. Two early examples include Berkshire Hathaway Inc. and Kohlberg Kravis Roberts & Co. (KKR) investing into MidAmerican Energy[6] of Des Moines, Iowa, and Dayton Power & Light[7] of Dayton, Ohio, respectively. Electric companies have always paid close attention to their shareholders and the equity markets, to be sure. But the scale of selling large portions of or entire companies could dramatically impact how power companies make investments and design marketing plans. The kinds of issues that drive mergers and acquisitions could start getting equal time with such managerial concerns as reliability and price risk.

The Big Tent Approach
to Portfolio Management

Utilities will gradually expand their approach to portfolio management to include physical assets, retail positions, and all relevant exposures. Rather than just managing electricity price risk, the "big tent" approach is often referred to as "enterprise risk management." Many factors will literally force managers to look at the big picture, least of which will be FASB 133. Another factor is diversification of electric companies, often through the purchase of entire natural gas companies. Traditional engineering functions such as generation optimization and congestion management might also benefit from market-driven risk principles, facilitating these issues being included in the portfolio management process.

In raising this "big tent," managers will face the problem of finding staff that understand the kinds of issues involved with integrating a multi-market portfolio and implementing the necessary technologies. The firm would have the operational risk of bringing together disparate data and systems into a single portfolio. The costs of such integration may well be greater than the perceived benefit. Of course, the manager must weigh this potential downside against the opportunity cost of not doing anything at all.

A Market in the Hand is Worth Two in the Bush

In the past few years, the energy and power risk management world has hosted countless seminars on markets closely related to electricity, including weather derivatives and bandwidth. These are excellent markets that offer excellent risk tools and trading opportunities. The problem is these new markets are not for everyone, particularly smaller power companies that have not yet even managed their core exposure of electricity price risk. Unless their corporate strategy dictates, managers must focus on their company's core markets and resist the temptation to enter peripheral markets with the hope of making some quick gains. Such managers should remember how hard it was to get the electricity desks up and running.

Finishing Old Business

Managers will continuously need to ensure that the firm maintains and complies with a decent Risk Management Policies and Procedures

(RMPP.) The manager will need to require, approve, and monitor the creation or implementation of the tools needed to properly populate the *Price-Risk Pyramid.* Persistent risk technology problems seem to involve building forward price curves (especially at the discrete daily level), creating energy-specific energy option models, and an over-reliance on Value-at-Risk (VaR) as the primary risk management tool.

Gosh Darn IT!

A manager's effectiveness will be highly dependent upon the quality of his/her information technology (IT), especially as it relates to the other major issues facing the industry. In order for a "big tent" approach to succeed in portfolio management, the IT system will need to integrate such traditionally disparate books as power, natural gas, physical generation, transmission, and retail exposures. Many companies continue to struggle with simple issues like single point deal capture, let alone integrating deal capture across multiple commodities traded at multiple locations.

From a technology point-of-view, many companies already operate legacy systems purchased in the mid-1990s that no longer meet the firm's overall system needs; each manager faced with this situation must choose between using the legacy system as the base for integration or replace the system with a new integrated framework. From a pure risk point-of-view, the accuracy of valuation models embedded within systems will also raise concerns. Legacy systems that do not properly handle energy risk will either need to be upgraded or replaced. Finally, the reliability of systems will depend heavily on their ability to respond to increasing demand. As mentioned in Chapter 11, the role of good database management may ultimately become the decisive factor in IT performance.

Keeping the Faith,
Spreading the Gospel

As a fitting conclusion to this book, the need for leadership is the final issue facing the power industry to complete the revolutionary promise of deregulation. As deregulation touches new departments or as new people are hired, the broad themes raised throughout this book will continue to command attention. They include the following:

- the revolutionary notion of "marking-to-market" liberating power companies from the regulated cost-driven mentality;
- how corporate objectives define trading strategies and their inherent risks;
- the role of an effective RMPP document;
- the value of forward-looking, quantitative financial modeling; and,
- the education of upper management as renaissance-style leaders who both understand technology and how it can help a company fulfill its objectives.

Managers must play a key role in energy risk management, keeping the faith in mark-to-market principles and spreading this type of awareness both within their organization and across the general industry.

ENDNOTES

[1] "Mother nature KOs San Diego market, price cap fervor stings like a bee," Electric Light & Power, August, 2000, page 1.

[2] "Outages prompt lawsuits, dismissals at major utilities," Electric Light & Power, September, 1999, page 1.

[3] Power Outage Study Team interim report, January, 2000, U.S. Dept. of Energy.

[4] "Calif. ISO approves plan to buy more 'peaking' power," October 4, 2000, Reuters.

[5] For a terrific history on this topic, see "The Greatest-Ever Bank Robbery: The Collapse of the Savings and Loan Industry" by Martin Mayer.

[6] Berkshire Hathaway Inc., Omaha, Nebraska businessman Walter Scott, Jr., and David L. Sokol, MidAmerican's chairman and chief executive officer announced the completion of its acquisition of MidAmerican in March 2000. See www.midamerican.com to review the press release.

[7] KKR announced its $550 million strategic investment into DP&L in March 2000. See www.waytogo.com to review the press release.

appendix

Items To Consider For Trading And Derivatives Policies, Guidelines, Controls, And Internal Procedures

by Andrea S. Kramer
Partner
Mcdermott, Will & Emery

Outline

ITEMS TO CONSIDER FOR TRADING AND DERIVATIVES POLICIES, GUIDELINES, CONTROLS, AND INTERNAL PROCEDURES

I. **RISK MANAGEMENT POLICY**

   A. Consideration For Organizational Structure and Responsibilities

      1. Board of Directors ("Board") Authorization

         a. Board should set out the risk management objectives for the Company before risk management strategy is implemented.

         b. Periodic Board review and approval of risk management policies and procedures (particularly those that define risk tolerance).

         c. Board should know what derivatives the Company uses and the attendant risks.

            (1) List of all authorized products

            (2) List of all authorized markets

            (3) Consider delegating product strategies

         d. General authorizing guidelines and procedures ("Guidelines") should be reviewed and approved by the Board, at least annually.

         e. Board should allocate sufficient resources to record, manage, and control derivatives risks.

         f. Board should be regularly informed of risk exposures and material risk management issues.

         g. Board should exercise or delegate overall supervision of operations, while leaving day-to-day operations to management. Provide that specified individuals or committees within management may approve exceptions to the quantitative guidelines in the Guidelines, with material exceptions reported to the Board.

         h. Board minutes should document the Board's involvement.

Items To Consider For Trading And Derivatives Policies, Guidelines, Controls, And Internal Procedures

(1) The Board should determine that mechanisms are in place so that information about risk-creating activities is reported to the appropriate risk monitoring and risk management personnel.

(2) The Board should provide for or designate an adequate level of professional expertise for risk monitoring and risk management. Adequate personnel with appropriate expertise should be committed to effectively implement the Company's risk monitoring and risk management systems and processes.

i. The Board should ensure that Company's risk monitoring and risk management operations have the necessary authority and resources to accomplish their management control objectives. The Board can delegate the following:

(1) The Board can impose specific constraints on the scope of the Company's permitted activities (such as; product, market, geographic, or trading strategy restrictions), and the Board should specify these restrictions. The Board can also approve only specific activities; specify the scope of authorized activity; designate the individuals with the authority to authorize activities; or restrict activities to particular products or markets.

(2) The Board should identify the scope (or the procedures for determining the scope) of authorized activities and any nonquantitative limitations on the scope of authorized activities.

(3) The Board should identify the quantitative guidelines for managing overall or constituent risk exposures.

(4) The Board should identify the significant structural elements of the risk monitoring and management systems and processes.

(5) The Board should identify the scope and frequency of management reports addressing risk exposures.

(6) The Board should identify the mechanisms for reviewing Guidelines.

2. Board Designation of Responsibilities to develop, implement, monitor, and enforce the policies and procedures might include some of the following:
   a. Board of Directors
   b. Risk Management Committee
   c. Chief Financial Officer
   d. Risk Manager
   e. Accounting Risk Manager
   f. Senior Vice President for Trading
   g. Program Manager
3. Risk Management Committee ("RMC")
   a. Members should be assigned based on responsibilities.
   b. The risk management function should be independent from the management of the trading activities.
      (1) Trading risks and profits and losses should be reported at least daily to managers who supervise —but do not themselves conduct—trading activities.
      (2) The head of the risk management function should have sufficient authority and stature to provide an effective independent assessment of risk exposure levels.
      (3) Trader's compensation should not be tied too closely to the profitability of trading.
      (4) Reports should allow management to evaluate risk exposures and the Company's overall risk profile.
   c. Risk management methods should be reviewed at least annually to evaluate the assumptions used to measure risk and limit exposures.
   d. There should be a formal review process for new products to develop appropriate policies and controls and to integrate new products into the risk management and measurement system.
   e. Responsibilities of the RMC to issue detailed implementation requirements should be clearly set out.
   f. Meetings of the the RMC should be regularly scheduled.
   g. Reporting requirements of the RMC should be clearly set

out.

B. Employee Requirements

1. Comprehensive background checks should be conducted prior to employment or involvement with trading operations.

   a. Prior and pending litigation

   b. Prior employment history

   c. Prior and pending disciplinary matters

      (1) Prior firms

      (2) Self-regulatory organizations (such as commodity and securities exchanges)

      (3) Government regulators (such as the SEC and CFTC)

2. Employees should be properly trained with the appropriate level of trading expertise for their responsibilities.

   a. Programs should be implemented for the training of personnel involved in derivatives transactions.

   b. Personnel should be trained as to the nature of the relevant markets and their responsibilities.

   c. Employees with authority to enter into trades:

      (1) Must have a working knowledge of the relevant market

      (2) Must have a familiarity with all derivatives that may be used

      (3) Must have a solid understanding of Company's specific exposures and hedging strategies

      (4) Must understand the risk exposures arising from the product in question

      (5) Must understand risk management guidelines

      (6) Must understand the management control procedures for documenting, recording, and reporting the transaction

3. For those traders with discretionary trading authority, individual trading limits must be specified.

   a. Limits on net open positions

   b. Limits on options and leveraged derivatives transactions

    c. Limits and trade restrictions in designated products

4. Restricted activities of any or all employees must be specified.

    a. Prohibition against disclosure of confidential or proprietary information

    b. Prohibition against trading for one's own account in designated products

    c. Noncompetition agreements, if any, are to be signed

    d. Prohibition against conflict of interest situations, including incentives, gratuities, travel, and entertainment received from third parties except for what is authorized in Employee Code of Conduct or the company's Ethics Policies

5. Employee Code of Conduct

    a. Authorized Transactions, Parameters, and Controls

        Each Trader is permitted to enter into those Authorized Transactions defined in the Risk Management Policy as those transactions that a particular Trader is authorized to enter into specifically authorized by the Appropriate Position for that Trader. No employee, designated as a Trader or otherwise, shall enter into any transaction that is not an Authorized Transaction. Exceptions from this prohibition can be made only with the prior written approval of the Appropriate Position.

    b. Prohibited Activities

        Employees shall not engage in any activity in contravention of Company Policies, including the Risk Management Policy.

    c. Employee Compliance

        Each and every Trading employee shall comply with all Company policies, including the Risk Management Policy (collectively "Company Policies"). Any employee who violates the terms or the spirit of Company Policies, including the Risk Management Policy or possesses knowledge that any other employee has done so, shall immediately report such violation to the Risk

Management Function.

d. Conflict of Interest

The Company's Ethics Policy, entitled "When Ethics is the Question," is expressly made a part of and incorporated by reference into the Risk Management Policy. Any violation of the Ethics Policy will be deemed to violate the Risk Management Policy.

e. Trading for Own Account

No employee shall, directly or indirectly, enter into, or hold any beneficial ownership interest in any transactions for any energy or energy-related product of any product of any type, without the prior written approval of the Appropriate Position.

f. Concealment of Trades

No employee shall, directly or indirectly, conceal or hide the execution of any trade, delay or improperly record any trade, misrepresent the accuracy of any information relating to any trade or contemplated trade, or conceal, misrepresent, or not disclose any information with respect to any trade or contemplated trade. Traders and other employees responsible for entering trade related information must ensure that all trades are documented in Trading Information System by the end of the day on which the trade was entered into. Failure to enter trade information on a timely basis will be considered to be a concealment of a trade and a violation of this Code of Conduct.

g. Disclosure of Confidential Information

No employee shall, directly or indirectly, publish, disclose, or otherwise divulge any oral or written information, including, but not limited to, information relating to any policies, transactions, positions, or Company objectives to any person that is not a Company employee or authorized agent, without the prior written consent of the Appropriate Position. All such written consents shall be provided to the Risk Management Position for filing.

h. Duty to Report Violations

Any employee who violates a term or the spirit of Company Policies, including the Risk Management Policy, or possesses knowledge that another employee has violated any term of the Risk Management Policy or Company Policies, must immediately report such violation to the Risk Management Function and to the Internal Auditor, as required by Appropriate Document – such as the Ethics Policy. In addition to the procedures specified in the business ethics and conflict of interest policy, the Risk Management Function shall submit a written report summarizing the violation to the Appropriate Position within five (5) business days of notice of the violation. The Appropriate Position of Trading Function can then take such action, which may include termination of employment, or any other action that it deems necessary to protect the best interests of the Company.

i. Disciplinary Action

Employees who breach the Risk Management Policy or Company Policies shall be subject to disciplinary action, including, but not limited to, removal of authority to trade, if relevant, suspension from duties, and/or immediate discharge from employment.

6. Obtain employee acknowledgments, annually in writing, as to compliance:

a. Obtained, read, and understood a copy of both the Company's Policies;

b. Agreed to comply with the [spirit, philosophy, and terms of] the Policies;

c. Met with senior management to discuss the employee's personal responsibilities as outlined in the Policy or attended a seminar on the policies and procedures at which the employee's responsibilities were discussed;

d. Acknowledged by his/her signature that a violation of the Policy or any direct or indirect actions that violate the policies and procedures could constitute grounds for termination of employment and criminal prosecution;

e. Agreed to abide by limitations on accepting gratuities and travel and entertainment;

f. Understand the confidential and proprietary nature of the information used in the trading and risk management activities, and agree to maintain such information as confidential, and acknowledge prohibition against communicating any confidential and proprietary information to third parties;

g. Agreed to report any violation of the [term or spirit] of the Company Policies, including this Policy;

h. Agreed that conversations may be monitored, recorded, and transcribed, and that all trading transactions will be conducted on recorded lines;

i. Agreed not to trade authorized products for any account other than the Company's account and to comply with all personal trading restrictions and limitations;

j. Agreed to abide by signed Noncompetition Agreements;

k. Agreed that the employee is employed by the Company at will and the Company may terminate the employee's employment without cause at any time [a different statement needed if employment contract is in place.]

l. The employee is responsible to maintain his or her Policy current by updating it with information that may be provided in electronic or hard copy format.

7. Disciplinary actions, including termination, can be taken for any violations.

C. Risk Exposure Guidelines

1. Set out risk exposure guidelines on risk exposures of the

overall physical and derivatives activities.

   a. Base risk exposure guidelines on factors such as the character of the risks being measured

   b. Base the risk exposure guidelines on the extent and nature of the derivative products utilized

   c. Base the risk exposure guidelines on the risk measurement methodology

   d. Base the risk exposure guidelines on the nature of Company's counterparties and their industry and credit rating categories

2. If specific risk exposure limits are not provided, set out quantitative guidelines sufficient to implement specific quantitative limits.

3. Address the degree to which derivatives risk exposures should be aggregated, for purposes of risk monitoring and risk management, with the risk exposures resulting from other trading activities.

D. Accounting and Tax

  1. Accounting Profit and Loss Policies and Controls

    a. Realized and unrealized gain and loss

     (1) Provide a detailed and comprehensive discussion of the procedures involved in the realized and unrealized gain/loss evaluation and recognition process.

     (2) Track the flow of information from the trade initiation phase through the general ledger.

    b. Immediate recognition/deferral

     (1) Set out policy for realizing and recognizing gains and losses.

     (2) Set out the means by which such information is accumulated, summarized and classified in the financial statements

     (3) Identify the criteria for applying hedge accounting treatment and the monitoring procedures required (such as correlation, effectiveness, and designation).

    c. Reconciliation with general ledger and cash positions

  2. Valuation Calculations

    a. Define the methodology used for measuring value:
- (1) The intervals for market risk sensitivity
- (2) Market risk limits
- (3) How a mark is made and valued
- (4) How the validity of a mark is confirmed

    b. Market risk calculations

    c. Stress testing:
- (1) To assess the probability of adverse events
- (2) To address plausible potential "worst-case" scenarios
- (3) To demonstrate where there may be too much exposure
- (4) To require a comprehensive knowledge of the composition of risk exposures

    d. Reporting:
- (1) Value at risk
- (2) Capital at risk
- (3) Exceptions and violations of the policies

    e. Procedures for exception and violations:
- (1) Consequences
- (2) Reporting and correction responsibilities
- (3) Use computer lock-outs and passwords to limit access to reporting of positions and corrections

    f. Market risk management reporting

3. Valuation Methodology Policies

    a. Establish systems and procedures to mark-to-market the value of products, positions, and portfolios on a timely basis.

    b. Establish frequency of mark-to-market calculations, with the frequency that derivatives positions are marked-to-market consistent with the Guidelines established by the Board. It should be based on
- (1) The volatility of the relevant market factor(s) and
- (2) The nature of the Company's risk profile

    c. The valuation policy should reflect fair market value and, where appropriate, should incorporate adjustments for credit quality, market liquidity, funding costs, and transaction administration costs.

(1) Pricing verification procedures

(2) Routine procedures should be in place to verify the prices assigned to particular derivative products to validate valuation methodologies on a periodic basis.

(3) Any assumptions (such as historic correlations and volatilities) used in valuing positions should be periodically evaluated and verified.

(4) Frequent pricing verification should be done for long-dated contracts and illiquid positions.

    d. Establish verification procedures for statistical and simulation models. Models that conduct "stress tests" and measure the impact of various market movements on the value of derivative positions should be subject to review and validation. Model verification procedures should include a comparison of model predictions against actual market performances. There should also be timely identification and correction of any deficiencies in the models.

  4. Tax Policies and Controls

    a. Tax aggregate hedge policy manuals, as required

    b. Same day identification requirements

    c. Tax accounting methods

E. Legal Review

  1. Evaluate counterparty capacity to enter into transactions.

  2. Evaluate counterparty authority to enter into transactions.

  3. Conduct periodic reviews of agreements for changes in market practices or the law.

  4. Establish procedures to monitor and address the risk that a transaction will be unenforceable because:

    a. Transaction documentation is inadequate.

    b. The counterparty lacks the requisite legal authority or is subject to other legal restrictions.

    c. The transaction is not permissible under applicable law.

    d. Applicable bankruptcy or insolvency laws may limit or alter contractual remedies.

F. Establish a System of Self-Protecting and Internal Controls
1. Establish Internal Controls
   a. Separation of functions and duties
   b. Complete separation of trading from back office and middle office operations
   c. Daily reevaluation of trading positions, including illiquid and long-dated contracts, should be independent of the trading personnel and management.
   d. Limit access to deal and system data. Computer system should have a lock-out feature and audit function using passwords.
   e. Independent validation process
   f. Integrated Company-wide system for measuring and limiting risk
   g. The structure and appropriate independence of the risk management processes and organization "checks and balances"
      (1) Dual entries
      (2) Reconciliations
      (3) Tickler systems
   h. Periodically confirm that adopted policies and procedures have been implemented.
   i. Controls should be in line with the scope, size, and complexity of the activities that have been authorized and the nature and extent of the Company's risks.
2. External Verification
   a. Confirmations
   b. Verification of Prices and Volatilities
   c. Authorizations
   d. Settlements
   e. External Audit Reports
   f. Internal Audit Reports
3. Establish a line function to monitor compliance with customer-appropriateness policies that is independent of the trader and marketer.

        a. Review customer mark-to-market exposures on a periodic basis.

        b. Provide for a post-trade look at each deal.

4. Establish a third-party review to audit policy compliance.

        a. Provide for internal audit review.

          (1) On a regular basis

          (2) To confirm compliance with all policies, procedures, and controls

        b. Establish auditing procedures for periodic review.

          (1) Review credit files for documentation of creditworthiness and evidence of appropriateness

          (2) Review marketing files for documentation and evidence of appropriateness

          (3) Review sales presentations (if any) to ensure they are clear, balanced, and reasonable

          (4) Review marketer's trading tapes for appropriateness of sales pitches

          (5) Employee compliance with trading limitations and conflict of interest policies

5. Steps to avoid a confrontation with a customer

        a. Select a course of action that minimizes the likelihood of disputes.

        b. Possible courses of action:

          (1) Do not enter into the transaction

          (2) Provide customer with additional information

          (3) Involve senior management at customer before entering into a transaction

          (4) Enter into a written agreement as to any advisory or fiduciary relationship if any to be established

G. Intercompany and Related Party Activities

1. Include procedures required when a trading company enters into transactions with or on behalf of other affiliated companies, including accounting, tax treatment, settlement procedures, and reporting procedures.

2. Apply the same standards and procedures to affiliated companies as are applied to third parties, including standards with respect to errors, audits, and out trades.

II. TRADING POLICIES

A. Operations

1. Trading authorizations, approvals, limits, and guidelines to designate authority to commit on trades. Procedures should authorize certain employees to enter into particular types of derivatives transactions, specify any quantitative limits on such authority, and provide for the oversight of the exercise of employee authority.

   a. Overall business strategies
   b. General risk management philosophy
   c. Risk tolerance
   d. Past performance and experience
   e. Financial condition and capital
   f. Internal expertise and experience
   g. Sophistication of risk monitoring and risk management systems
   h. Regulatory and organizational constraints
   i. Approvals and authorized products
      (1) Authorized products
         (a) Physicals
         (b) Over-the-counter (OTC) derivatives
         (c) Exchange-traded products
      (2) Unauthorized products (possibly leveraged transactions and/or compound options might be listed as unauthorized for certain employees)
         (a) Physicals
         (b) OTC derivatives
         (c) Exchange-traded products
   j. Approved trading volume limits
   k. Limits on net open position
   l. Approval levels needed for trades over a certain size:
      (1) Dollar amount
      (2) Quantity limit
      (3) Time period
   m. Set actions to be taken if approved limits are exceeded

        (1) Who takes the actions?

        (2) How are violations reported?

        (3) How are violations corrected?

    n. Immediate withdrawal of trading authority for terminated employees and immediate notification of such withdrawal to all counterparties and brokers

2. Exchange-Traded Futures and Options on Futures

    a. Identify approved types of exchange-traded products.

    b. Set out guidelines for monitoring government regulations that may apply to operations.

    c. Identify brokers for various exchange-traded transactions.

        (1) Approved limits

        (2) Fees they charge for various transactions

        (3) Margin requirements

        (4) Procedures for verifying broker margin calculations

        (5) Procedures for follow up and trade settlement

        (6) Procedures to comply with the Company's conflict of interest, gift, and gratuity policies

3. OTC Swaps, Forwards, and Options

    a. Set out the various types of OTC products.

    b. Credit risk management policies and procedures with respect to OTC products

4. New Product Approval

    a. Set out the process for new product approval.

    b. Set out the reporting requirements for new products.

    c. Set out the monitoring requirements for new products.

5. Monitoring of Operations

    a. Address the flow and documentation of information into and out of the trading desk; the supervision of personnel engaged in derivatives and physical trading activities; identify those documents used to capture trade information; identify the computer systems involved in processing data; and identify those reports generating realized and unrealized gain/loss analysis, end of day positions, broker reconciliation, sensitivity analysis, credit considerations, and other management analysis such as "by trader" profit and loss.

    b. Overall monitoring

(1) Procedures should adequately identify and address any deficiencies in the Company's operating systems (such as database management, trade entry, trade processing, trade confirmation, payment, delivery, receipt, collateral management, valuation, and related information systems).

(2) Procedures should be implemented to contain losses from unidentified deficiencies.

(3) Operational risk measurement and management procedures should, as appropriate, incorporate the use of disaster recovery planning or related techniques for reducing the Company's exposure to operational risks.

c. Trading

(1) Set out method for monitoring quantitative compliance with risk measurement and controls.

(2) Set out how trades are initiated.

(3) Required approvals and authorizations

(4) Limit transactions to approved counterparties.

(5) Trade execution requirements, including time stamping and other audit trail requirements

(6) How transactions are recorded

(7) Set out how a new counterparty can be approved.

d. Deal input, edits, and audits

(1) Set out how a trade ticket is inputted into the reporting system.

(2) Set out how a ticket is reviewed.

(3) Set out how trades can be amended—and by whom—and the procedures for protecting the audit trail and position control.

(4) Set out how trades can be reversed and the procedures for protecting audit trail and position control.

(5) Set out how exceptions and changes to open transactions must be reported and monitored. Assure adequate lock-out functions on the computer systems and assure that trade blotters and computer tracking system both accurately reflect the transactions.

    e. Confirmations
       (1) For physical transactions
       (2) For OTC financial transactions
       (3) For exchange-traded futures and options on futures
    f. Address the structural elements of risk monitoring and risk management.
       (1) Establish an independent monitoring process with all appropriate checks and balances for all risk monitoring activities.
          (a) Define a risk monitoring process that is independent from the Company's business and trading units that create those risks that are being monitored.
          (b) Establish organizational checks and balances to protect against irregularities or inconsistencies in risk measurement and to ensure that derivatives risks are uniformly and accurately identified and evaluated.
       (2) Provide for the appropriate degree of risk management independence. Define the risk management function to be performed by specified committees or individuals that is independent from the business or trading units that create risks.
       (3) Establish authority, resources, and information reporting requirements.
       (4) Establish analytics for the middle office and position control to track patterns, as well as single day valuation and variation patterns.
          (a) Track patterns by product, desk, and individual traders.
          (b) Variations should be tracked intra-day, daily, weekly, and against historical averages.
       (5) Confirm on a regular basis the valuation of illiquid and long-dated contracts and positions.
       (6) Reconcile cash and general ledger positions with mark-to-market values.

    g. Procedures should provide for adequate documentation of the terms of transactions and other relevant information with respect to such transactions.

        (1) Such documentation should be appropriately maintained and made available to internal auditors, independent auditors, and other authorized examiners.

        (2) Operational systems should provide for the effective tracking and processing of derivative transactions from initiation to settlement.

B. Administration

    1. Master Agreements and Netting Agreements

        a. Physical transactions

            (1) Set out approved terms and conditions for the form and substance of any master agreements or netting agreements.

            (2) Prohibit transactions without either a master agreement or a netting agreement in place.

            (3) Set out procedures for negotiating and executing agreements with counterparties.

            (4) List all approved counterparties or necessary credit characteristics for approval and monitor carefully.

            (5) Set out the verification process for confirming and approving physical transactions.

        b. OTC financials

            (1) Set out approved terms and conditions for the form and substance of any master agreements or netting agreements.

            (2) Prohibit transactions without either a master agreement or a netting agreement in place.

            (3) Set out procedures for negotiating and executing agreements with counterparties.

            (4) List all approved counterparties or necessary credit characteristics for approval and monitor carefully.

         (5) Set out the verification process for confirming and approving swap and OTC derivative transactions, including approval levels for contracts with increased price and market liquidity risks.

   c. Exchange-traded futures and options on futures

         (1) Set out approved terms and conditions for the form and substance of any master agreements or netting agreements.

         (2) Prohibit transactions without a master agreement or a netting agreement in place.

         (3) Set out procedures for negotiating and executing agreements with counterparties.

         (4) List all approved counterparties or necessary credit characteristics for approval.

   d. Other transactions

         (1) Set out approved terms and conditions for the form and substance of any master agreements or netting agreements.

         (2) Prohibit transactions without either a master agreement or a netting agreement in place.

         (3) Set out procedures for negotiating and executing agreements with counterparties.

         (4) List all approved counterparties or necessary credit characteristics for approval and monitor carefully.

2. Scheduling Procedures

   a. Set out any scheduling procedures and requirements unique to physical transfers of commodities.

   b. Match delivery points.

   c. Arrange physical movements or book-out transactions.

   d. Coordinate delivery requirements with affiliates.

3. Settlement Procedures

   a. Set out responsibilities and procedures to liquidate and settle contracts with counterparties and brokers.

   b. Settlement procedures might include how to calculate margin, who is responsible for verifying the margin calculations, and procedures to process and approve margin payments.

4. Computer Data
   a. Computer pricing models should be integrated with the trading system.
   b. Computer pricing models should be used to confirm pricing.
   c. Computer data processes should implement all policies and procedures to protect data from accidental loss or unauthorized manipulation.

C. Accounting and Tax
   1. Accounting Profit and Loss Policies and Controls
      a. Realized and unrealized gain and loss
         (1) Provide a detailed and comprehensive discussion of the procedures involved in the realized and unrealized gain/loss evaluation and recognition process.
         (2) Track the flow of information from the trade initiation phase through the general ledger.
      b. Immediate recognition/deferral
         (1) Set out policy for realizing and recognizing gains and losses.
         (2) The means by which such information is accumulated, summarized, and classified in the financial statements
         (3) Identify the criteria for applying hedge accounting treatment and the monitoring procedures required (such as correlation, effectiveness, and designation)
      c. Reconciliation with general ledger and cash positions
   2. Valuation Calculations
      a. Define the methodology used for measuring value
         (1) The intervals for market risk sensitivity
         (2) Market risk limits
         (3) How a mark is made and valued
         (4) How the validity of a mark is confirmed
      b. Market risk calculations
      c. Stress testing
         (1) To assess the probability of adverse events
         (2) To address plausible potential "worst-case" scenarios
         (3) To demonstrate where there may be too much exposure
         (4) To require a comprehensive knowledge of the composition of risk exposures

    d. Reporting
- (1) Value at risk
- (2) Capital at risk
- (3) Exceptions and violations of the policies

    e. Procedures for exception and violations
- (1) Consequences
- (2) Reporting and correction responsibilities
- (3) Use computer lock-outs and passwords to limit access to reporting of positions and corrections

    f. Market risk management reporting

3. Valuation Methodology Policies

    a. Establish systems and procedures to mark-to-market the value of products, positions, and portfolios on a timely basis

    b. Establish frequency of mark-to-market calculations. The frequency with which derivatives positions are marked-to-market should be consistent with the Guidelines established by the Board and should be based on:
- (1) The volatility of the relevant market factor(s) and
- (2) The nature of Company's risk profile

    c. The valuation policy should reflect fair market value and, where appropriate, should incorporate adjustments for credit quality, market liquidity, funding costs, and transaction administration costs.

    d. Pricing verification procedures
- (1) Routine procedures should be in place to verify the prices assigned to particular derivative products to validate valuation methodologies on a periodic basis.
- (2) Any assumptions (such as historic correlations and volatilities) used in valuing positions should be periodically evaluated and verified.
- (3) Frequent pricing verification for long-dated contracts and illiquid positions.

    e. Establish verification procedures for statistical and simulation models. Models that conduct "stress tests" and measure the impact of various market movements on the value of derivative positions should be subject to review and validation. Model verification procedures should include a comparison of model predictions against actual market performances. There should also be timely identification and correction of any deficiencies in the models.

    4. Tax Policies and Controls

      a. Tax aggregate hedge policy manuals, where appropriate

      b. Same day identification requirements

      c. Tax accounting methods

D. Legal Review

    1. Evaluate counterparty capacity to enter into transactions.

    2. Evaluate counterparty authority to enter into transactions.

    3. Conduct periodic reviews of agreements for changes in market practices or the law.

    4. Establish procedures to monitor and address the risk that a transaction will be unenforceable because:

      a. Transaction documentation is inadequate.

      b. The counterparty lacks the requisite legal authority, or is subject to other legal restrictions.

      c. The transaction is not permissible under applicable law.

      d. Applicable bankruptcy or insolvency laws may limit or alter contractual remedies.

III. CREDIT POLICIES AND RISK MANAGEMENT PROCEDURES

A. Address Credit Exposures Across All Companies and Business Activities.

    1. Company can have a portfolio of interrelated credit exposures across its companies and business activities.

    2. Want to be sure the management of credit risk and exposure are performed in a consistent manner by all subsidiaries and affiliates.

    3. Should delegate to affiliates the operational aspects of credit risk management.

    4. Company should do the following for all affiliates:

      a. Aggregate credit exposure by counterparty on a corporate wide basis

      b. Establish corporate wide counterparty concentration limits

      c. Monitor counterparty concentration levels and periodic review

      d. Manage allocation of parent guarantees and monitor usage by companies and business activities

      e. Monitor each company's credit quality of portfolios

      f. Review and modify internal credit routines of counterparties by affiliates

      g. Develop, review, update credit reserving methodology built into the mark-to-market accounting system.

B. Establish Process for Selection, Approval, and Continuation of Relationship with Counterparties.

    1. Counterparty risk limits by counterparty (notional amounts may not accurately reflect risk of counterparty)

    2. Counterparty credit standards with creditworthiness determination (including any requirements for credit enhancements, including third party guarantees, letters of credit, or collateral support of any type)

    3. Risk ratings, assignment, and monitoring counterparty credit limits

    4. Evaluate extension of credit

      a. Current credit exposure

      b. Potential credit exposure

    5. Update credit limits and reapprove credit limits on a periodic basis

    6. Credit concentration by counterparty

    7. Customer derivatives policies (formal and informal)

    8. Generic risk disclosure statements (if applicable)

C. Evaluate Customer Appropriateness as a Counterparty

    1. Provide clear policies and procedures with respect to appropriateness of any third party customer.

    2. Establish management's philosophy:

      a. To "know the customer" and establish the proposed transaction suitable for the customer

      b. To promote strong customer relationships ("relationship oriented," not transaction oriented)

      c. To observe a standard of good faith and fair dealings when marketing, negotiating, entering into, and performing transactions, as well as when carrying out all contractual duties

        (1) To refrain from making misrepresentations

        (2) There might be an implied contractual duty to disclose information to a customer if the Company has superior knowledge, the information is not readily available to the customer, or the customer is acting on the basis of a mistake

    d. To fairly disclose information to the customer if the customer is justified in relying on that information

    e. To foster policies and procedures to reduce the risks of misunderstandings and disputes

3. Define personnel responsibilities to ensure customer appropriateness.

    a. Credit officers

    b. Verify customer's legal and financial ability and willingness to perform obligations

4. Verify customer's goals and objectives if the customer is not sophisticated.

5. Approve a trading line.

6. Approve a credit line.

7. Ongoing review of customer transactions

8. Responsibility of marketers and traders

    a. To ensure appropriateness of deals, given customer's sophistication and the level of complexity of the transaction

    b. To determine adequate credit line is available before executing any transactions

D. Establish Documentation Requirements for Customer Appropriateness

1. Maintain customer profiles.

2. Certain types of customers may require specialized formal documentation (to assure legal capacity and authority).

    a. Customers in regulated industries

        (1) Public utilities

        (2) Insurance companies

    b. Statutorily created entities (to determine that the customer has the constitutional or statutory authority to execute the transactions)

  (1) Cities and countries

  (2) Special local government districts and authorities (such as airports, terminals, certain hospitals, and certain utilities)

  (3) State treasuries

  (4) Pension funds

  (5) Endowments and foundations

  (6) College and university operating funds

  (7) Government sponsored entities

 c. Pooled investment vehicles

  (1) Commodity pools

  (2) Mutual funds

  (3) Money market funds

  (4) Hedge funds

 d. Nonfinancial corporations

  (1) Publicly held

  (2) Privately held

 e. Financial corporations

  (1) Banks and thrifts

  (2) Nonbanks (financial institutions other than banks, insurance companies, and security firms)

  (3) Credit unions

 f. Insurance companies

3. Use standard customer questionnaires.

4. Maintain adequate credit file documentation, addressing:

 a. Financial capacity and creditworthiness

 b. Business characteristics

 c. Customer goals and objectives

 d. Expected types of derivatives to be used

 e. Customer contracts

 f. Customer approval authorities

5. Maintain adequate marketing file documentation, including:

 a. Customer profile form

 b. Customer questionnaire

 c. All written agreements

     d. All transaction confirmations

     e. All deal term sheets

     f. Sales presentations, if applicable, which clearly state that the customer makes its own judgments

     g. Analyses of different scenarios, if applicable, which are truthful and will be corrected if inaccurate (there may be a duty to correct)

     h. All correspondence must be accurate and not intentionally misleading.

E. Address Customer Disclosure Requirements

  1. Establish different levels of disclosure based on

     a. Customer sophistication

     b. Transaction complexity

  2. Sophisticated customers (such as professionals, market makers, dealers, and customers that "shop the market" and "compare prices") might only need to receive a trade confirmation.

     a. Courts have been reluctant to hold dealers liable for anything beyond statements made if the customer is "sophisticated."

     b. Dealer cannot misrepresent a transaction or its terms.

     c. Dealers are not usually liable for omissions unless other factors are present (such as a particularly complex payment formula or leverage).

     d. Tends to be sufficient if the customer is sophisticated and statements were accurate at the time made

  3. Less sophisticated customers might need to be provided with a detailed analysis of price sensitivity over a broad range of price movements up and down.

  4. Customer disclosures

     a. Should be clear and understandable

     b. Should not be intentionally misleading

     c. Communications should not be misconstrued as recommendations

     d. Customer makes its own informed decisions

5. Should clarify material terms
   a. Identify and agree on all material terms.
   b. Customer should seek additional clarification if necessary.
   c. If customer does not seek additional clarification, customer may be deemed to have sufficient information.
   d. Any sensitivity and scenario analyses should cover a broad range of outcomes.
6. Disclaimers should be made as to term-sheets, sales presentations, marketing data, and mark-to-market valuations.
   a. Act in good faith to perform the calculations accurately.
   b. Base calculations on good faith assumptions and not with a view to presenting a misleading picture.
7. Calculations should also include a legend that
   a. Identifies the assumptions used
   b. Describes market factors that may affect the analysis
   c. Discloses that a variety of assumptions and market factors may affect the analysis
8. Make clear that Company does not provide recommendations or investment advice unless a written agreement is entered into with the customer to establish an advisory or fiduciary relationship (generally a contractual duty of care or has explicitly assumed a role that puts it in a position of controlling transactions or advising with respect to transactions).
9. Clarify quotations and valuations
   a. Clarify whether quotation is an indicative price quote.
   b. Clarify whether quotation is a firm price quote.
   c. Clarify if mid-market valuation
   d. Disclose that valuation may vary from indicative or firm price quotations.
   e. Disclose that valuations may vary from other dealers.
10. Acknowledge that a transaction can be interrelated with other transactions and instruments so that some positions may be (or appear to be) in conflict with other transactions.
11. Provide generic risk disclosure statements for less sophisticated customers.

      a. To notify less sophisticated customer that transaction is arm's length, and that customer should not rely on the Company for trading advice

      b. To identify principal risks

      c. To clarify the nature of the relationship

      d. To clarify that any information provided to a customer is to assist that customer in its own decision-making processes

F. Process for Selection of Brokers

    1. Broker credit standards with credit worthiness determination (including any requirements for third party guarantees, letters of credit, or collateral support of any type)

    2. Assignment and monitoring of risk ratings

    3. Extension of credit

    4. Margin requirements

    5. Standard contract provisions and settlement terms

    6. Broker certification of compliance with Company's conflict of interest policies

G. Establish Methodology to Measure Credit Risk

H. Document the Requirements to Meet Credit Risk Management Requirements

    1. Credit support documents

    2. Master agreements or netting agreements

I. Reporting of Credit Risk Management

    1. Credit expenses

    2. Counterparty reports

J. Require Trades to be Made Only With Pre-Approved Counterparties with Pre-Set Credit Limits

K. Set Out How Exceptions to Credit Limits are Approved.

L. Set Out Process for Reporting Exceptions to Credit Limits and Monitoring Exceptions.

M. Counterparty Credit Procedures

    1. Purpose

    2. Procedure Text/Credit Culture

    3. General Credit Considerations

4. Market Participants/Related Considerations
5. Credit Information Gathering
6. Credit Approvals
7. Financial Assessment Tools
8. Frequency of Credit Review
9. Counterparty Credit Documentation
10. Internal Counterparty Grading System and Credit Controls
11. Financial Analysis Spreadsheet
12. Monitoring
    a. Credit Usage
    b. Credit Exposure
    c. Credit Quality
    d. Contract Compliance
13. List of Reports

IV. **FRAMEWORK TO EVALUATE CUSTOMER APPROPRI-ATENESS FOR EACH TRANSACTION**
  A. Evaluate Customer Sophistication
    1. Is the customer sophisticated with respect to this particular transaction?
      a. Knowledge about the relevant market
      b. Access to information
    2. Is the customer sophisticated in one market but unsophisticated in another market?
    3. Items to evaluate customer sophistication
      a. Historical trading patterns
      b. Prior use of these products
      c. Intended use of the products
      d. Ability to value the transactions
      e. Is the source for the transaction an idea from the customer or the Company's trader or marketer?
      f. Customer's asset size
      g. Customer's earnings performance
  B. Understand Customer Needs
    1. Obtain basic information with respect to the customer's industry, business, financial condition, cash flow, and financing needs.

2. The marketer who maintains contact with the customer should understand the customer.
3. For a less sophisticated customer
   a. Understand the customer's strategies and objectives
      (1) Underlying business activity
      (2) Purpose of transaction
   b. Understand the customer's risk exposures to the degree possible (this may be difficult if the customer views its risks as proprietary information)
      (1) Market risks
      (2) Industry risks
      (3) Financial risks
   c. Understand services desired by customer.
      (1) One way or two-way price information
      (2) Simple or complex transactions
   d. Understand products desired by customer.
      (1) Simple
      (2) Plain vanilla
      (3) Structured
      (4) Leveraged
C. Evaluate Complexity of the Transaction to Ascertain that the Customer is Sufficiently Sophisticated to Understand the Transactions.
   1. Use of leverage: Does the transaction involve the use of either explicit or implicit leverage?
   2. Path dependency: Does the transaction contain time or price-related triggering events which could materially alter the nature of the transaction?
   3. Transparency of transaction: Is the true economic substance of the transaction easily determined from the structure of the transaction without significant analysis?
   4. Fragmentation or inability to determine the whole structure: Is the transaction constructed so that no one document describes the whole transaction, making it possible for a reader to review documents for a segment of the transaction and not understand that it is part of a larger transaction?

5. Consistency of transaction with industry practice: Is the transaction unusual in the client's industry?
6. Credit exposure relative to capital and earnings of customer: Will the transaction have a significant impact on the customer's financial condition or results and will that impact need to be disclosed?
7. Existence of regulatory, legal, tax, or accounting guidance: Is applicable regulatory, legal, tax, and accounting guidance clear with respect to the transaction?
8. Probability of event risk (regulatory, legal, tax, or accounting): Are the rules governing the transaction predictable, or could the transaction be subject to sudden application of different standards because of political or social developments?
9. Number of legal jurisdictions involved: Does the transaction cross multiple jurisdictions, resulting in the need for separate legal opinions in each? Does this make the oversight process more difficult?

D. Determine Appropriate Level of Company Contact with Customer's Senior Management.
   1. Require customer contacts to have sufficient authority to enter into transactions.
   2. Obtain signed resolutions specifically naming authorized employees.
   3. Determine level of necessary contact with customer's senior management, based on customer's sophistication and the complexity of the transaction.
   4. Some transactions may require contact with customer's management that is more senior than those individual Company traders or marketers generally works with (or a decision not to enter into the transactions) including:
      a. Transactions where a customer clearly does not appear to have the capability to understand and make independent decisions about a transaction
      b. Transactions where a customer has the capability to understand and evaluate a transaction but where the risks

posed by the transaction appear to be materially larger in relation to the size and nature of the customer and its prior transactions

    c. Transactions where a customer has the capacity to understand and evaluate a transaction but nevertheless appears to be relying on the Company for investment advice or recommendations

V. ONGOING TRAINING PROGRAMS TO EVALUATE CUSTOMER APPROPRIATENESS

Address the nature of the market, the responsibilities of the employees, and the need to identify circumstances that may present special situations.

A. Marketers

B. Credit Officers

C. Risk Managers

D. Legal Staff

E. Tax and Accounting

VI. BACK OFFICE POLICIES AND PROCEDURES

A. Deal Input, Edits, and Audits

    1. Set out how a trade ticket is inputted into the reporting system.

    2. Set out how a ticket is reviewed.

    3. Set out how trades can be amended—and by whom—and the procedures for protecting the audit trail and position control.

    4. Set out how trades can be reversed and the procedures for protecting audit trail and position control.

    5. Set out how exceptions and changes to open transactions must be reported and monitored. Assure adequate lock-out functions on the computer systems and assure that trade blotters and computer tracking system both accurately reflect the transactions.

B. Confirmations

    1. For physical transactions

    2. For OTC financial transactions

    3. For exchange-traded futures and options on futures

C. Structural Elements of Risk Monitoring and Risk Management.

    1. Establish an independent monitoring process with all appropriate checks and balances for all risk monitoring activities.

    a. Define a risk monitoring process that is independent from the Company's business and trading units that create those risks that are being monitored.

    b. Establish organizational checks and balances to protect against irregularities or inconsistencies in risk measurement and to ensure that derivatives risks are uniformly and accurately identified and evaluated.

    c. Provide for the appropriate degree of risk management independence. Define the risk management function to be performed by specified committees or individuals that is either independent from or senior to the business or trading units that create risks.

2. Establish authority, resources, and information reporting requirements.

3. Establish analytics for the middle office and position control to track patterns, as well as single day valuation and variations patterns.

    a. Track patterns by product, desk, and individual traders.

    b. Variations should be tracked intra-day, daily, weekly, and against historical averages.

4. Confirm on a regular basis the valuation of illiquid and long-dated contracts and positions.

5. Reconcile cash and general ledger positions with mark-to-market values.

D. Adequate Documentation

1. Such documentation should be appropriately maintained and should be made available to internal auditors, independent auditors, and other authorized examiners.

2. Operational systems should provide for the effective tracking and processing of derivative transactions from initiations from initiation to settlement

E. Accounts Payable and Cash Disbursements Procedures and Controls: Include a detailed and comprehensive discussion of the flow of transactions, duties, controls and levels of authorization over the Accounts Payable/Cash Disbursements process. Provide flow charts depicting movement through the accounting system and the various sources generating payables and cash disbursements.

1. Physical Transactions
2. OTC Financials
3. Exchange Traded Futures and Options
4. Other Transactions
5. Wire Transfer Procedures and Controls
6. Standing Payment Instructions

F. Billing, Accounts Receivable, and Cash Receipts Procedures and Controls: Include a detailed and comprehensive discussion of the flow of transactions, duties, controls, and safeguarding of asset considerations involved in the billing and receipt of funds from counterparties and brokers.

G. Records and Reports (Internal and External): Include formats of financial statements and disclosures for management/internal reporting as well as any external reporting to regulatory agencies, such as, the SEC, CFTC, and other regulators. Such reporting might be monthly, quarterly, and annually. Some reporting might also be necessary for tax filings.

1. Records
   (Records creation and maintenance procedures should be reviewed to determine the retention of documentation with respect to derivatives transactions.)
2. Reports
   a. Management reports
   b. Board reports
3. Scope and frequency of reporting
   a. The Guidelines should identify the type, scope, and frequency of reports to be prepared in connection with the firm's risk monitoring and risk management systems and processes and to be made available for review by the Board and senior management.
   b. Such reports should contain information regarding the Company's positions and risk exposures to facilitate effective oversight of the risk monitoring and risk management functions.
   c. The Board should review the scope and frequency of reporting as business and market circumstances change.

    4. Daily reconciliation of positions, equity, and margins
       a. Conducted by someone without trading responsibilities
       b. Completed prior to the start of business on the next trading day
    5. Reconciliation of trading systems to the general ledger
       a. Standard accounting formation to serve trading and accounting
       b. Track open and closed positions

VII. DISCLOSURE OBLIGATIONS
    A. On the Financial Statements
    B. To Comply with SEC and CFTC Disclosure Rules
    C. To Comply with Rules of Applicable Self Regulatory Organizations and Exchanges

ABBREVIATIONS AND NOTATIONS

5x16: The Monday-through-Friday on-peak hours excluding holidays
5x8,2x24: The off-peak hours
6x16: The Monday-through-Saturday period of on-peak hours
7x24: The full-week around-the-clock period
8760: The 24 hourly periods for every day of the 365-day year

X: Chi
Δ : Delta
Γ: Gamma
V : Nu
Ω: Omega
ρ : Rho or Correlation
Φ: Phi

Ψ: Psi
θ : Theta
τ : Time to expiration
Π: Portfolio value
$\tilde{Z}$: A stochastic variable

ATM: At-the-Money
CBoT: Chicago Board of Trade
CFTC: Commodity Futures Trading Commission
CMO: Collateralized Mortgage Obligation
COB: California-Oregon Border
Co-DOT: Co-Dependent Option Tree
df: Discounting factor
DBA: Database Administrator
DLL: Dynamic Link Library
DSM: Demand Side Management
EaR: Earnings at Risk
EFP: Exchange of Future for Physical
F: Forward Price
FASB: Financial Accounting Standards Board
GARCH: Generalized Autoregressive Conditional Heteroskedasticity
IPP: Independent Power Producer
ISO: Independent System Operator
IT: Information Technology
K: Option Strike Price
LMP: Locational Marginal Pricing
MBA: Masters (Degree) in Business Administration
MtM: Marking-to-Market
MVA: Minimum Variance Analysis
MWh: Megawatt Hour
NERC: North American Electric Reliability Council
NPV: Net Present Value
NYMEX: New York Mercantile Exchange
O: Option or Option Value Price
OTC: Over-the-Counter

PJM: Pennsylvania-Jersey-Maryland
PUHCA: Public Utility Holding Company Act of 1935
PURPA: Public Utility Regulatory Policies Act of 1978
PV: Parity Value, Present Value or Palo Verde
RMC: Risk Management Committee
RMPP: Risk Management Policies and Procedures
S: Spot Price or Swap Price
SEC: Securities and Exchange Commission
SME: Second Moment Equivalence
STD: Standard Deviation
t: Time of Observation
T: Time of Expiration
VaR: Value-at-Risk
VP: Vice President
WTI: West Texas Intermediate, a grade of crude oil

TERMS

5x8,2x24 Market: A market based on a contract that specifies delivery of power during the eight off-peak hours of the five business days of the week as well as the full 24 hours of the weekend days and holidays. The days of delivery are usually adjusted for holidays. Commonly referred to as an "off-peak" market.

5x16 Markets: A market based on a contract that specifies delivery of power during the 16 peak hours of the five business days of the week. The days of delivery are adjusted for holidays. Commonly referred to as an "on-peak" market.

7x24 Markets: A market based on a contract that specifies delivery of power during the 24 hours of each day of the week. The days of delivery are usually adjusted for holidays.

A

American Option: A general type of option for which the buyer has the right to exercise or strike the option at any time prior to the contract's expiration date.

Analyst: A general job title for someone who performs analytical support for the trading desk, risk manager, or other function.

Analytics: The set of models, techniques, and computer software designed to value and analyze the risk sensitivities of contracts, derivatives, assets, and any position in a portfolio.

Arbitrage: A trade or position that provides a guaranteed profit without any risk. (Can also be used as a verb.)

Arbitrage-Free: An assumption that a market, position, or model does not carry any inconsistencies (in pricing, structuring, or other variables) that would result in an opportunity for an arbitrage.

Arbitrage Strategy: A general strategy of making money off of arbitrage or pseudo-arbitrage trading and positions. One of the four *Risk-Return Strategies* (Pilipovic, 1998, p.199-203).

Asian Option: "Asian options have a payoff that depends on the average value of the underlying asset over some period before expiry." (Wilmott, p. 187). Also see *Truncated Asian Option*.

Ask or Ask Price: The price asked by the seller of a contract. The counterpart to *Bid Price*.

Asset: The unit of value that is either delivered (such as a commodity or stock certificate) or represented by derivative contract.

Asset Arbitrage: A pseudo-arbitrage strategy in which a company manages its generation assets in a way to exploit market price opportunities.

Assets as Options: The concept of applying real options theory to valuing physical assets such as generation plants as their equivalent financial options and integrating these positions into one's general portfolio.

Assumption: A theoretical idea, abstraction, or expression of a market condition that is useful in the creation or application of a model or methodology.

At-the-Money (ATM): An expression for describing the relative value of an option that has a strike price (K) that equals the current price of the underlying asset. If the option were being valued at expiration with exercise into delivery, one would use the spot price $(S=K)$, where spot price is the price for next day delivery. Were the option being valued prior to expiration, one would compare the strike price to the forward price $(F=K)$ corresponding to day of delivery. Ideally, in energy markets, this comparison should include relative discounting to delivery vs. payment dates.

Auctions: A market mechanism in which counterparties place bid prices (or ask prices) in a static exchange with settlement prices skewed toward the highest (or lowest) prices.

B

Back Office: A set of business functions including trade confirmations, accounting, and other processes that support the trading desk in the *Front Office*. Part of the *Front/Middle/Back Office* model.

Back-to-Back Trading: A process in which a company that buys (or sells) into a particular position will then sell (or buy) the identical position. A common technique in a *Market Maker Strategy.*

Backwardation: An expression for describing a market condition observable in that market's forward price curve in which the spot price is higher than the short-term forward prices.

Baseload: In the context of swing options, load-curtailment contracts or a structured product, the amount of fixed-volume power that is to be delivered and valued as a swap.

Baseload Swap: A swap that covers the fixed-volume portion of a structured product.

Basis: The geographic variation in value between similar assets that differ in some way, most typically geographic location. This basis value can be embedded within a single position asset if that position derives part of its value from the differential between two markets.

Basis Option: An option on a basis.

Basis Risk: The risk of change in the basis value embedded within a position.

Basis Spread: The difference in value between similar assets that differ in some singular way, most typically geographic location; the value of a basis.

Bermuda Option: Options that "allow exercise on specific dates, or in specified periods." (Wilmott, p. 32.) Very similar to a cap contract.

Bid or Bid Price: The price offered by the buyer of a contract. The counterpart to *Ask Price.*

Bid-Ask Spread: The difference between the bid and ask prices. The relative size of this spread reflects liquidity; the smaller the spread the higher the liquidity.

Bilateral Trading: Direct trading between two counterparties.

Binomial Tree Methodology: An option valuation tree in which two simulations (or branches) emulate from each node. One simulation implements a probability *(p)* of the forward price increasing and the other with a corresponding probability *(1-p)* of the forward price decreasing. Also see *Tree Methodology* and *Trinomial Tree Methodology*.

Black '76 Model: See *Black Model*.

Black Model: A descendent of the Black-Scholes Model derived to value options on forward positions. Also known as the *Black '76 Model*.

Black-Scholes Model: An option valuation model created by Fisher Black and Martin Scholes. Appropriate for options on spot positions consistent with the assumptions of lognormal price behavior and constant volatility.

Black-Scholes Volatility: The volatility implied from option prices using the Black-Scholes Model.

Book: A subset of the total portfolio containing confirmed deals. Books are usually associated with a unique market but can also share markets (such as the case of basis books.) Books can also be organized by strategy, asset optimization, trader, trading group, or other business function. When used as a verb, "to book" means to commit a contract to a portfolio or portfolio system.

Boption: A basis option.

Broker: An individual or company that fosters bilateral trading by publishing market price indications and putting counterparties together.

Brownian Motion: A price process in which movement is random and there is equal chance of the price going up or down. If one plotted a histogram of all the price steps, the distribution would look like a normal distribution. Also referred to as the "random walk."

Bucket: A clustering of information or values. See *Strike Bucket* and *Time Bucket* for examples.

C

Calibration: The process of determining the value of a parameter (or parameters) given the final result. Similar to the process of implying.

Call: An option that allows the owner the right to purchase an asset at the specified strike price.

Cap: A structured product that contains a strip of multiple call option contracts with identical specifications but staggered expirations. Each of the individual option contracts is called a "caplet".

Capacity: Generally refers to the maximum available generation volume of a single plant or a region.

Caplet: One of the individual option contracts comprising a *cap* contract.

Cash Desk: The trading desk that handles very short-term (i.e. daily, weekly, and perhaps balance-of-month) deals. Converse to *Term Desk*.

Cash Settlement (or Cash Settled): A contract that settles with the counterparties exchanging cash. Converse of *Physical Settlement.*

Chi (X): A risk sensitivity measurement of the imput on the value of a contract, position, or portfolio given a one-unit change in the quantity-price correlation.

Churn: When a single contract or kind of contract is bought and sold numerous times. A high churn ratio is an indicator of liquidity.

Clearinghouse or Clearinghouse Function: The function at a trading exchange that guarantees fulfillment of the obligations of all parties who enter into contracts through that exchange. A clearinghouse eliminates bilateral trading risk.

Co-Dependent American Option: An American-style option with multiple exercise rights in which the value of each exercise right is dependent on the others. Also known as a *Price Swing Option.*

Co-Dependent Option Time (Co-DOT) Methodology: A pricing model designed by Dragana Pilipovic to value price swing options.

Collar: "A collar is a combination of a long position in a cap and a short position in a floor." (Hull, p. 378).

Commodity: An asset such as electricity that is traded but also consumable.

Concentric Circles Model: A model for organizing a business with trading and risk management operations.

Confidence Interval: The probability measure used in specifying variable values within a distribution. In the context of *Value-at-Risk (VaR)*, describes the probability with which the VaR number is reported.

Confirmation: The process in which counterparties check that a trade has occurred and confirm the contractual details.

Contango: An expression for describing a market condition observable in that market's forward price curve in which the spot price is lower than the forward prices.

Contingent Liability: A potential obligation that may or may not become an actual obligation. See *Option*.

Continuous Hedging: The process of continuously analyzing risks and actively trading contracts to hedge those risks.

Contract: A deal that is defined by a contract legal document.

Contract Terms: The standardized contractual terms.

Convenience Yield: The value of holding a commodity or asset.

Convexity: Non-linearity. Describes anything with curvature or skew. Within the context of an option's value, the change in value of an option following an increase of underlying price will not necessary equal the change associated with a decrease in underlying price.

Coordinating Council: A National Electric Reliability Council (NERC) term for a sub-area of a NERC region.

Correlation (ρ): A measure of how the value of one variable changes if another variable is changed. In the world of risk, the correlation is typically calculated using price-returns rather than the prices themselves.

Cost-Plus-Return: A valuation method in which a contract, position, or asset is valued as the cost of its production plus some profit ratio. Contrasts with *Mark-to-Market*.

Cost of Carry: The cost of holding a commodity or asset.

Cost of Money: The time value of money as it relates to holding or financing a contract, commodity, position, or other asset.

Cost of Risk: The cost that reflects the premium associated with off-setting the inherent risk of a contract, commodity, position, or asset.

Counterparty: The person or company on the other side of a bilateral contract or position.

Covered Position: An option position that also includes the underlying asset, as would be the case where a party that sold a call option on an asset also purchased the asset. (Contradicts with *naked position*.)

Crack-Spread Option: An option on the spread between crude oil and the commodities created at the refinery, such as heating oil and gasoline.

Credit Enhancement: A technique or product that either reduces the likelihood of contract default or guarantees payment or delivery in the event of default.

Credit Risk: The probable change in (or sensitivity to) value due to a counterparty defaulting on a contract.

Cross-Gamma: The change in the delta (Δ) due to another market price changing.

Cross-Market Correlation: The correlation of price-returns for two different markets.

D

Daily Settlement: A process in which choices or delivery occur every day according to an agreed upon calendar schedule.

Day-Ahead Market: The spot market for power to be delivered the next qualified delivery date.

Deal: A generic phrase used for a contract, position, or quote.

Deal Capture: The process of recording trades at the time of inception into the trading and portfolio management system.

Decomposition: The process of analyzing a portfolio in order to identify the impact of individual variables, risks, or contracts.

Deep-In-the-Money: An expression for describing the relative value of an option that has a strike price (K) that is so much less than current price of the underlying asset that there is little chance the underlying price will approach the strike price before expiration.

Delivery: The process of one counterparty providing the other counterparty a commodity at the contractually-specified location or region. Delivery may occur at a single time or over a delivery period.

Delivery Expiration Date: The date of each delivery leg in a physically-settled contract. For a contract in a market with day-ahead spot markets, the delivery expiration date is the date prior to the actual date of delivery.

Delivery-into-Next-Day Market: See *Day-Ahead Market.*

Delta (Δ): A first-order risk sensitivity measurement of the impact on the value of a contract, position, or portfolio given a one-unit change in the underlying price. A member of the measurements known as the Greeks. When the unit is a dollar, as is standard, also known as the *Dollar Delta.*

Delta Hedging: The process of measuring the delta (Δ) of a contract or portfolio, identifying hedge contracts that offset the existing delta, and entering the optimal number of hedge contracts that will either eliminate or minimize the existing delta risk.

Delta Neutral: A position with a delta risk of zero.

Demand Side Management (DSM): A practice in which end users of electricity (i.e. the demand side) are encouraged or incented to reduce their demand of power for either economic or conservation purposes.

Demand Swing Option: A swing option in which one of the counterparties will execute out of need for power as opposed to taking advantage of market price movements (also known as *non-ruthless exercise.*) Converse to *Price Swing Option.*

Deregulation: The process of a government relaxing legal constraints on a particular market or industry.

Derivative: A contract, position, or asset that derives its value from some other underlying asset or combination of assets.

Desk: The office and or group of people performing trading, analysis, and/or risk management.

Deterministic Process: A process with a known behavior or outcome about which there is no uncertainty. Synonymous with *Drift.* Converse to *Stochastic Process.*

Discount Factor (df): A multiplier reflecting the time value of money.

Discounting: The process of calculating the time value of money. Also describes adjusting future cash flows by discount factors.

Discounting Rate (r): The interest rate used for calculating discount factors.

Discrete: The most detailed available level of analysis or analytical output.

Discrete Daily Forward Price: The forward price for a single date in the future.

Discrete Volatility: The particular volatility in three dimensions: by strike price or strike bucket; by time of observation; and by the underlying forward price's time or time bucket of expiration.

Distribution: The probabilities or occurrences of various outcomes. When graphed, distributions often look like bell curves but may take many different shapes. Characteristics of a distribution may be described using *moments*.

Distribution Analysis: The statistical analysis of a price or other variable distribution and describing that distribution in terms of its *moments*.

Diversification: The process of adding different types of positions with different, uncorrelated behaviors to a portfolio.

Dollar Delta, $\Delta_\$$: The delta measurement for a single-unit change of one dollar.

Downside: The portion of a potential payoff that shows a loss.

Drift: A deterministic or expected price change. Also see *Deterministic Process*.

Driver: A process that affects or "drives" market prices.

Dynamic Link Library (DLL): A kind of computer program that is utilized by other computer programs.

E

Early Exercise: When the holder of an American-style option strikes the option prior to the contract's final expiration date.

Earnings at Risk (EaR): The maximum shortfall of earnings, relative to a specified budget. Much like Value-at-Risk (VaR), may be calculated as a function of a statistical confidence level.

Economic Exercise: See *Ruthless Exercise*.

Efficient Market Theory: A theory that market prices include all necessary information and expectations from all market participants.

Embedded Option: A choice within a contract or asset that adds value to the position, but is not explicitly labeled as an option contract.

End User: A company that consumes a commodity or asset being traded in a marketplace.

Energy Risk: The risk associated with energy positions or portfolios, especially those risks not commonly seen in non-energy markets.

Engine: A software program that calculates or quantifies the value or risk of a position, book, or portfolio.

Equilibrium Price (L): An average price around which spot prices trade or to which forward prices converge. In the Pilipovic Model for the Forward Price Curve, it represents the long-term price to which prices revert.

Error Term: In the case of an approximation or expectation, the error term is the difference between the actual value compared with the approximating or expected value.

European Option: A general type of option for which the buyer has the right to exercise or strike the option only on the contract's expiration date.

Exchange: An organization that provides centralized trading of standardized contracts and performs the clearinghouse function.

Exercise: When the holder of an option right uses that right. Synonymous with *Strike*.

Exercise Price: See *Strike Price*.

Exotic: A contract, structured product or position that is unusual, complex, or non-standardized. Converse of *vanilla*.

Exposure: A position that is subject to change.

Expectation: A general sense of price behavior. In financial modeling, refers to a mark-to-market expression of the range of possible prices or price returns.

Expiration: A date to which some activity is linked. An option expiration is when the option right expires. Trading expiration is the last day on which a contract may be traded.

Expiry: The expiration date of an option and the final exercise date.

Exploratory Trade: A trade entered as part of the price discovery process or as training prior to full market participation.

F

Factor: A stochastic process represented by an equation with a stochastic variable.

FASB 133: A rule promulgated by the Financial Accounting Standards Board (FASB) requiring the distinction between speculative and hedge trading.

Fat Tails of a Distribution: When the extreme right and left sides of a plotted distribution suggest a large probability of extreme values. A "fat" tail suggests a relatively high probability of an extreme occurrence at that side of the distribution.

Fee: A fixed or deterministic value associated with the price of a contract.

Feedstock: The energy used to generate a different energy.

Financial Engineering: The application of mathematics for the valuation of derivatives and the measurement of risk. Not used very often in the world of energy risk, the term "financial engineering" is more common in money markets as symbolized by the International Association of Financial Engineers, a group comprised of academics and practitioners.

Financial Settlement: See *Cash Settlement*.

Firm Contract: A traditional utility contract that obliges both delivery and payment. Synonymous with *Forward Contract* and converse of *non-firm*.

First Moment (M1): A measure of the mean of a distribution.

First-Order Risk: The risk sensitivity of a position or portfolio given a change in an input variable. May be calculated as the first derivative of a position or portfolio's value relative to that variable. *Delta* (Δ) is an example of a first-order risk.

Fish Flush: A phenomenon often observable in the forward price curve for markets containing hydroelectric units that must release stored water for purposes of ecological conservation. Can appear as a form of third seasonality within the forward price curve.

Fixed-for-Floating: The contractual relationship that characterizes a swap in which one counterparty pays a fixed price for an asset or commodity, while the other counterparty either pays (or delivers) the asset or commodity that has floating value in the open market.

Fixed-Income Derivative: A derivative on a fixed-income product such as a bond.

Flat: Constant or a line without slope.

Floating Price: A price that is not fixed and can change with the market.

Floor: A structured product that contains a strip of multiple put option contracts with identical specifications but staggered expirations.

Forecasting: The process of predicting a particular outcome. Traditionally associated with fundamental analysis.

Forward Contract: A fixed-price contract for which no premium is paid up front. Special cases include a *Future* and a *Swap*.

Forward Price (F): The price for an asset that one would contract for "today" for delivery (and payment) of that asset at some time in the future.

Forward Strip: The presence of equivalent standardized contracts available for different periods going forward.

Fourth Moment (M4): A measure of the tails of a distribution. Related to *Kurtosis*.

Frictionless Markets: "Markets where there are no restrictions nor costs to trading assets." (Jarrow and Turnbull, p. 671.)

Front/Middle/Back Office Model: A model from the financial markets in which duties and functions are organized into three general sectors: a front office where trading occurs; a middle office that provides analytical support and risk management; and a back office that performs such administrative duties as confirmations.

Front Office: The sector of the trading operation where the trading occurs. Part of the *Front/Middle/Back Office* model.

Full Requirements Contract: A fixed-price, variable volume contract that is common in regulated power markets.

Fundamental Analysis and Modeling: The process of analyzing and modeling the fundamental processes that influence a variable. Contrasts with quantitative modeling, which analyzes and models the variable itself.

Fungibility: The degree to which an asset may be replaced by another asset.

Futures Contract: A standardized forward contract offered at an exchange with a clearinghouse function and margin accounts.

G

Gamma (Γ): A second-order risk sensitivity measurement of the impact on the delta (Δ) of a contract, position, or portfolio given a one-unit change in the underlying price. A member of the measurements known as the Greeks.

Gamma Criterion: The principle that all managers and decision makers at a company with market price risk should understand all the basic concepts of risk management necessary to understand the definition and potential impact of gamma (Γ) risk.

Generalized Autoregressive Conditional Heteroskedasticity (GARCH): An econometric volatility methodology.

Gas Peaker: A gas-fired generation unit primarily used to supply electricity during peak market conditions.

Generation Asset: A facility used to generate electricity.

Generator: A company with the primary purpose of generating electricity.

Granularity: The level of detail for which data are being dissected, analyzed, valued, or reported. The finer the detail, the greater granularity.

Greek: A risk-sensitivity measure that is symbolized by letter(s) from the Greek alphabet, including delta (Δ) and gamma (Γ).

H

Hedge or Hedge Contract: A contract used for the purpose of offsetting the risk of a pre-existing position or portfolio.

Hedge Fund: A trading house that trades on its own portfolio.

Hedge Ratio: The maximum variance ratio of hedge contracts to contracts in the portfolio. In the case of an option, the option's delta.

Hedging: The process of analyzing existing risk levels and entering hedging contracts to achieve desired risk levels.

Hedging Horizon: The last date of the period of time over which hedging is to be performed.

Historical Analysis: Analysis that depends on historical data and not on forward-looking market data and expectations.

Hockey Stick Payoff Diagram: A common shape within a payoff diagram for a call or put option in which part of the diagram is flat and another part is sloped, thus resembling the shaft and blade of a hockey stick.

Holiday: In electricity and commodity markets, a predetermined date on which an otherwise regularly scheduled delivery does not occur.

Horizon: A point in forward time that defines the final point or date for analysis.

Human Risk: The risk due to human error, illegal behavior, or other problems associated with individuals in the trading and risk management units.

I

Illiquidity: See *Liquidity*.

Implied Values: Values that are "backed out" or implied from market prices, generally by using valuation models.

Implied Volatility: A marked-to-market volatility implied from actual market option quotes.

In-the-Money: An expression for describing the relative value of a call/put option that has a strike price (K) that is less/more than the current price of the underlying asset. If a call option were being valued at expiration, one would use the spot price ($S>K$). Were the call option being valued prior to expiration, one would compare the strike price to the forward price ($F>K$).

Input: A variable to be entered into an equation. In valuation, inputs include forward prices, volatilities, and correlations.

Intra-Market Correlation ($\varsigma^{F1,F2}$): The correlation between price returns within a particular market's forward price curve. Could be the correlation between spot and some forward date, between particular time buckets, or between some other time periods.

Intrinsic Value of an Option: "The payoff that would be received if the underlying is at its current level, when the option expires." (Wilmott, p. 26.)

J

Java Moment: An expression used in this book to alert the reader to get a cup of "java" or coffee in preparation for an intellectually challenging or information-intense concept in the forthcoming paragraph.

Juice: Slang for electricity.

Jump Diffusion: A description of price behavior in which price jumps do not stay at their elevated level, but rather diffuse. Can also be an element of modeling for either valuation or risk assessment.

K

Kurtosis: Describes the tails of a distribution. Related to the "fourth moment" in distribution analysis.

L

Lag: A period of time between two dates such as between the delivery date and the payment date.

Leg: A portion of a contract's delivery or payment cycle.

Linearity: The degree to which a process is fixed, predictable, equally true regardless of next step or direction taken, or represented by a straight line.

Liquidity: The relative amount of units being traded of an asset in a particular market. A measure of quality, high liquidity is considered good for price discovery, whereas illiquidity is not.

Liquidity Risk: The risk of an asset's value changing due to liquidity issues such as improper price discovery, decreases in liquidity, and undue influence of market power.

Load: Generally refers to the volume taken or required by an end user, but can also be used to describe other types of quantities.

Load Curtailment Contract: A contract that allows the supplier to curtail or not deliver all or a portion of power contracted for delivery.

Locational Marginal Pricing (LMP): A method of pricing power as a function of location within a larger transmission system broken down into nodes.

Lognormal (LN): The behavior of a variable for which the log of its function is normally distributed. Lognormal prices are always positive.

Long: A position in which an asset or right is owned.

Long Term: A period of forward time starting with a few days, a few weeks, or even a few months, and then extending beyond. Each company and market will have a different definition. In the context of the Pilipovic Model for the Forward Price Curve, it covers the period after reversion to the equilibrium price behavior.

Look-back Option: An option with settlement as a function of past price behavior.

M

Margin Account: An account used by the clearinghouse at an exchange for managing an individual's exposure to their open interest contracts. Each participant deposits a certain amount into their margin account; the balance of that account tracks the value of the contract, with a gain entitling a withdrawal of the difference; while a loss requires a deposit of additional funds.

Margining: The process of tracking the current values of open interest contracts at an exchange and ensuring the counterparties maintain their margin accounts.

Market: In the context of trading and risk management, a *market* describes something containing enough traders to support meaningful activity of a particular *asset*. It contains enough participants—both buyers and sellers—to support meaningful activity (typically measured by *liquidity* or the volume of contracts being traded) of a particular contract, commodity, or other asset of value. In the energy sector, a "market" represents the commodity or asset that forms the basis for standardized trading. For a particular asset, a market is usually defined by a geographical delivery point or area; in addition, the market is further tied to a particular delivery schedule with standardized contract specifications.

Market Caps: Predetermined price levels that a centralized authority sets as a maximum price that can be paid for a commodity.

Market-Implied Volatility: See *Implied Volatility*.

Market Maker: A company or individual that both buys and sells contracts in order to make money off the fees or the bid/ask spread.

Market Maker Strategy: A trading strategy in which a company generates profits from fees and/or associated bid/ask spreads from deals with counterparties. One of the four *Risk-Return Strategies*. (Pilipovic, 1998, p. 199-203.)

Market Risk: The probable change in value of (or sensitivity to) a contract, position, or portfolio due to general changes in market conditions. While often used interchangeably with price risk, market risk does include non-price risks.

Marketing Risk: The general risk to a company or the market perception of a company due to improper or illegal marketing efforts.

Mark-to-Market: See *Marking-to-Market*.

Marking-to-Cost: The process of valuing a position or portfolio based on cost of production or replication. See *Cost-Plus-Return*.

Marking-to-Market (MTM): The process of valuing a position or portfolio against market clearing-price or other market signals.

Markov Process: A "particular type of stochastic process where only the present value of a variable is relevant for predicting the future. The past history of the variable and the way in which the present has emerged from the past are irrelevant." Hull (p. 191).

Master Agreement: A standardized agreement to which other agreements or contracts are referred.

Mean: Describes the average of a distribution. Related to the "first moment" in distribution analysis.

Mean Reversion: The price behavior in which spot and forward prices revert to an equilibrium or "mean" level, typically a price in energy markets or a yield in other markets.

Merchant Power: The business of generating electricity by companies that do not fit the traditional electric utility profile.

Middle Office: Part of the *Front/Middle/Back Office* model.

Minimum Variance Analysis (MVA): A mathematical procedure of calculating the number of given hedge contracts to be bought (or sold) that would minimize the variance of a portfolio.

Model: A theoretical or mathematical technique for replicating reality.

Modeling: The process of creating models.

Modeling Risk: The probable change in value of (or sensitivity to) a contract, position, or portfolio due to changes in modeling variables or models.

Model-Implied Volatility: A volatility implied from market prices that is dependent on a model to accommodate for missing or inadequate market price information.

Moment: A parameter for describing the shape of a distribution. See *First Moment, Second Moment, Third Moment,* and *Fourth Moment.*

Monte Carlo Simulation: Simulation of market price behavior in order to observe possible portfolio or individual position values.

Monte Carlo Value-at-Risk (VaR): A VaR methodology that uses Monte Carlo simulation to generate portfolio value distributions on which to apply the desired confidence intervals.

Monthly Settlement: The process in which decisions or delivery are made once a month with delivery occurring for the entire month according to an agreed-upon calendar schedule.

N

Naked Option: An option position that is not covered by the underlying asset, as would be the case where a party sold a call option on an asset without already owning that asset. (The opposite of a *Covered Position.*)

North American Electric Reliability Council (NERC): An organization of American electricity companies.

Near-the-Money: An expression for describing the relative value of an option that has a strike price (K) that is generally near (but not equal to) the current price of the underlying asset.

Net Present Value (NPV): A single-figure estimate—adjusted to the costs of inflation—of value of an asset over the life of that asset.

Netting Agreement: A contingency agreement in which long and short positions are allowed to offset each other (i.e., to "net out") in the event of either counterparty defaulting.

New York Mercantile Exchange (NYMEX): An important exchange where major U.S. electricity, natural gas, and other energy contracts are traded.

No-Arbitrage Assumption: The assumption that an efficient market is free of arbitrage opportunities.

Node: *In Locational Marginal Pricing (LMP)*, an individual delivery (and therefore valuation) point. In a tree valuation methodology, an individual simulation point.

Non-Firm Contract: A traditional power industry expression for a variable-volume contract where the seller (or a buyer) has the right to change the contract quantity. Converse to *Firm Contract*.

Non-Linearity: Converse to *Linearity*.

Non-Ruthless Exercise: The exercise of an option right for reasons other than taking advantage of market price movements. In energy markets, typically associated with exercising out of need for the commodity. Also known as non-economic exercise. Converse to *Ruthless Exercise*. Also see *Demand Swing Option*.

Normal Distribution: "This is the standard bell-shaped, symmetric probability distribution." (Jarrow and Turnbull, p. 672). A normally distributed variable has an equal probability of going up as it does down.

Normalization: "The conversion of a value expressed in one set of terms into another set of terms." (Pilipovic, 1998, p. 233.)

Notional: The number of units associated with a position or contract. If applied to an option, represents the potential value or units that might be executed.

Nu (V): Quantity gamma.

O

Observation Date: See *Time of Observation*.

Objective: The expression of a company's financial desires articulated at the highest levels and implemented in the form of strategies.

Off-peak: The hours of lowest demand. Can be referred to as the "*5x8,2x24*" market for the night hours of five business days and the full weekend days. All the hours not covered by the on-peak hours.

Offsetting Position: A position that is the converse of another position. See *Back-to-Back Trading*.

Omega (Ω): Quantity risk.

On-peak: The hours of highest demand during the business day (typically the 16 hours between 6:00 am and 10:59 pm). The Monday-through-Friday contract is known as the "5x16" market, whereas the Monday-through-Saturday market, common in the western U.S. markets, is referred to as the "6x16" market.

Open Interest: Describes the volume of contracts that have been entered into (generally on an exchange) and have not yet expired.

Operational Risk: The probable change in value of (or sensitivity to) a contract, position, or portfolio due to unexpected failures in operational systems such as computer systems.

Opportunity Cost: The cost of doing one thing (such as entering into a contract or a business) at the detriment of not doing something else (such as doing nothing or entering into a different contract or business).

Option: A contract or asset that carries choice or a contingent liability.

Option Right: The contractual right provided to the option buyer. Typically involves the right to purchase (or sell) an asset or commodity at the strike price (K), but could involve other rights such as setting different volumes.

Option Underlying: The asset or price against which an option's strike price is compared.

Outcome: In a payoff diagram, an outcome is a potential underlying value that may occur at expiration. Plotted along the x-axis of the payoff or profit diagram.

Out-of-the-Money: An expression for describing the relative value of an call/put option that has a strike price (K) that is higher/lower than the current price of the underlying asset. If a call option were being valued at expiration, one would use the spot price ($S<K$). Were a call option being valued prior to expiration, one would compare the strike price to the forward price ($F<K$).

Over-the-Counter (OTC) Market: A market traded outside a traditional exchange. Contracts may be standardized or customized. Communication is achieved either by telephone or the Internet, with brokers playing a facilitory role. Trades are performed on a bilateral basis.

P

P&L: See *Profit & Loss*.

P&L Decomposition: The process of analyzing a portfolio's profit & loss statement in order to identify the impact of individual variables, risks, or contracts.

Parity Value: The value of option at expiration for a particular outcome of the underlying market.

Payoff Diagram: A plot of "the value of an option at expiry as a function of the underlying." (Wilmott, p. 27). Unlike a profit diagram, the payoff diagram does not include any premium paid for options.

Peak: A period of greatest demand for electricity or another commodity. Typically associated with higher price levels.

Peaker Plant: An electric generation facility used to serve peak load.

Phi (Φ): Quantity vega.

Physical Asset: A generation plant, transmission system, or other real asset. Converse of *Financial Asset*.

Physical Settlement (or Physically Settled): The process in which a contract settles where one counterparty delivers the commodity while the other pays cash. Converse to *Cash Settlement*.

Pilipovic Model for the Forward Price Curve: A two-factor price-mean reverting model with a seasonality function published by Dragana Pilipovic in 1995.

Plug and Chug: A process of plugging in different coefficients for parameters in order to match a result. May be performed manually or by a computer program.

Policies: The portion of the *Risk Management Policies and Procedures* (RMPP) that provides general guidelines, which are approved (and best understood) by upper management. In contrast, the *Procedures* delineate details on implementing the *Policies*.

Portfolio (Π): Represents the firm's total collection of contracts and assets. Can be organized into sub-portfolios and/or books. The overall value of a particular portfolio is often symbolized by the Greek letter pi, π.

Portfolio Analysis: The process of valuing portfolios of contracts or positions. Also includes the process of measuring, controlling, and hedging the risks of such portfolios.

Position: A individual exposure that exists within one's portfolio. May be a financial contract, generation unit, or other asset included and managed within the portfolio.

Power: In this book, used inter-changeably with *electricity*. Many professionals prefer to make a distinction between the two, but that will not be the case in this book.

Power Marketer: A person or firm buying and selling power; generally implies that the firm does not own or control generating assets.

Premium (K): The fee paid for buying an option.

Present Value: See *Net Present Value*.

Price Behavior: The pattern(s) that price returns exhibit over time. Can be assumed to be continued in the future. Can be analyzed using time series analysis or distribution analysis and expressed using quantitative models.

Price Discovery: The process of ascertaining the price of a particular asset. The quality of such price discovery is correlated with liquidity.

Price Elasticity: The measure of responsiveness by market participants to respond to changes in market conditions in terms of setting market prices and altering consumption.

Price Mean-Reversion: The price behavior in which spot and forward prices revert to an equilibrium or "mean" price.

Price Risk: The probable change in value of (or sensitivity to) a contract, position, or portfolio due to changes in market prices.

Price-Risk Pyramid: A framework that places the general functions of risk management into a hierarchical pyramid formed by a market input layer (forward prices, volatilities, and correlations) at the bottom; valuation (swap, option, and asset valuation) in the middle; and risk management at the top.

Price Spike: An unexpected jump in market prices.

Price Swing Option: A swing option in which the option holder will execute in order to take advantage of market price movements (also known as *Ruthless Exercise*.) Converse to *Demand Swing Option*.

Probability (*p*): The percentage chance of a particular outcome.

Probability Distribution: A graphical plot of all possible outcomes (*x*-axis) by the associated probabilities (*y*-axis).

Procedures: The portion of the *Risk Management Policies and Procedures* (RMPP) that provides specific rules for operating a trading and risk management operation. Upper management may delegate design and monitoring of the *Procedures*. The *Procedures* delineate details on implementing the *Policies*.

Profit & Loss (P&L): The net profit or loss of a position, book, or portfolio.

Profit Diagram: The payoff diagram adjusted for any premiums paid for the contracts.

Prompt: An adjective to describe the "next" period. For example, the *Prompt Month* is the next full month.

Prompt Contract: The next available contract that is still available for trading.

Prompt Month: The next full month.

Psi (Ψ): Cross-market correlation sensitivity.

Put: An option that allows the owner the right to sell an asset at the specified strike price (K).

Put-Call Parity: The no-arbitrage relationship between a call and a put on the same underlying asset.

Q

Quant: Nickname for *Quantitative Analyst*.

Quantitative Analysis and Modeling: The process of analyzing and modeling price or other variable behavior using stochastic principles.

Quantitative Analyst: A risk professional who uses and/or designs mathematical and statistical models to measure or quantify the values of and risk implied by a position, book, or portfolio.

Quanto Option: A cross-currency option.

Quantity Risk: See *Volumetric Risk*.

Quote: A price indication for a particular contract.

R

Rainbow Option: An option that depends on two or more underlying variables.

Random Process: A process that does not follow a purely deterministic path.

Random Walk: See *Brownian Motion.*

Real Option: A physical or "real" asset or business exposure with embedded optionality value that can be valued using option models.

Real Time: A process that occurs in present time or reflects the status of activity as it occurs, with little or no delay in reporting time.

Region: The geographic point or area relative to which the asset is valued.

Reliability: The degree to which a commodity, particularly electricity, will be available and deliverable to an individual counterparty or the general market. In American markets, generally refers to the obligation of a regulated utility to prevent blackouts and other disruptions.

Reliability Region: A multi-state region defined by the North American Electric Reliability Council (NERC) organized to promote and enhance reliability.

Remainder of Week Contract: A contract that covers delivery of energy during the remaining qualifying delivery days of the week.

Residual Risk: The risk that remains in a book or portfolio after the hedge contracts have been entered.

Retail: Relating to deals with end users; generally outside the wholesale market.

Return: Change in value, typically expressed as a percentage. Can be a profit or loss.

Rho (ρ): A first-order risk sensitivity measurement of the impact on the value of a contract, position, or portfolio given a one-unit change in the interest rate. A member of the measurements known as the "Greeks."

Risk: The impact of unexpected change.

Risk-Adjusted: A value or measure that takes into account the impact of risk (e.g., market price behavior.)

Risk Engine: See *Engine*.

Risk Limit: A specific value promulgated within the *Risk Management Policies and Procedures* (RMPP) that represents the maximum or minimum for a particular variable that may be associated with a contract, trader, counterparty, book, portfolio, or some other measure of analysis.

Risk Management: The set of skills and processes for measuring, controlling, and hedging risk.

Risk Management Policies and Procedures (RMPP): The document written for and approved by the Board of Directors (or delegated executive manager) that sets forth the policies and procedures governing the trading, risk management, and marketing operation.

Risk Manager: An individual with the duties to measure existing risk sensitivities, compare existing risk to desired risk, and recommend hedges to reconcile differences between existing and objective risk levels.

Risk Measurement: The process of measuring the impact on the value of a contract or portfolio given a change in some variable.

Risk-Return Strategy: The type of trading activities that a company will employ to meet their general financial objectives.

Risk Sensitivity Analysis: A form of risk measurement that calculates the change in value of a position or portfolio given a one-unit change in some input. (See the "Greeks.")

RiskMetrics: A data-providing service first introduced by JP Morgan in 1994. (Wilmott, p. 593).

Rocket Scientist: See *Quantitative Analyst.*

Rolling Hedge: A hedging strategy for a longer-dated position that is based on continuous renewal of short-dated hedge contracts.

Rollover: Generally refers to when some date or reference changes due to the passage of time. In the futures market, refers to the date when the prompt month contract expires and a new prompt month is designated. (For example, during the course of January, the prompt month is *February*. At the end of January, however, the *February* contract expires, causing a rollover to March as the prompt month.) In portfolio analysis, rollover refers to the process of changing the *Observation Date* and revaluing the portfolio accordingly.

Rollover Date: The date when rollover occurs.

Ruthless Exercise: The process of a holder of an option right exercising that right when optimal to do so in order to take advantage of market prices. The type of exercise associated with the *Price Swing Option*. Synonymous with *Economic Exercise*. Converse of *Non-Ruthless Exercise*.

S

Second Moment (*M2*): A measure of the width of a distribution. Related to *Variance and Volatility*.

Second Moment Equivalence (SME): A methodology for valuing European-type options. Utilizes the lognormal price approximation to create equivalent second moments that then may be adjusted for actual volatility term structure.

Second-Order Risk: The risk sensitivity of a first-order risk given a change in the underlying variable. May be calculated as the second-order derivative of a position or portfolio's value relative to the variable. As an example, gamma (Γ) is a portfolio or contract's second-order risk to price.

Sensitivity: The degree to which the value of a position or portfolio will change given a change in some variable.

Settlement: The process in which cash payments or physical delivery occurs for a given contract. See *Cash Settlement* and *Physical Settlement*.

Short: A position in which an asset or right is not owned.

Short Term: A period of forward time starting with the current or "spot" time going out anywhere between a few days and a few weeks. Each company will have a different definition. In the context of the Pilipovic Model for the Forward Price Curve, covers the period between spot price behavior until the reversion to the equilibrium price behavior (i.e., the period of mean reversion.)

Shoulder Months: The period immediately before and after a peak period. Typically the autumn and the spring. Synonymous with *Wing Months*.

Skew: Describes how a distribution is skewed around its mean. Related to the "third moment" of distribution analysis.

Sleeve: A trading practice involving a middleman assuming obligations from one party and then immediately selling those obligations to an undesirable third party or vice versa.

Source Code: The raw computer code before it is compiled to create a software application.

Spark Spread: A contract that derives its value from the spread between electricity and natural gas prices, commonly based on the heat-exchange rate. Typically the contract is valued as a function of buying enough units of natural gas to generate a single unit of power. Can be contracted for physical or financial settlement.

Speculation: A bet against the market price.

Speculation Strategy: A trading strategy in which the company generates profits from assuming risk in the marketplace. One of the four *Risk-Return Strategies*. (Pilipovic, 1998, p. 199-203).

Spike: A unexpected jump in spot or forward prices.

Split Personality of Energies: A characterization of the fact that energy prices behave one way over the short-term and in a different way over the long-term. In other words, energy forward price markets exhibit very low intra-market correlations between short- and long-term forwards.

Spot Market: The market where a contract, commodity, or asset is traded for its most immediate or next-available contracting and delivery. The immediacy of delivery is a function of the market characteristics. In American power markets, the spot market is generally regarded as the *delivery-into-next-day* or *day-ahead* market.

Spot Price: The price of a contract, commodity, or asset in the spot market.

Spread: The difference in price for two contracts, commodities, positions, or assets.

Spread Option: An option on two contracts, commodities, positions or assets. See *Basis Option, Crack-Spread Option,* and *Spark-Spread Option.*

Standard Deviation (STD): A statistical measure of the width of a distribution. Equals the square root of the *Variance*.

Standardized Contracts: Contracts with specifications that are well known to market participants and are commonly traded.

Stochastic Behavior: A behavior with a random component.

Stochastic Hat (~): A mathematical symbol (also known as a tilde) that denotes stochastic behavior when placed on tope of a variable; e.g., $\tilde{z}$.

Stochastic Variable: A variable with random price behavior. Mathematically denoted with a stochastic "hat" (e.g., $\tilde{z}$).

Storability: The degree to which a commodity or asset may be stored, and to a lesser extent, the cost-efficiency of such storage.

Straddle Option: A structured product with a long call and a long put at the same strike prices.

Strangle Option: A structured product with a long call and a long put at the different strike prices.

Strategy: The specific set of actions to be taken to accomplish a company's general objectives.

Stress Testing: A form of risk measurement that calculates the change in a contract or portfolio value given a change in a variable that is assumed to replicate a highly stressful condition.

Strike: *Verb*: To exercise an option right. *Noun*: see *Strike Price*.

Strike Bucket: A range of strike prices. The strike bucket framework would include all potential strike prices organized into strike buckets.

Strike Price (K): The price set in an option price for which the underlying asset will be bought (or sold) upon exercise.

Strike Structure: Describes how the volatility of an option changes as a function of a contract's strike price.

Strip: A set of similar contracts with different expirations.

Structured Product: A non-standardized derivative contract that is complex, unusual, or combines standard contracts in some unique manner.

Sub-Portfolio: A sub-portfolio is any combination of deals or books that represent a sub-set of the portfolio. (Also see *Book*.)

Swap: A contract that exchanges a floating position for a fixed position. In power markets, a swap exchanges a fixed-price for some period of delivery of power that has a floating commodity value for each date or increment over the delivery period. If swap is traded on an exchange, it is called a "futures" contract. In financial markets, the definition of a swap is constrained to a "financial contract which obligates both counterparties to a series of cash payments for a fixed period of time" (Jarrow and Turnbull, p. 674.)

Swing Option: An American-style, variable-volume option that allows the buyer a certain number of "swing rights" over the term of the contract. Typically, each swing right is for next-day delivery that may be exercised for any qualified delivery date; only one swing right may be executed on any single day. May be structured as a pure option or embedded within a baseload swap.

Synthetic Position: A portfolio whose payoffs replicate that of a standard contract. As an example, a portfolio that owns an asset and owns a put option represents a synthetic call option.

361

Systematic Risk: A risk measure calculated for all books within a portfolio as a function of a single market or underlying variable.

T

Tails of a Distribution: The extreme right and left sides of a plotted distribution that represent extreme values for that distribution. Measured by the *fourth moment* or *kurtosis*. A "fat" tail suggests a relatively high probability of an extreme occurrence at that side of the distribution.

Taylor Series Expansion: An expansion that expresses the change in a value in terms of its first, second, and higher order sensitivities (i.e., the "Greeks").

Technical Analysis: The process of predicting prices by extending patterns seen in past price behavior.

Tenor: The frequency with which some process occurs. For example, a daily-settled option has a daily tenor.

Term: As it relates to time, represents the forward time covered by a particular contract or position. As it relates to the trading desk, relates to expiration dates of one or two months forward and beyond. As it relates to contract specifications, can either express the forward time covered by the contract or any individual detail within the contract itself.

Term Desk: A trading desk that handles longer-term contracts (typically one or two months forward and beyond.) Contrasts with *Cash Desk*.

Term Structure: The behavior of a market or market variable over the forward term. For example, see *Volatility Term Structure*.

Theta (Θ): The first-order risk sensitivity measurement of the impact on the value of a contract, position, or portfolio given a one-unit change in time (typically one day.) A member of the measurements known as the "Greeks."

Third Moment (M3): A measure of how a distribution is skewed to the left or right of the First Moment (or mean.) Related to *Skew*.

Tick: The smallest unit used to delineate allowable price values in a market.

Time Bucket (TB): A particular period of forward time, with the full horizon of forward time organized into a time bucket framework.

Time Decay: The loss of optionality value as time passes and the option approaches expiration.

Time Horizon: The last date of forward time used for analysis.

Time of Expiration (T): The time at which a contract or position stops trading or is exercised.

Time of Observation (t): The time at which one values a position, book or portfolio based using the market expectations at that moment of observation. Synonymous with *Observation Date*.

Time Value of Money: The value of money held over a period of time. Related to *Discount Rate* or interest rate.

Trading Expiration: The last day on which a contract may be traded.

Treasury Strategy: A conservative trading strategy in which one is primarily focused on stabilizing profits and/or minimizing risks. One of the four *Risk-Return Strategies*. (Pilipovic, 1998, p. 199-203).

Tree Methodology: A method for valuing options that involves building a tree of forward prices with associated probabilities.

Trinomial Tree Methodology: An option valuation tree in which three branches emulate from each node. Also see *Binomial Tree Methodology* and *Tree Methodology*.

Truncated Asian Option: A special version of an Asian option common in energy markets in which exercise occurs prior to delivery and delivery is over a period of time.

U

Underlying: A market or asset upon which an analysis, value, or behavior is based. Also see *Option Underlying*.

Underlying Price: The spot or forward price for the underlying asset in an option or a position upon which analysis or behavior is based.

Upside: The portion of a potential or actual payoff that shows a gain.

Utility: The vernacular for the traditional sense of an electric company whose core competence is generating power. Note that a more formal definition would include issues such as monopolist servicing and non-electricity related services such as water and telecommunications.

Utility Function: A model designed to model the optional utilization of a portfolio given risk and reward objectives.

V

Valuation: The determination of the value of a position or asset at the time of observation.

Value-at-Risk (VaR): A form of a single-figure estimate of risk measurement that calculates loss in value of a portfolio given a probability and a time horizon.

Vanilla: Simple, well-known, or standardized. Converse of *Exotic*.

Variable Volume Option: See *Swing Option*.

Variance: A statistical measure of how data within a distribution are dispersed around the mean. The square root of the variance equals the *Standard Deviation*.

Vega: A first-order risk measurement of the impact on the value of a contract, position, or portfolio given a one-unit change in the volatility of the underlying. A member of the measurements known as the "Greeks."

Volatility (σ): Measures the magnitude of percentage changes in prices over time, in annualized terms. It equals the price return's standard deviation over time. Measures the expected range or band within which the forward price path, as it converges into spot prices, may occur within some confidence interval. For example, if the prices were normally distributed, the volatility would define the range of upward and downward movement 66% of the time.

Volatility Smile: A pattern often seen when plotting volatility by strike price. In this pattern for a simple call option, for example, the volatility for the at-the-money strike price (i.e., the at-the-money volatility) is the lowest, with volatilities growing as the strike price increases (i.e., becoming "in-the-money") and as the strike price decreases (i.e., becoming "out of the money").

Volatility Term Structure: The behavior of volatility across forward time.

Volume: The amount of power or commodity specified by a contract.

Volumetric Risk: The risk of the volume of a contract or position changing from the current expectation. Can be expressed as a change in value or change in units.

W

Warrant: A call option "issued by a company on its own equity." (Wilmott, p. 40).

Weather Derivative: A derivative based on a temperature or other climate-related variable as the underlying variable.

What If? **Analysis:** Similar to *Stress Testing*.

Wholesale Market: The market in which energy is traded in bulk between generators, distributors, and other non-retail players.

Wing Months: See *Shoulder Months*.

Y

Yield: The rate of return.

Yield-Mean Reverting: A mean-reversion process in which the market reverts to an equilibrium yield.

Z

Zero-Premium Option: A structured product in which the option premium is embedded within a fixed-price cash flow. Also known as an "pay-as-you-go" contract.

bibliography

Arthur, Brian, *Increasing Returns and Path Dependence in the Economy*, The University of Michigan Press, 1994.

Bachelier, Louis, "Theorie de la Speculation," *Annales de l'Ecole Normale Superierure* 17 (1900). Translated in A.J. Bones, *The Random Character of Stock Market Prices*, edited by Paul H. Cotner, MIT Press, Cambridge, Mass, 1967.

Baily, Jeff, *City Electricity Trader Worked Briefly for Firm that is Involved in Defaults*, Wall Street Journal, August 5, 1998.

Bernstein, Peter, *Against the Gods: The Remarkable Story of Risk*, John Wiley & Sons, 1996.

Bhansali, Vineer, *Pricing and Managing Exotic and Hybrid Options*, Irwin Library, McGraw-Hill, 1998.

Black, Fisher and Scholes, Myron, "The Pricing of Options and Corporation Liabilities", *The Journal of Political Economy*, May-June 1973

Derman, Emanuel, *The Future of Modeling*, Risk Magazine, December 1997, p. 164.

Dixit, Avinash K. and Pindyck, Robert S., *Investment Under Uncertainty*, Princeton University Press, 1994.

Hackett Fischer, David, *The Great Wave, Price Revolutions and the Rhythms of History*, Oxford University Press, 1996.

Hull, John C., *Options, Futures, and Other Derivative Securities*, Prentice-Hall, Inc., Englewood Cliffs, NJ, 1993.

Jarrow, Robert and Turnbull, Stuart, *Derivative Securities*, South-Western College Publishing, 1996.

Jorion, Philippe, *Value at Risk: The New Benchmark for Managing Financial Risk*, McGraw-Hill, 2nd Edition, 2000.

Jorion, Phillippe and Roper, Robert *Big Bets Gone Bad: Derivatives and Bankruptcy in Orange County*, Academic Press, 1995.

Kranhold, Kathryn and Ershwiller, John *Out of Power: How a Smaller Dealer in Electricity Ruled Midwestern Market*, Wall Street Journal, September 1, 1998.

Knecht, G. Bruce, *Wisconsin Fund Posts $95 Million Loss From Unauthorized Use of Derivatives*, Wall Street Journal, March 24, 1995.

Marzio, Peter, *Iron Laces One* Dedication Brochure, Allen Center, Houston, Texas, November 17, 1983.

Moore, Geoffrey, *Crossing the Chasm: Marketing and Selling High-Tech Products to Mainstream Customers*. HarperBusiness, New York NY, 1999 (revised edition.)

Natenberg, Sheldon, *Option Volatility & Pricing : Advanced Trading Strategies and Techniques*, Probus Publishing Company, 1994.

Nelken, Israel, *Pricing, Hedging, and Trading Exotic Options*, Irwin Library of Investment and Finance, McGraw-Hill, 2000.

Pilipovic, Dragana, *Energy Risk: Valuing and Managing Energy Derivatives*, McGraw-Hill, 1998.

Pilipovic, Dragana, and Wengler, John, *Forward Roll*, Energy Risk magazine, August, 1995.

Ibid, *Assets as Options*, Derivatives Strategy, December 1999.

Ibid, *Basis for Boptions*, Energy +Power Risk Management, December 1998/January 1999.

Ibid, *Debut of Two New Seasonality Functions*, The Desk, July 1, 1998.

Ibid, *Getting into the Swing*, Energy +Power Risk Management, March 1998.

Ibid, *The Power Greeks*, The Desk, November 1998

Ibid, *The VaR Vacuum*, Energy +Power Risk Management, November 1999.

Ibid, *Volatility, the Fuel for Option Engines*, Commodities Now, March 1999.

Risk Publications, *Energy Modelling and the Management of Uncertainty*, July 1999.

Ibid, *Managing Energy Price Risk*, Risk Publications, 1995.

Ibid, *The U.S. Power Market: Restructuring and Risk Management*, Risk Publications, 1997.

Trigeorgis, Lenos, *Real Options : Managerial Flexibility and Strategy in Resource Allocation*, MIT Press, 1996.

Waldrop, M. Mitchell, *Complexity, The Emerging Science at the Edge of Order and Chaos*, Simon and Schuster, 1992.

Wilmott, Paul, *Derivatives: The Theory and Practice of Financial Engineering*, John Wiley & Sons, 1998.

index

A

5x16 market, 321, 323

5x8, 2x24 market, 321, 323

6x16 (definition), 321

7x24 market, 321, 323

8760 (definition), 321

Account management, 207

Account setup, 207

Accounting and tax, 58, 294-296, 305-307, 317

Accounts payable/cash disbursement, 318-319

Allowed contracts, 146

Alternative strategies, 72-75, 81-84: treasury, 72-74; speculation, 72-75; arbitrage, 72-73, 81; market maker, 72-73, 82-84

American option, 133-134, 324

American power tradition, 33-35

Analysis by market prices, 104-106

Analyst, 98-99, 324: role of, 98-99

Analytics, 324

Approved counterparties, 146

Arbitrage, 72-73, 81, 112, 147, 200, 324-325

Arbitrage strategy, 72-73, 81, 147, 200, 324

Arbitrage-free, 324

Articulating objectives, 201

H

I

M

P

Q

R

Other titles offered by PennWell...

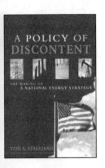

A Policy of Discontent: The Making of a National Energy Strategy
by Vito A. Stagliano
446 pages, hardcover
$39.95 US/CAN
$54.95 Intl
ISBN: 0-87814-817-5

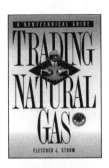

Trading Natural Gas: A Nontechnical Guide
by Fletcher J. Sturm
206 pages, hardcover
$64.95 US/CAN
$79.95 Intl
ISBN: 0-87814-709-8

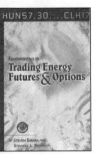

Fundamentals of Trading Energy Futures & Options
by Steven Errera and Stewart Brown
253 pages, hardcover
$64.95 US/CAN
$79.95 Intl
ISBN: 0-87814-760-8

Energy Marketing Handbook
by Denise Warkentin
197 pages, hardcover
$64.95 US/CAN
$79.95 Intl
ISBN: 0-87814-604-0

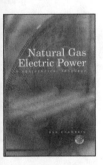

Natural Gas & Electric Power in Nontechnical Language
by Ann Chambers
258 pages, hardcover
$64.95 US/CAN
$79.95 Intl
ISBN: 0-87814-761-6

Electric Power Industry in Nontechnical Language
by Denise Warkentin
239 pages, hardcover
$64.95 US/CAN
$79.95 Intl
ISBN: 0-87814-719-5

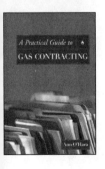

A Practical Guide to Gas Contracting
by Ann O'Hara
467 pages, hardcover
$64.95 US/CAN
$79.95 Intl
ISBN: 0-87814-764-0

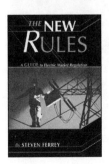

The New Rules: A Guide to Electric Market Regulation
by Steven Ferrey
370 pages, hardcover
$64.95 US/CAN
$79.95 Intl
ISBN: 0-87814-790-X

To purchase a PennWell book...

Visit our online store www.pennwell-store.com, or
Call 1.800.752.9764 (US) or +1.918.831.9421 (Intl), or
Fax 1.877.218.1348 (US) or +1.918.831.9555 (Intl)